ZIONISM IN THE AGE OF THE DICTATORS

Zionism in the Age of the Dictators

Lenni Brenner

CROOM HELM
London & Canberra

LAWRENCE HILL
Westport, Connecticut

©1983 Lenni Brenner
Croom Helm Ltd, Provident House, Burrell Row, Beckenham, Kent BR3 1AT

British Library Cataloguing in Publication Data

Brenner, Lenni
    Zionism in the age of the dictators.
    1. Zionism – History
    I. Title
    956.94′001   DS149
    ISBN 0-7099-0628-5

Published in the United States by
Lawrence Hill & Company, Publishers, Inc.
520 Riverside Avenue, Westport, Connecticut 06880

Library of Congress Cataloging in Publication Data

Brenner, Lenni, 1937-
    Zionism in the age of the dictators.

    Includes bibliographical references and index.
    1. Zionism—Controversial literature. 2. Jews—
Politics and government. 3. Holocaust, Jewish (1939-
1945) I. Title.
DS149.B845   1983   956.94′001   82-23369
ISBN 0-88208-163-2
ISBN 0-88208-164-0 (pbk.)

Typeset by Mayhew Typesetting, Bristol
Printed in the United States of America

CONTENTS

PREFACE

Why another book on the Second World War, which is probably the most written about subject in human history? Why another book on the Holocaust, which has been movingly described by many survivors and scholars? As a general subject, the age of the dictators, the world war, and the Holocaust have indeed been covered — but has the inter-action between Zionism and Fascism and Nazism been adequately explored? And if not, why not?

The answer is quite simple. Different aspects of the general subject have been dealt with, but there is no equivalent of the present work, one that attempts to present an overview of the movement's world activities during that epoch. Of course, that is not an accident, but rather a sign that there is much that is politically embarrassing to be found in that record.

Dealing with the issues brings difficult problems, one of the most difficult arising out of the emotions evoked by the Holocaust. Can there by any doubt that many of the United Nations delegates who voted for the creation of an Israeli state, in 1947, were motivated by a desire to somehow compensate the surviving Jews for the Holocaust? They, and many of Israel's other well-wishers, cathected the state with the powerful human feelings they had toward the victims of Hitler's monstrous crimes. But therein was their error: they based their support for Israel and Zionism on what Hitler had done *to* the Jews, rather than on what the Zionists had done *for* the Jews. To say that such an approach is intellectually and politically impermissable does not denigrate the deep feelings produced by the Holocaust.

Zionism, however, is an ideology, and its chronicles are to be examined with the same critical eye that readers should bring to the history of any political tendency. Zionism is not now, nor was it ever, co-extensive with either Judaism or the Jewish people. The vast majority of Hitler's Jewish victims were not Zionists. It is equally true, as readers are invited to see for themselves, that the majority of the Jews of Poland, in particular, had repudiated Zionism on the eve of the Holocaust, that they abhorred the politics of Menachem Begin, in September 1939, one of the leaders of the self-styled 'Zionist-Revision-ist' movement in the Polish capital. As an anti-Zionist Jew, the author is inured to the charge that anti-Zionism is equivalent to anti-Semitism and 'Jewish self-hatred'.

It is scarcely necessary to add that all attempts to equate Jews and Zionists, and therefore to attack Jews as such, are criminal, and are to be sternly repelled. There cannot be even the slightest confusion between the struggle against Zionism and hostility to either Jews or Judaism. Zionism thrives on the fears that Jews have of another Holocaust. The Palestinian people are deeply appreciative of the firm support given them by progressive Jews, whether religious – as with Mrs Ruth Blau, Elmer Berger, Moshe Menuhin, or Israel Shahak – or atheist – as with Felicia Langer and Lea Tsemel and others on the left. Neither nationality nor theology nor social theory can, in any way, be allowed to become a stumbling block before the feet of those Jews, in Israel or elsewhere, who are determined to walk with the Palestinian people against injustice and racism. It can be said, with scientific certainty, that, without the unbreakable unity of Arab and Jewish progressives, victory over Zionism is not merely difficult, it is impossible.

Unless this book were to become an encyclopedia, the material had necessarily to be selected, with all due care, so that a rounded picture might come forth. It is inevitable that the scholars of the several subjects dealt with will complain that not enough attention had been devoted to their particular specialties. And they will be correct, to be sure; whole books have been written on particular facets of the broader problems dealt with herein, and the reader is invited to delve further into the sources cited in the footnotes. An additional difficulty arises out of the fact that so much of the original material is in a host of languages that few readers are likely to know. Therefore, wherever possible, English sources and translations are cited, thus giving sceptical readers a genuine opportunity to verify the research apparatus relied upon.

As readers are committed to discovering by reading this book, the consequences of Zionist ideology deserve study and exposure. That is what is attempted here. As an unabashed anti-Zionist, I clearly conclude that Zionism is wholly incorrect; but that is my conclusion drawn from the evidence. The conclusions are, in short, my own. As for the persuasiveness of the arguments used in arriving at them, readers are invited to judge for themselves.

ABBREVIATIONS

AJC	American Jewish Committee – bourgeois assimilationist organisation.
AJC	American Jewish Congress – Zionist organisation identified with rabbi Stephen Wise.
AK	*Armia Krajowa* (Home Army) – Polish underground affiliated to the government-in-exile.
BUF	British Union of Fascists.
CID	British Criminal Investigation Division.
CPUSA	Communist Party of USA.
CV	*Centralverein* (Central Union of German Citizens of the Jewish Faith) – assimilationist defence organisation.
DDP	*Deutsche Demokratische Partei* (German Democratic Party).
Endeks	National Democrats – anti-Semitic Polish party.
HOG	*Hitachdut Olei Germania* (German Immigrants' Association in Palestine).
ILP	Independent Labour Party – British socialist organisation.
INTRIA	International Trade and Investment Agency – Zionist-organised company selling German goods in Britain.
JFO	Jewish Fighting Organisation – underground movement in the Warsaw ghetto.
JLC	Jewish Labor Committee – anti-Zionist labour union organisation in America.
JNF	Jewish National Fund – Zionist agricultural fund.
JnP	*Judische-nationale Partei* (Jewish National Party) – Austrian Zionist party.
JPC	Jewish People's Council – community defence group against Mosleyites in Britain.
JWV	Jewish War Veterans – right-wing American ex-serviceman's grouping.
KB	*Korpus Bezpieczenstwa* (Security Corps) – Polish underground movement friendly to the Revisionists.
KPD	*Kommunistische Partei Deutschlands* (Communist Party of Germany).
KPP	*Kommunistyczna Partja Polski* (Communist Party of Poland).
Naras	National Radicals – extreme anti-Semitic Polish party.

NEMICO	Near and Middle East Commercial Corporation – Zionist company selling German goods in the Middle East.
NPP	National Peasant Party – Romanian party.
NSDAP	*Nationalsozialistische Deutsche Arbeiterpartei* (National Socialist German Workers' Party).
NZO	New Zionist Organisation – Revisionist international organisation.
POUM	*Partido Obrero de Unificación Marxista* (Workers' Party of Marxist Unity) – Spanish left-wing party.
PPS	*Polska Partja Socjalistyczna* (Polish Socialist Party).
SD	*Sicherheitsdienst* (Security Service of the SS).
SPD	*Sozialdemokratische Partei Deutschlands* (Social Democratic Party of Germany).
SS	*Schutzstaffel* (Protection Corps).
SWP	Socialist Workers Party – American Trotskyist party.
VnJ	*Verband nationaldeutscher Juden* (Union of National-German Jews) – pro-Nazi Jewish assimilationist movement.
WJC	World Jewish Congress.
WZO	World Zionist Organisation.
ZOA	Zionist Organisation of America – a right-wing Zionist movement.
ZVfD	*Zionistische Vereinigung für Deutschland* (Zionist Federation of Germany).

GLOSSARY OF JEWISH AND ZIONIST ORGANISATIONS

Agudas Yisrael   Union of Israel – an anti-Zionist Orthodox movement.

Alliance Israélite Universelle   French Jewish philanthropy.

American Jewish Committee   Right-wing assimilationist grouping.

American Jewish Congress   Zionist-dominated organisation identified with rabbi Stephen Wise.

American Jewish Joint Distribution Committee   Major bourgeois overseas charity.

Anglo-Palestine Bank   Zionist bank in Palestine.

Betar   Revisionist youth organisation. See Revisionists.

B'nai B'rith   Sons of the Covenant – conservative assimilationist fraternal order.

Board of Deputies of British Jews   Major Jewish organisation in Britain.

Brit HaBiryonim   Union of Terrorists – Revisionist Fascist organisation.

Brith HaChayal   Union of Soldiers.

Brith Hashomrim   Union of Watchmen – Revisionist organisation in Nazi Germany.

Bund   General Jewish Workers League – Yiddish socialist movement in Russia and Poland; anti-Zionist.

Central Bureau for the Settlement of German Jews   Headed by Chaim Weizmann, it organised German immigration to Palestine.

Centralverein   Central Union of German Citizens of the Jewish Faith – defence organisation of assimilationist bourgeoisie.

Comité des Délégations Juives   Committee of Jewish Delegations – post-First World War international Jewish defence organisation dominated by Zionists.

Emergency Committee for Zionist Affairs   Official voice of World Zionist Organisation in the United States during the Second World War.

Far Eastern Jewish Council   Organisation of Japanese collaborators.

General Zionists   Bourgeois Zionists divided into rival factions.

Gentile Friends of Zionism   Pro-Palestine Committee in Austria.

Ha'avara Ltd.   Trading company set up by World Zionist Organisation to trade with Nazi Germany.

Hadassah   Zionist women's organisation.

Haganah   Underground militia in Palestine, dominated by Labour Zionists.

Ha Note'a Ltd.   Citrus corporation in Palestine which entered into trade agreement with Nazi Germany.

HaPoel   The Worker – Labour Zionist sports movement.

Hashomer Hatzair   Young Watchmen – left Zionist youth movement.

HeChalutz   Pioneers – Labour Zionist youth movement.

Histadrut   General Federation of Jewish Labour in Palestine.

Hitachdut Olei Germania   German Immigrants' Association in Palestine.

International Trade and Investment Agency   British affiliate of Ha'avara Ltd.

Irgun Zvei Leumi   National Military Organisation – Revisionist underground.

Jabotinsky Institute   Revisionist research centre.

Jewish Agency for Palestine   Central office of World Zionist Organisation in Palestine; originally it nominally included non-Zionist sympathisers.

Jewish Colonial Trust   Zionist bank.

Jewish Fighting Organisation   One of two Jewish underground movements in the Warsaw ghetto, incorporating the left-Zionist youth groups, the Bund and the Communists.

Jewish Labor Committee   American organisation, dominated by Bundist sympathisers, anti-Zionist in 1930s.

Jewish Legion   Zionist military organisation in British Army during conquest of Palestine in the First World War.

Jewish National Fund   Zionist land fund.

Jewish Party (Romania)   Zionist party.

Jewish People's Committee (USA)   Communist front group.

Jewish People's Council   Community defence movement against Mosleyites in Britain.

Jewish Telegraphic Agency   Zionist news service.

Jewish War Veterans   Right-wing American ex-servicemen's organisation.

Joint Boycott Council of the American Jewish Congress and the Jewish Labor Committee   Anti-Nazi boycott organisation.

Judenrat   Jewish Council – Nazi puppet council in the ghettos.

Judenstaat Partei   Jewish State Party – Revisionist splinter group, post-1934, loyal to World Zionist Organisation.

Judische-nationale Partei   Jewish National Party – Austrian Zionist party.

Judischer Verlag   Jewish publishers – German Zionist publishing house.

Judische Volkspartei   Jewish People's Party – right-wing party in German Jewish communal politics, dominated by Zionists.

Keren Hayesod   Palestine Foundation Fund.

Labour Zionists   See *Poale Zion*.

Left *Poale Zion*   Labour Zionist splinter grouping with a strong Yiddishist orientation.

Leo Baeck Institute   German Jewish exile research organisation.

Lohamei Herut Yisrael   Fighters for the Freedom of Israel – Stern Gang-Revisionist splinter group.

Maccabi   Zionist sports organisation.

Minorities Bloc   Coalition of bourgeois nationalists in Poland set up by Polish Zionists.

Mizrachi   Religious Zionist party.

Mossad   Bureau in charge of illegal immigration for World Zionist Organisation.

Naftali Botwin Company   Yiddish-speaking unit with International Brigades in Spain.

Nationale Jugend Herzlia   Revisionist youth movement in Nazi Germany.

Near and Middle East Commercial Corporation (NEMICO)   Affiliated to Ha'avara Ltd.

New Zionist Organisation   Revisionist international organisation set up in 1935.

Non-Sectarian Anti-Nazi League   Anti-Nazi boycott organisation of the 1930s.

Ordener grupe   Defence groups of the Bund in Poland.

Organisation of Jewish Centre Party Voters   Grouping of Jewish capitalists who voted for Catholic Centre Party.

Palestine Labour Party   Labour Zionist party in Palestine; see *Poale Zion*.

Palestine Offices   Fourteen world-wide offices for immigration to Palestine.

Poale Zion   Workers of Zion – Labour Zionists.

Polish Zionist Organisation   Mainline Zionist federation.

Radical Zionists   Bourgeois Zionist faction, later merged with a faction of the General Zionists.

Reichstag Elections Committee   Short-lived Jewish bourgeois grouping for 1930 election.

Reichsverband judischer Kulturebunde   German Union of Jewish Culture Leagues — segregationist organisation established by Nazis.

Reichsvertretung der deutschen Juden   Reich Representation of Jews in Germany — united organisation of Jewish bourgeoisie under the Nazis.

Revisionists   Political party established by Vladimir Jabotinsky in 1925.

Staatszionistische Organisation   State Zionist Organisation — Revisionist movement in Nazi Germany, technically unaffiliated to world Revisionist movement.

Stern Gang   *Lohamei Herut Yisrael* — Fighters for the Freedom of Israel.

Swit   Dawn — Revisionist underground movement in Poland under the Nazis.

Tnuat HaHerut   Freedom Movement — Revisionist party in Israel, founded by Menachem Begin.

United Jewish Parties   Czechoslovakian Jewish electoral bloc including Zionists.

Vaad Hazalah   Jewish Agency's Rescue Committee during the Holocaust.

Vaad Leumi   National Council — semi-government of Zionist settlement under the British.

Working Group   Jewish rescue group in Slovakia.

World Jewish Congress   Pro-Zionist Jewish defence organisation established in 1936.

World Zionist Organisation   Central body of Zionist movement.

Yad Vashem Remembrance Authority   Israeli Holocaust Institute.

Židovska Strana   Jewish Party — Zionist party in Czechoslovakia.

Zion Mule Corp   Zionist unit with British Army in the First World War.

Zionist Organisation of America   Equivalent of General Zionists.

Zionistische Vereinigung für Deutschland   Zionist Federation of Germany.

ZIONISM IN THE AGE OF THE DICTATORS

1 ZIONISM AND ANTI-SEMITISM PRIOR TO THE HOLOCAUST

From the French Revolution to the unification of Germany and Italy it appeared that the future foretold the continuing emancipation of Jewry in the wake of the further development of capitalism and its liberal and modernist values. Even the Russian pogroms of the 1880s could be seen as the last gasp of a dying feudal past, rather than a harbinger of things to come. Yet by 1896, when Theodor Herzl published his *Jewish State*, such an optimistic scenario could no longer be realistically envisioned. In 1895 he personally had seen the Parisian mob howling for the death of Dreyfus. That same year he heard the wild cheers of middle-class Vienna as they greeted the anti-Semitic Karl Lueger after he had swept the election for *burgomeister*.

Born amidst a wave of defeats for the Jews, not only in backward Russia, but in the very centres of industrial Europe, modern Zionism's pretensions were the noblest conceivable: the redemption of the downtrodden Jewish people in their own land. But from the very beginning the movement represented the conviction of a portion of the Jewish middle class that the future belonged to the Jew-haters, that anti-Semitism was inevitable, and natural. Firmly convinced that anti-Semitism could not be beaten, the new World Zionist Organisation never fought it. Accommodation to anti-Semitism — and pragmatic utilisation of it for the purpose of obtaining a Jewish state — became the central stratagems of the movement, and it remained loyal to its earliest conceptions down to and through the Holocaust. In June 1895, in his very first entry in his new Zionist *Diary*, Herzl laid down this fixed axiom of Zionism:

> In Paris, as I have said, I achieved a freer attitude toward anti-Semitism, which I now began to understand historically and to pardon. Above all, I recognized the emptiness and futility of trying to 'combat' anti-Semitism.[1]

In the severest sense, Herzl was a man of his time and class; a monarchist who believed the best ruler *'un bon tyran'*.[2] His *Jewish State* baldly proclaimed: 'Nor are the present-day nations really fit for democracy, and I believe they will become ever less fit for it . . . I have no

1

faith in the political virtue of our people, because we are no better than the rest of modern man.'[3]

His universal pessimism caused him to misjudge totally the political environment of late-nineteenth-century Western Europe. In particular, Herzl misunderstood the Dreyfus case. The secrecy of the trial, and Dreyfus's soldierly insistence on his innocence, convinced many that an injustice was done. The case aroused a huge surge of Gentile support. Kings discussed it and feared for the sanity of France; Jews in remote hamlets in the Pripet Marches prayed for Emile Zola. The intellectuals of France rallied to Dreyfus's side. The socialist movement brought over the working people. The right wing of French society was discredited, the army stained, the Church disestablished. Anti-Semitism in France was driven into isolation lasting until Hitler's conquest. Yet Herzl, the most famous journalist in Vienna, did nothing to mobilise even one demonstration on behalf of Dreyfus. When he discussed the matter, it was always as a horrible example and never as a rallying cause. In 1899 the outcry compelled a retrial. A court martial affirmed the captain's guilt, 5 to 2, but found extenuating circumstances and reduced his sentence to ten years. But Herzl saw only defeat and depreciated the significance of the vast Gentile sympathy for the Jewish victim.

> If a dumb beast were tortured in public, would not the crowd send up a cry of indignation? This is the meaning of the pro-Dreyfus sentiment in non-French countries, if indeed it is as widespread as many Jews estimate . . . To put it in a nutshell, we might say that the injustice committed against Dreyfus is so great that we forget that we are dealing with a Jew . . . is anyone presumptuous enough to claim that of any seven people two, or even one, favor the Jews? . . . Dreyfus represents a bastion that has been and still is a point of struggle. Unless we are deceived, that bastion is lost![4]

The French government understood realities better than Herzl and acted to head off further agitation by reducing the balance of the sentence. Given the success of the struggle for Dreyfus, French Jewry — right and left — saw Zionism as irrelevant. Herzl savaged them in his *Diary*: 'They seek protection from the Socialists and the destroyers of the present civil order . . . Truly they are not Jews any more. To be sure, they are no Frenchmen either. They will probably become the leaders of European anarchism.'[5]

Herzl's first opportunity to develop his own pragmatic strategy of non-resistance to anti-Semitism, coupled with emigration of a portion of the Jews to a Jewish state-in-the-making, came with Karl Lueger's success in Vienna. The demagogue's victory there was the first major triumph of the new wave of specifically anti-Semitic parties in Europe, but the Habsburgs strenuously opposed the new mayor-elect. Some 8 per cent of their generals were Jews. Jews were conspicuous as regime loyalists amidst the sea of irredentist nationalities tearing the Austro-Hungarian Empire apart. Anti-Semitism could only cause problems for the already weak dynasty. Twice the Emperor refused to confirm Lueger in office. Herzl was one of the few Jews in Vienna who favoured confirmation. Rather than attempting to organise opposition to the Christian Social demagogue, he met the Prime Minister, Count Casimir Badeni, on 3 November 1895 and told him 'boldly' to accommodate Lueger:

> I think that Lueger's election as Mayor must be accepted. If you fail to do it the first time, then you will not be able to confirm on any subsequent occasion, and if you fail to accede the third time – the dragoons will have to ride. The Count smiled: 'So!' – with a *goguenard* [scoffing] expression.[6]

It was poverty in the Habsburgs' Galicia, as well as discrimination in Russia, that was driving Jews into Vienna and further into Western Europe and America. They brought anti-Semitism with them in their luggage. The new immigrants became a 'problem' to the rulers of the host societies, and to the already established local Jewries, who feared the rise of native anti-Semitism. Herzl had a ready-made answer to the immigrant wave that he thought would please both the upper class of the indigenous Jews and the ruling class of Western capitalism: he would oblige them by taking the poor Jews off their hands. He wrote to Badeni: 'What I propose is . . . not in any sense the emigration of all the Jews . . . Through the door which I am trying to push open for the poor masses of Jews a Christian statesman who rightly seizes the idea, will step forward into world-history.'[7]

His first efforts at diverting the wind of opposition to Jewish immigration into Zionism's sails utterly failed, but that did not prevent him from trying again. In 1902 the British Parliament debated an Aliens Exclusion Bill aimed at the migrants, and Herzl travelled to London to testify on the Bill. Rather than pass it, he argued, the British government should support Zionism. He met Lord Rothschild but, in spite of all his public talk about the rejuvenation of Jewry, he dispensed with such cant in private conversation, telling Rothschild that he 'would incidentally be one of those wicked persons to whom English Jews might well erect a monument because I saved them from an influx of East European Jews, and also perhaps from anti-Semitism'.[8]

In his autobiography, *Trial and Error*, written in 1949, Chaim Weizmann – then the first President of the new Israeli state – looked back at the controversy over the Aliens Bill. An immigrant to Britain himself, the brilliant young chemist was already, in 1902, one of the leading intellectuals of the new Zionist movement. He had met Sir William Evans Gordon, author of the anti-Jewish legislation; even with hindsight, with the Holocaust fresh in his mind, the then President of Israel still insisted that:

> our people were rather hard on him [Evans Gordon]. The Aliens Bill in England, and the movement which grew up around it were natural phenomena . . . Whenever the quantity of Jews in any country reaches the saturation point, that country reacts against them . . . The fact that the actual number of Jews in England, and even their proportion to the total population, was smaller than in other countries was irrelevant; the determining factor in this matter is not the solubility of the Jews, but the solvent power of the country . . . this cannot be looked upon as anti-Semitism in the ordinary or vulgar sense of that word; it is a universal social and economic concomitant of Jewish immigration, and we cannot shake it off . . . though my views on immigration naturally were in sharp conflict with his, we discussed these problems in a quite objective and even friendly way.[9]

For all his talk about sharp conflict with Evans Gordon, there is no sign that Weizmann ever tried to mobilise the public against him. What did Weizmann say to him in their 'friendly' discussion? Neither chose to tell us, but we can legitimately surmise: as with the master Herzl, so with his disciple Weizmann. We can reasonably conjecture that the avowed devotee of pragmatic accommodation asked the anti-Semite for his support of Zionism. Never once, then or in the future, did Weizmann ever try to rally the Jewish masses against anti-Semitism.

'Taking the Jews away from the Revolutionary Parties'

Herzl had originally hoped to convince the Sultan of Turkey to grant him Palestine as an autonomous statelet in return for the World Zionist Organisation (WZO) taking up the Turkish Empire's foreign debts. It soon became quite apparent that his hopes were unreal. Abdul Hamid knew well enough that autonomy always led to independence, and he was determined to hold on to the rest of his empire. The WZO had no army, it could never seize the country on its own. Its only chance lay in getting a European power to pressure the Sultan on Zionism's behalf. A Zionist colony would then be under the power's protection and the Zionists would be its agents within the decomposing Ottoman realm. For the rest of his life Herzl worked towards this goal, and he turned, first, to Germany. Of course, the Kaiser was far from a Nazi; he never dreamt of killing Jews, and he permitted them complete economic freedom, but nevertheless he froze them totally out of the officer corps and foreign office and there was severe discrimination throughout the civil service. By the end of the 1890s Kaiser Wilhelm became seriously concerned about the ever-growing socialist movement, and Zionism attracted him as he was convinced the Jews were behind his enemies. He naively believed that 'the Social Democratic elements will stream into Palestine'.[10] He gave Herzl an audience in Constantinople on 19 October 1898. At this meeting the Zionist leader asked for his personal intervention with the Sultan and the formation of a chartered company under German protection. A sphere of influence in Palestine had attractions enough, but Herzl had grasped that he had another bait that he could dangle before potential right-wing patrons: 'I explained that we were taking the Jews away from the revolutionary parties.'[11]

In spite of the Kaiser's deep interest in getting rid of the Jews, nothing could be done through Berlin. His diplomats always knew the Sultan would never agree to the scheme. In addition, the German Foreign Minister was not as foolish as his master. He knew Germany's Jews would never voluntarily leave their homeland.

Herzl looked elsewhere, even turning to the tsarist regime for support. In Russia Zionism had first been tolerated; emigration was what was wanted. For a time Sergei Zubatov, chief of the Moscow detective bureau, had developed a strategy of secretly dividing the Tsar's opponents. Because of their double oppression, the Jewish workers had produced Russia's first mass socialist organisation, the General Jewish Workers League, the *Bund*. Zubatov instructed his Jewish agents to mobilise groups of the new *Poale Zion* (Workers of Zion) to oppose the revolutionaries.[12] (Zionism is not a monolithic movement, and almost from the beginning the WZO has been divided into officially recognised factions. For a list of the Zionist and Jewish organisations found herein, see pp. ix–xii). But when elements within the Zionist ranks responded to the pressures of the repressive regime and the rising discontent, and began to concern themselves about Jewish rights in Russia, the Zionist bank – the Jewish Colonial Trust – was banned. This brought Herzl to St Petersburg for meetings with Count Sergei Witte, the Finance Minister, and Vyacheslav von Plevhe, the Minister of the Interior. It was von Plevhe who had organised the first pogrom in twenty years, at Kishenev in Bessarabia on Easter 1903. Forty-five people died and over a thousand were injured; Kishenev produced dread and rage among Jews.

Herzl's parley with the murderous von Plevhe was opposed even by most Zionists. He went to Petersburg to get the Colonial Trust re-opened, to ask that Jewish taxes be used to subsidise emigration and for intercession with the Turks. As a sweetener for his Jewish critics, he pleaded, not for the abolition of the Pale of Settlement, the western provinces where the Jews were confined, but for its enlargement 'to demonstrate clearly the humane character of these steps', he suggested.[13] 'This would,' he urged, 'put an end to certain agitation.'[14] Von Plevhe met him on 8 August and again on 13 August. The events are known from Herzl's *Diary*. Von Plevhe explained his concern about the new direction he saw Zionism taking:

> Lately the situation has grown even worse because the Jews have been joining the revolutionary parties. We used to be sympathetic to your Zionist movement, as long as it worked toward emigration. You do not have to justify the movement to me. *Vous prêchez à un converti* [You are preaching to a convert]. But ever since the Minsk conference we have noticed *un changement des gros bonnets* [a change of big-wigs]. There is less talk now of Palestinian Zionism than there is about culture, organisation and Jewish nationalism. This does not suit us.[15]

Herzl did get the Colonial Trust reopened and a letter of endorsement for Zionism from von Plevhe, but the support was given solely on the proviso that the movement confine itself to emigration and avoid taking up national rights inside Russia. In return Herzl sent von Plevhe a copy of a letter to Lord Rothschild suggesting that: 'It would substantially contribute to the further improvement of the situation if the pro-Jewish papers stopped using such an odious tone toward Russia. We ought to try to work toward that end in the near future.'[16]

Herzl then spoke publicly, in Russia, against attempts to organise socialist groupings within Russian Zionism:

> In Palestine ... our land, such a party would vitalise our political life — and then I shall determine my own attitude toward it. You do me an injustice if you say that I am opposed to progressive social ideas. But, now, in our present condition, it is too soon to deal with such matters. They are extraneous. Zionism demands complete, not partial involvement.[17]

Back in the West, Herzl went even further in his collaboration with tsarism. That summer, during the World Zionist Congress in Basle, he had a secret meeting with Chaim Zhitlovsky, then a leading figure in the Social Revolutionary Party. (World Zionist Congresses are held every two years, in odd years; the 1903 Congress was the sixth.) Later Zhitlovsky wrote of this extraordinary conversation. The Zionist told him that:

> I have just come from Plevhe. I have his positive, binding promise that in 15 years, at the maximum, he will effectuate for us a charter for Palestine. But this is tied to one condition: the Jewish revolutionaries shall cease their struggle against the Russian government. If in 15 years from the time of the agreement Plevhe does not effectuate the charter, they become free again to do what they consider necessary.[18]

Naturally Zhitlovsky scornfully rejected the proposition. The Jewish revolutionaries were not about to call off the struggle for elementary human rights in return for a vague promise of a Zionist state in the distant future. The Russian naturally had a few choice words to say about the founder of the WZO:

> [He] was, in general, too 'loyal' to the ruling authorities — as is proper for a diplomat who has to deal with the powers-that-be — for him ever to be interested in revolutionists and involve them in his calculations . . . He made the journey, of course, not in order to intercede for the people of Israel and to awaken compassion for us in Plevhe's heart. He traveled as a politician who does not concern himself with sentiments, but *interests* . . . Herzl's 'politics' is built on pure diplomacy, which seriously believes that the political history of humanity is made by a few people, a few leaders, and that

what they arrange among themselves becomes the content of political history.[19]

Was there any justification for Herzl's meetings with von Plevhe? There can be only one opinion. Even Weizmann was later to write that 'the step was not only humiliating, but utterly pointless . . . unreality could go no further'.[20] The Tsar had not the slightest influence with the Turks, who saw him as their enemy. At the same time, in 1903, Herzl accepted an even more surreal proposition from Britain for a Zionist colony in the Kenya Highlands as a substitute for Palestine. Russian Zionists began to object to these bizarre discussions, and they threatened to leave the WZO, if 'Uganda' was even considered. Herzl had a vision of himself as a Jewish Cecil Rhodes; it hardly mattered to him where his colony was to be situated, but to most Russian Zionists the movement was an extension of their biblical heritage and Africa meant nothing to them. A deranged Russian Zionist tried to assassinate Herzl's lieutenant, Max Nordau, and only Herzl's premature death prevented an internal collapse of the movement.

However, direct contacts with tsarism did not stop with Herzl. By 1908 the ranks were willing to allow Herzl's successor, David Wolffsohn, to meet the Prime Minister, Piotr Stolypin, and Foreign Minister Alexandr Izvolsky, over renewed harassment of the Colonial Trust bank. Izvolsky quickly came to terms on the minimal request and indeed had a friendly discussion with the WZO's leader: 'I might almost say that I made a Zionist of him,' wrote Wolffsohn triumphantly.[21] But, needless to say, Wolffsohn's visit led to no changes in Russia's anti-Jewish legislation.

The First World War

Zionism's egregious diplomatic record in the pre-war period did not stop the WZO from trying to take advantage of the débâcle of the First World War. Most Zionists were pro-German out of aversion to tsarism as the most anti-Semitic of the contending forces. The WZO's headquarters in Berlin tried to get Germany and Turkey to support Zionism in Palestine as a propaganda ploy to rally world Jewry to their side. Others saw that Turkey was weak and certain to be dismembered in the war. They argued that, if they backed the Allies, Zionism might be set up in Palestine as a reward. To these, it hardly mattered that the Jews of Russia, that is the majority of world Jewry, stood to gain nothing by the victory of their oppressor and his foreign allies. Weizmann, domiciled in London, sought to win over the British politicians. He had already made contact with Arthur Balfour, who, as Prime Minister, had spoken against Jewish immigration, in 1905. Weizmann knew the full extent of Balfour's anti-Semitism, as he had unburdened himself of his philosophy to the Zionist on 12 December 1914. In a private letter, Weizmann wrote: 'He told me how he had once had a long talk with Cosima Wagner at Bayreuth and that he shared many of her anti-Semitic postulates.'[22]

While Weizmann intrigued with the politicians in London, Vladimir Jabotinsky had obtained tsarist support for a volunteer Jewish Legion to help Britain take Palestine. There were thousands of young Jews in Britain, still Russian citizens, who were threatened with deportation to tsarist Russia by Herbert Samuel, the Jewish Home Secretary, if they did not 'volunteer' for the British Army. They were not intimidated; they would fight neither for the Tsar nor his ally, and the government backed down. The legion idea was a way out for the embarrassed Allies.

The Turks helped make the scheme into a reality by expelling all Russian Jews from Palestine as enemy aliens. They were also unwilling to fight directly for tsarism, but their Zionism led them to follow Jabotinsky's co-thinker Yosef Trumpeldor into a Zion Mule Corps with the British at Gallipoli. Later Jabotinsky proudly boasted of how the Mule Corps – and the aid of the anti-Semites in Petersburg – helped him to obtain his goal:

it was that 'donkey battalion' from Alexandria, ridiculed by all the wits in Israel, which opened before me the doors of the government offices of Whitehall. The Minister of Foreign Affairs in St Petersburg wrote about it to Count Benkendoff, the Russian Ambassador in London; the Russian Embassy forwarded reports on it to the British Foreign Office; the chief Counsellor of the Embassy, the late Constantine Nabokov, who afterward succeeded the Ambassador, arranged for me meetings with British ministers.[23]

The Balfour Declaration and the Fight against Bolshevism

The end of the war saw both Jewry and Zionism in a totally new world. The WZO's manoeuvres had finally paid off – for Zionism, but not for Jewry. The Balfour Declaration was the price that London was prepared to pay to have American Jewry use its influence to bring the United States into the war, and to keep Russian Jewry loyal to the Allies. But although the declaration gave Zionism the military and political backing of the British Empire, it had not the slightest effect on the course of events in the former Tsarist Empire, the heartland of Jewry. Bolshevism, an ideology principally opposed to Zionism, had seized power in Petersburg and was being challenged by White Guard tsarists and Ukrainian, Polish and Baltic forces financed by Britain, the United States, France and Japan. The counter-revolution consisted of many elements which had a long tradition of anti-Semitism and pogroms. This continued, and even developed further, during the civil war and at least 60,000 Jews were killed by the anti-Bolshevik forces. Although the Balfour Declaration gave Zionism the lukewarm support of the backers of the White Guardist pogromists, it did nothing to curb the pogroms. The declaration was, at best, a vague pledge to allow the WZO to try to build a national home in Palestine. The content of that commitment was as yet completely undefined. The WZO's leaders understood that the British government saw the crushing of the Bolsheviks as its top priority, and that they had to be on their best behaviour, not merely in terms of insignificant Palestine, but in their activities in the volatile East European arena.

Western historians call the Bolshevik revolution the Russian Revolution, but the Bolsheviks themselves regarded it as triggering a worldwide revolt. So also did the capitalists of Britain, France and America, who saw the Communist success galvanising the left wing of their own working classes. Like all social orders that cannot admit the fact that the masses have justification to revolt, they sought to explain the upheavals, to themselves as well as the people, in terms of a conspiracy – of the Jews. On 8 February 1920, Winston Churchill, then the Secretary for War, told readers of the *Illustrated Sunday Herald* about 'Trotsky . . . [and] . . . his schemes of a world-wide communistic state under Jewish domination'. However, Churchill had his chosen Jewish opponents of Bolshevism – the Zionists. He wrote hotly of 'the fury with which Trotsky has attacked the Zionists generally, and Dr Weizmann in particular'. 'Trotsky,' Churchill declared, was 'directly thwarted and hindered by this new ideal . . . The struggle which is now beginning between the Zionist and Bolshevik Jews is little less than a struggle for the soul of the Jewish people.'[24]

The British strategy of using both anti-Semites and Zionists against 'Trotsky' rested ultimately on Zionism's willingness to co-operate with Britain in spite of the British involvement with the White Russian pogromists. The WZO did not want pogroms in Eastern Europe, but it did nothing to mobilise world Jewry on behalf of the Jews beleaguered there. Weizmann's statements at the time, as well as his memoirs, tell us how they saw the situation. He appeared at the Versailles Conference on 23 February 1919. Once again he enunciated the traditional line on Jewry shared by both anti-Semites and Zionists. It was not the Jews who really had problems, it was the Jews who were the problem:

> Jewry and Judaism were in a frightfully weakened condition, pre-senting, to themselves and to the nations, a problem very difficult of solution. There was, I said, no hope at all of such a solution — since the Jewish problem revolved fundamentally round the home-lessness of the Jewish people — without the creation of a National Home.[25]

The Jews, of course, presented no real problem — neither to the nations nor to 'themselves' — but Weizmann had a solution to the non-existent 'problem'. Once again Zionism offered itself to the assembled capitalist powers as an anti-revolutionary movement. Zionism would 'transform Jewish energy into a constructive force instead of its being dissipated in destructive tendencies'.[26] Even in his later years Weizmann could still only see the Jewish tragedy during the Russian Revolution through the Zionist end of the telescope:

> Between the Balfour Declaration and the accession of the Bolsheviks to power, Russian Jewry had subscribed the then enormous sum of 30 million rubles for an agricultural bank in Palestine; but this, with much else, had now to be written off . . . Polish Jewry . . . was still suffering so much in the separate Russo-Polish War, that it was incapable of making any appreciable contribution to the tasks which lay ahead of us.[27]

Weizmann saw Zionism as weak in all respects with only a toe-hold in Palestine. Eastern Europe was 'a tragedy which the Zionist move-ment was at the moment powerless to relieve'.[28] Others were not so torpid. The British trade unions organised an embargo of arms ship-ments to the Whites. French Communists staged a mutiny in the French Black Sea fleet. And, of course, it was the Red Army that tried to protect the Jews against their White murderers. But the WZO never used its influence, either in the Anglo-Jewish community or in the seats of power, to back up the militant unionists. Weizmann completely shared the anti-Communist mentality of his British patrons. He never changed his opinion on the period. Even in *Trial and Error*, he still sounded like a high Tory writing of 'a time when the horrors of the Bolshevik revolution were fresh in *everyone's* mind' (my emphasis).[29]

The Minority Treaties at the Versailles Peace Conference

Russia was out of control, but the Allies and their local clients still dominated the rest of Eastern Europe; now that the WZO had been converted by the Balfour Declaration into an official Voice of Israel, it could no longer remain taciturn about the fate of the huge Jewish communities there. It had to act as their spokesman. What it wanted was for the Jews to be recognised as a nation with autonomy for its separate schools and language institutions, as well as for the Jewish sabbath to be recognised as their day of rest. Since reliance on imperialism was the backbone of Zionist strategy, the *Comité des Délégations Juives* – essentially the WZO in tandem with the American Jewish Committee – presented a memorandum on national autonomy to the Versailles Conference. All the new successor states to the fallen empires, but neither Germany nor Russia, were to be compelled to sign minority-rights treaties as a precondition of diplomatic recognition. At first the idea was taken up by the Allies, who realised that minority rights were essential if the tangled national chauvinists of Eastern Europe were not to tear each other to pieces and pave the way for a Bolshevik take-over. One by one the Poles, the Hungarians and the Romanians signed, but their signatures were meaningless. The rapidly growing Christian middle classes in these countries saw the Jews as their entrenched competitors and were determined to dislodge them. The Pole who signed their treaty was the country's most notorious anti-Semite, the Hungarians declared their treaty day a day of national mourning and the Romanians refused to sign until the clauses guaranteeing sabbath rights and Jewish schools were deleted from their treaty.

There never was the slightest chance of success for the utopian plan. Balfour soon realised what problems the treaties would create for the Allies in Eastern Europe. On 22 October, he told the League of Nations that the accusing states would be assuming a thankless duty if they attempted to enforce the treaty obligations. He then argued that since the treaties preceded the League, it should not obligate itself to enforce them.[30] The assembled lawyers then accepted legal responsibility for the treaties, but provided no enforcement machinery.

Jews could not be bothered to use the meaningless treaties. Only three collective petitions were ever sent in. In the 1920s Hungary was found to have a *numerus clausus* in its universities. In 1933 the still-weak Hitler felt compelled to honour the German–Polish Minority Convention, which was the only such treaty applicable to Germany, and 10,000 Jews in Upper Silesia retained all civil rights until treaty term in July 1937.[31] Romania was found guilty of revoking Jewish citizen rights in 1937. Such petty legalistic victories changed nothing in the long run.

The only way the Jews could have had any success in fighting for their rights in Eastern Europe was in alliance with the working-class movements which, in all these countries, saw anti-Semitism for what it was: an ideological razor in the hands of their own capitalist enemies. But although social revolution meant equality for the Jews as Jews, it also meant the expropriation of the Jewish middle class as capitalists. That was unaccceptable to the local affiliates of the WZO, who were largely middle class in composition with virtually no working-class following. The world Zionist movement, always concerned for British ruling-class opinion, never pushed its local groupings in the direction of the left, although the radicals were the only mass force on the ground that was prepared to defend the Jews. Instead, the WZO leaders concluded that they lacked the strength to struggle simultaneously for Jewish rights in the Diaspora and build the new Zion, and by the 1920s they abandoned all pretence of action on behalf of Diaspora Jewry *in situ*, leaving their local affiliates − and the Jewish communities in these countries − to fend for themselves.

The Zionist Alliance with Anti-Semitism in Eastern Europe

Most of the Jews in Eastern Europe did not see the Bolsheviks as the ogres that Churchill and Weizmann believed them to be. Under Lenin the Bolsheviks not only gave the Jews complete equality, but they even set up schools and, ultimately, courts in Yiddish; however, they were absolutely opposed to Zionism and all ideological nationalism. The Bolsheviks taught that the revolution required the unity of the workers of all nations against the capitalists. The nationalists separated 'their' workers from their class fellows. Bolshevism specifically opposed Zionism as pro-British and as fundamentally anti-Arab. The local Zionist leadership was therefore forced to turn to the nationalists as possible allies. In the Ukraine that meant Simon Petliura's *Rada*

(Council), which, like the Zionists, recruited on strictly ethnic lines: no Russians, no Poles and no Jews.

Ukrainia

The Rada was based on village schoolteachers and other language enthusiasts, steeped in the 'glorious' history of the Ukraine – that is Bogdan Zinovy Chmielnicki's seventeenth-century Cossack revolt against Poland, during which the enraged peasantry massacred 100,000 Jews whom they saw as middlemen working for the Polish *Pans* (nobles). Nationalist ideology reinforced the 'Christ-killer' venom which was poured into the illiterate rural masses by the old regime. Anti-Semitic outbreaks were inevitable in such an ideological climate, but the Zionists were taken in by promises of national autonomy, and rushed into the Rada. In January 1919 Abraham Revusky of the Poale Zion took office as Petliura's Minister for Jewish Affairs.[32] Meir Grossmann of the Ukrainian Zionist Executive went abroad to rally Jewish support for the anti-Bolshevik regime.[33]

The inevitable pogroms started with the first Ukrainian defeat at the hands of the Red Army in January 1919, and Revusky was compelled to resign within a month when Petliura did nothing to stop the atrocities. In many respects the Petliura episode destroyed the mass base of Zionism amongst Soviet Jews. Churchill lost his gamble: Trotsky, not Weizmann and not Revusky, was to win the soul of the Jewish masses.

Lithuania

Lithuanian Zionist involvement with the anti-Semites was likewise a failure, although, fortunately, Lithuania did not generate significant pogroms. The nationalists there were in an extremely weak position. Not only did they face a threat from Communism, they also had to struggle against Poland in a dispute over the territory around Vilna. They felt compelled to work with the Zionists, as they needed the support of the considerable Jewish minority in Vilna, and they also overestimated Zionist influence with the Allied powers whose diplomatic assent was a requirement if they were ever to gain the city. In December 1918 three Zionists entered the provisional government of Antanas Smetona and Augustinas Voldemaras. Jacob Wigodski became Minister for Jewish Affairs, N. Rachmilovitch became Vice-Minister for Trade and Shimshon Rosenbaum was appointed Vice-Minister for Foreign Affairs.

The bait again was autonomy. Jews would be given proportional representation in government, full rights for Yiddish, and a Jewish

National Council would be given the right of compulsory taxation of all Jews for religious and cultural affairs. Non-payment of tax would only be allowed for converts. Max Soloveitchik, who succeeded Wigodski at the Jewish Ministry, enthused that 'Lithuania is the creative source of the future forms of Jewish living'.[34]

By April 1922 the Lithuanian government felt it could begin to move against the Jews. The Vilna Corridor was definitely lost to Poland and the Polish Army stood between Communism and the Lithuanian border. Smetona's first move was to refuse to guarantee the institutions of autonomy in the constitution. Soloveitchik resigned in protest, and went to join the WZO Executive in London. The local Zionists tried to deal with the problem by forming an electoral bloc with the Polish, German and Russian minorities. This little extra muscle made the government slow its pace, and Rosenbaum was given the Jewish Ministry by Ernestas Galvanauskas, the new Prime Minister. By 1923 the onslaught began again with parliamentary speeches in Yiddish being forbidden. By June 1924 the Jewish Ministry was abolished; by July Yiddish store signs were outlawed; in September the police scattered the National Council, and Rosenbaum and Rachmilovitch moved to Palestine. By 1926 Smetona had set up a semi-Fascist regime which lasted until the Second World War take-over by Stalin. In later days Voldemaras and Galvanauskas openly assumed the role of Nazi agents in Lithuanian politics.

Zionist Accommodation with Anti-Semitism

The essentials of Zionist doctrine on anti-Semitism were laid down well before the Holocaust: anti-Semitism was inevitable and could not be fought; the solution was the emigration of unwanted Jews to a Jewish state-in-the-making. The inability of the Zionist movement to take Palestine militarily compelled it to look for imperial patronage, which it expected to be motivated by anti-Semitism to some degree. Zionists additionally saw revolutionary Marxism as an assimilationist enemy which persuaded them to ally against it with their fellow separatists of the anti-Semitic right-wing nationalist movements in Eastern Europe.

Herzl and his successors were proven correct. It was an anti-Semite, Balfour, who enabled Zionism to entrench itself in Palestine. Although Israel was ultimately established through armed revolt against Britain, if it had not been for the presence of the British Army during the early years of the Mandate, the Palestinians would not have had the slightest problem pushing Zionism out.

But we are victims here of a sleight-of-hand trick. Balfour did give Zionism its toe-hold in Palestine, but did the British Mandate protect the Jews against their enemies in Europe?

Anti-Semitism could always be fought. It was not only fought, it was defeated in France, Russia and the Ukraine without any help from the World Zionist Organisation. Had the people of those countries followed the dictates of the Zionists, the anti-Semites would never have been defeated.

The policies of the early WZO were continued, in all essentials, by Chaim Weizmann, the main leader of the organisation during the Hitler epoch. Those elements in the WZO who wanted to make a stand against Nazism in the 1930s always found their main internal enemy in the President of their own movement. Nahum Goldmann, himself to become a post-Holocaust President of the WZO, later described in a speech the fierce arguments on the subject between Weizmann and rabbi Stephen Wise, a leading figure in American Zionism:

> I remember very violent discussions between him and Weizmann, who was a very great leader in his own right, but who rejected every interest in other things. He did take an interest in saving German Jews in the period of the first years of Nazism but World Jewish Congress, fight for Jewish rights, not that he denied their need, but he could not spare the time from his Zionist work. Stephen Wise argued with him 'but it is part and parcel of the same problem. If you lose the Jewish Diaspora you will not have a Palestine and you can only deal with the totality of Jewish life.'[35]

Such was Zionism, and such its leading figure, when Adolf Hitler strode on to the stage of history.

Notes

1. Marvin Lowenthal (ed.), *The Diaries of Theodor Herzl*, p. 6.
2. Desmond Stewart, *Theodor Herzl*, p. 141.
3. Ludwig Lewisohn (ed.), *Theodor Herzl: A Portrait*, pp. 293–4.
4. Ibid., pp. 219–20.
5. Raphael Patai (ed.), *The Complete Diaries of Theodor Herzl*, vol. II, pp. 672–3.
6. Lowenthal, *Diaries of Theodor Herzl*, p. 71.
7. Ibid., p. 100.
8. Ibid., p. 366.

9. Chaim Weizmann, *Trial and Error*, pp. 90–1.

10. David Yisraeli, 'Germany and Zionism', *Germany and the Middle East, 1835-1939* (Tel Aviv University, 1975), p. 142.

11. Patai, *Complete Diaries of Theodor Herzl*, vol. III, p. 729.

12. George Gapon, *The Story of My Life*, p. 94.

13. Patai, *Complete Diaries of Theodor Herzl*, vol. IV, p. 1521.

14. Ibid.

15. Ibid., p. 1525.

16. Ibid., p. 1538.

17. Amos Elon, *Herzl*, pp. 381–2.

18. Samuel Portnoy (ed.), *Vladimir Medem – The Life and Soul of a Legendary Jewish Socialist*, pp. 295–8.

19. Ibid.

20. Weizmann, *Trial and Error*, p. 82.

21. Emil Cohen, *David Wolffsohn*, p. 196.

22. Meyer Weisgal (ed.), *The Letters and Papers of Chaim Weizmann, Letters*, vol. VII, p. 81. After the Holocaust Weizmann could not reveal the anti-Semitism of Zionism's great patron. He changed the record in *Trial and Error*: 'Mr Balfour mentioned that, two years before, he had been in Bayreuth, and that he had talked with Frau Cosima Wagner, the widow of the composer, who had raised the subject of the Jews. I interrupted Mr Balfour . . .' (p. 153).

23. Vladimir Jabotinsky, *The Story of the Jewish Legion*, p. 74.

24. Winston Churchill, 'Zionism versus Bolshevism', *Illustrated Sunday Herald* (8 February 1920), p. 5.

25. Weizmann, *Trial and Error*, p. 243.

26. Leonard Stein, *The Balfour Declaration*, p. 348.

27. Weizmann, *Trial and Error*, pp. 240–1.

28. Ibid., p. 242.

29. Ibid., p. 218.

30. Jacob Robinson *et al.*, *Were the Minority Treaties a Failure?*, pp. 79–80.

31. Jacob Robinson, *And the Crooked shall be made Straight*, p. 72.

32. 'Abraham Revusky', *Encyclopedia Judaica*, vol. 14, col. 134.

33. 'Meir Grossmann', *Encyclopedia Judaica*, vol. 7, col. 938.

34. Samuel Gringauz, 'Jewish National Autonomy in Lithuania (1918-1925)', *Jewish Social Studies* (July 1952), p. 237.

35. Nahum Goldmann, 'Dr Stephen S. Wise', *A Galaxy of American Zionist Rishonim*, pp. 17–18.

2   *BLUT UND BODEN* (BLOOD AND SOIL): THE ROOTS OF ZIONIST RACISM

It was anti-Semitism — alone — that generated Zionism. Herzl could not ground his movement in anything positively Jewish. Although he sought the support of the rabbis, he personally was not devout. He had no special concern for Palestine, the ancient homeland; he was quite eager to accept the Kenya Highlands, at least on a temporary basis. He had no interest in Hebrew; he saw his Jewish state as a linguistic Switzerland. He had to think of race, for it was in the air; the Teutonic anti-Semites were talking of the Jews as a race, but he soon discarded the doctrine, and gave a paradoxical discussion with Israel Zangwill, one of his earliest adherents, as the instance for his rejection. He portrayed the Anglo-Jewish writer as:

> of the long-nosed Negro type, with wooly deep-black hair . . . He maintains, however, the racial point of view — something I can't accept, for I have merely to look at him and at myself. All I say is: we are an historical unit, one nation with anthropological diversities.[1]

Unconcerned with religion, he even proposed that an atheist, the then world-famous author, Max Nordau, should succeed him as the WZO's President. Again, the disciple was less liberal than the master. Nordau was married to a Christian, and was afraid that his wife would be resented by the Orthodox among the ranks.[2] He was already married when he converted to Zionism and, despite his own Gentile wife, he soon became a confirmed Jewish racist. On 21 December 1903 he gave an interview to Eduard Drumont's rabid anti-Semitic newspaper, *La Libre Parole*, in which he said that Zionism was 'not a question of religion, but exclusively of race, and there is no one with whom I am in greater agreement on this point than M. Drumont'.[3]

Although only one national branch of the WZO (the Dutch Federation in 1913) ever went to the trouble of trying formally to exclude Jews living in mixed marriages, cosmopolitan Zionism died an early death with Herzl in 1904.[4] The WZO as such never had to take a position against mixed marriage; those who believed in it rarely thought to join the obviously unsympathetic Zionists. The movement in Eastern

Europe, its mass base, shared the spontaneous folk-religious prejudices of the Orthodox communities around them. Although the ancient Jews had seen proselytising and marriages to Gentiles as adding to their strength, latter pressure from the Catholic Church caused the rabbis to begin to see converts as a 'troublesome itch' and they abandoned proselytising. With the centuries, self-segregation became the hallmark of the Jews. In time the masses came to see mixed marriage as treason to Orthodoxy. Although in the West some Jews modified the religion and formed 'Reform' sects and others abandoned the God of their forefathers, the traffic was essentially away from Judaism. Few joined the Jewish world either by conversion or marriage. If Western Zionism developed in a more secular atmosphere than that of Eastern Europe, the bulk of its members still saw mixed marriage as leading Jews away from the community rather than bringing new additions to it.

The German university graduates, who took over the Zionist movement after Herzl's death, developed the modernist–racist ideology of Jewish separatism. They had been powerfully influenced by their pan-Germanic fellow students of the *wandervogel* (wandering birds or free spirits) who dominated the German campuses before 1914. These chauvinists rejected the Jews as not being of Germanic *blut*; therefore they could never be part of the German *volk* and were thoroughly alien to the Teutonic *boden* or soil. All Jewish students were compelled to grapple with these concepts which surrounded them. A few moved left and joined the Social Democrats. To them this was just more bourgeois nationalism and was to be fought as such. Most remained conventionally *Kaiser-treu*, stout nationalists who insisted that a thousand years on the German *boden* had made them into 'Germans of the Mosaic persuasion'. But a portion of the Jewish students adopted the *wandervogel* ideology whole and simply translated it into Zionist terminology. They agreed with the anti-Semites on several key points: the Jews were not part of the German *volk* and, of course, Jews and Germans should not mix sexually, not for the traditional religious reasons, but for the sake of their own unique *blut*. Not being of Teutonic *blut*, they perforce had to have their own *boden*: Palestine.

At first glance it would appear strange that middle-class Jewish students should be so influenced by anti-Semitic thought, especially as at the same time, socialism, with its assimilationist attitudes towards the Jews, was gaining considerable support in the society around them. However, socialism appealed primarily to the workers, not to the middle class. In their environment chauvinism predominated; although intellectually they repudiated their connection with the German people, in fact they never emancipated themselves from the German capitalist class, and throughout the First World War the German Zionists passionately supported their own government. For all their grandiose intellectual pretensions, their *voelkisch* Zionism was simply an imitation of German nationalist ideology. Thus the young philosopher Martin Buber was able to combine Zionism with ardent German patriotism during the First World War. In his book *Drei Reden uber das Judentum*, published in 1911, Buber spoke of a youth who:

> senses in this immortality of the generations a community of blood, which he feels to be the antecedents of his I, its perseverance in the infinite past. To that is added the discovery, promoted by this awareness, that blood is a deep rooted nurturing force within individual man; that the deepest layers of our being are determined by blood; that our innermost thinking and our will are colored by it. Now he finds that the world around him is the world of imprints and influences, whereas blood is the realm of a substance capable of being imprinted and influenced, a substance absorbing and assimilating all into its own form . . . Whoever, faced with the choice between environment and substance, decides for substance will henceforth have to be a Jew truly from within, to live as a Jew with all the contradiction, all the tragedy, and all the future promise of his blood.[5]

The Jews had been in Europe for milleniums, far longer than, say, the Magyars. No one would dream of referring to the Hungarians as Asiatics, yet, to Buber, the Jews of Europe were still Asians and presumably always would be. You could get the Jew out of Palestine, but you could never get Palestine out of the Jew. In 1916 he wrote that the Jew:

> was driven out of his land and dispersed throughout the lands of the Occident . . . yet, despite all this, he has remained an Oriental . . . One can detect all this in the most assimilated Jew, if one knows how to gain access to his soul . . . the immortal Jewish unitary drive — this will come into being only after the continuity of life in Palestine . . . Once it comes into contact with its maternal soil, it will once more become creative.[6]

However, Buber's *voelkisch* Zionism, with its assorted strands of mystical enthusiasm, was too spiritual to appeal to a wide following. What was needed was a popular Zionist version of the social-Darwinism which had swept the bourgeois intellectual world in the wake of Europe's imperial conquests in Africa and the East. The Zionist version of this notion was developed by the Austrian anthropologist Ignatz Zollschan. To him the secret value of Judaism was that it had, albeit inadvertently, worked to produce a wonder of wonders:

> a nation of pure blood, not tainted by diseases of excess or immorality, of a highly developed sense of family purity, and of deeply rooted virtuous habits would develop an exceptional intellectual activity. Furthermore, the prohibition against mixed marriage provided that these highest ethnical treasures should not be lost, through the admixture of less carefully bred races . . . there resulted that natural selection which has no parallel in the history of the human race . . . If a race that is so highly gifted were to have the opportunity of again developing its original power, nothing could equal it as far as cultural value is concerned.[7]

Even Albert Einstein subscribed to the Zionist race conceptions and in so doing he reinforced racism, lending it the prestige of his reputation. His own contributions to the discussion sound suitably profound, but they are based on the same nonsense.

> Nations with a racial difference appear to have instincts which work against their fusion. The assimilation of the Jews to the European nations . . . could not eradicate the feeling of lack of kinship between them and those among whom they lived. In the last resort, the instinctive feeling of lack of kinship is referable to the law of the conservation of energy. For this reason it cannot be eradicated by any amount of well meant pressure.[8]

Buber, Zollschan and Einstein were but three among the classic Zionists who pontificated learnedly on race purity. But for sheer fanaticism few could match the American Maurice Samuel. A well-known writer in his day − later, in the 1940s, he was to work with Weizmann on the latter's autobiography − Samuel addressed the American public in 1927 in his *I, the Jew*. He denounced with horror a town which he readily conceded that he only knew by repute − and that the evidence would make us think was the free-living artists' colony at Taos, New Mexico:

> there came together into this small place, representatives of the
> African Negro, the American and Chinese Mongol, the Semite and
> the Aryan . . . free intermarriage had set in . . . Why does this pic-
> ture, part actual, part fanciful, fill me with a strange loathing,
> suggest the obscene, the obscurely beastly? . . . Why then does that
> village which my fancy conjures up call to mind a heap of reptiles
> breeding uglily in a bucket?[9]

'To be a Good Zionist one must be Somewhat of an Anti-Semite'

Although *blut* was a recurrent theme in pre-Holocaust Zionist literature, it was not as central to its message as *boden*. As long as America's
shores remained open, Europe's Jews asked: if anti-Semitism could not
be fought on its home ground, why should they not just follow the
crowd to America? The Zionist response was double-barrelled: anti-
Semitism would accompany the Jews wherever they went and, what
was more, it was the Jews who had created anti-Semitism by their own
characteristics. The root cause of anti-Semitism, Zionists insisted, was
the Jews' exile existence. Jews lived parasitically off their 'hosts'. There
were virtually no Jewish peasants in the Diaspora. The Jews lived in
cities, they were alienated from manual labour or, more bluntly, they
shunned it and preoccupied themselves with intellectual or commercial
concerns. At best, their claims of patriotism were hollow as they
wandered eternally from country to country. And when they fancied
themselves as socialists and internationalists, in reality they were still
no more than the middlemen of the revolution, fighting 'other people's
battles'. These tenets combined were known as *shelilat ha'galut* (the
Negation of the Diaspora), and were held by the entire spectrum of
Zionists who varied only on matters of detail. They were argued
vigorously in the Zionist press, where the distinctive quality of many
articles was their hostility to the entire Jewish people. Anyone reading
these pieces without knowing their source would have automatically
assumed that they came from the anti-Semitic press. The *Weltanschauung* of the youth organisation *Hashomer Hatzair* (Young Watchmen), originally composed in 1917, but republished again as late as
1936, was typical of these effusions:

> The Jew is a caricature of a normal, natural human being, both

physically and spiritually. As an individual in society he revolts
and throws off the harness of social obligations, knows no order
nor discipline.[10]

Similarly, in 1935 an American, Ben Frommer, a writer for the ultra-
right Zionist–Revisionists, could declare of no less than 16 million of
his fellow Jews that:

> The fact is undeniable that the Jews collectively are unhealthy and
> neurotic. Those professional Jews who, wounded to the quick,
> indignantly deny this truth are the greatest enemies of their race,
> for they thereby lead them to search for false solutions, or at most
> palliatives.[11]

This style of Jewish self-hatred permeated a great deal of Zionist
writing. In 1934 Yehezkel Kaufman, then famous as a scholar of
biblical history at Jerusalem's Hebrew University and himself a Zionist,
though an opponent of the bizarre theory of the Negation of the
Diaspora, aroused furious controversy by culling the Hebrew literature
for yet worse examples. In Hebrew the ranters could really attack their
fellow Jews without fear of being accused of providing ammunition
for the Jew-haters. Kaufman's *Hurban Hanefesh* (Holocaust of the
Soul) cited three of the classic Zionist thinkers. For Micah Yosef
Berdichevsky the Jews were 'not a nation, not a people, not human'.
To Yosef Chaim Brenner they were nothing more than 'Gypsies, filthy
dogs, inhuman, wounded, dogs'. To A.D. Gordon his people were no
better than 'parasites, people fundamentally useless.'[12]

Naturally Maurice Samuel had to apply his fine hand to concocting
libels against his fellow Jews. In 1924, in his work *You Gentiles*, he
fabricated a Jewry driven by its own sinister demiurge to oppose the
Christian social order:

> We Jews, we the destroyers, will remain the destroyers forever.
> NOTHING that you will do will meet our needs and demands. We will
> forever destroy because we need a world of our own, a God-world,
> which is not your nature to build . . . those of us who fail to under-
> stand that truth will always be found in alliance with your rebellious
> factions, until disillusionment comes, the wretched fate which scat-
> tered us through your midst has thrust this unwelcome role upon
> us.[13]

Labour Zionism produced its own unique brand of Jewish self-hatred. In spite of its name and pretensions, Labour Zionism was never able to win over any significant section of the Jewish working class in any country cf the Diaspora. Its members had a self-defeating argument: they claimed that the Jewish workers were in 'marginal' industries, such as the needle trades, which were unessential to the economy of the 'host' nations, and therefore the Jewish workers would always be marginal to the working-class movement in the countries of their abode. Jewish workers, it was claimed, could only wage a 'healthy' class struggle in their own land. Naturally poor Jews showed little interest in a so-called labour movement that did not tell them to put their all into fighting in the immediate present for better conditions, but rather to concern themselves about far-off Palestine. Paradoxically, Labour Zionism's primary appeal was to those young middle-class Jews who sought to break with their class origins, but were not prepared to go over to the workers of the country of their habitation. Labour Zionism became a kind of counter-culture sect, denouncing Jewish Marxists for their internationalism, and the Jewish middle class as parasitic exploiters of the 'host' nations. In effect they translated traditional anti-Semitism into Yiddish: the Jews were in the wrong countries in the wrong occupations and had the wrong politics. It took the Holocaust to bring these Jeremiahs to their senses. Only then did they appreciate the common voice in their own message and the Nazis' anti-Jewish propaganda. In March 1942 Chaim Greenberg, then the editor of New York's Labour Zionist organ, *Jewish Frontier*, painfully admitted that, indeed, there had been:

> a time when it used to be fashionable for Zionist speakers (including the writer) to declare from the platform that 'To be a good Zionist one must be somewhat of an anti-Semite' . . . To this day Labor Zionist circles are under the influence of the idea that the Return to Zion involved a process of purification from our economic uncleanliness. Whosoever doesn't engage in so-called 'productive' manual labor is believed to be a sinner against Israel and against mankind.[14]

'Grist to the Mills of Nazi Propaganda'

If, without further facts, anyone were told that the early Zionists were racists, it would be automatic to assume this to be a part of the colonialist aspects of Zionism in Palestine. In reality this is not so;

blut Zionism would have evolved even if Palestine were to have been completely empty. Enthusiasm for *blut und boden* were part of Zionism before the first modern Zionist ever left Europe.

Race Zionism was a curious offshoot of racial anti-Semitism. True, these Zionists argued, the Jews were a pure race, certainly purer than, say, the Germans who, as even the pan-Germanics conceded, had a huge admixture of Slavic blood. But to these Zionists, even their racial purity could not overcome the one flaw in Jewish existence: they did not have their own Jewish *boden*. If the Teutonic racists could see themselves as *ubermenchen* (supermen), these Hebrew racists did not see the Jews in that light; rather, it was the reverse. They believed that because they lacked their own *boden* the Jews were *untermenchen* and therefore, for their 'hosts', little more than leeches: the world pest.

If one believes in the validity of racial exclusiveness, it is difficult to object to anyone else's racism. If one believes further that it is impossible for any people to be healthy except in their own homeland, then one cannot object to anyone else excluding 'aliens' from their territory. In fact the average Zionist never thought of himself as leaving civilised Europe for the wilds of Palestine. In life it is obvious that Zionist *blut und boden* provided an excellent rationale for not fighting anti-Semitism on its home ground. It was not the fault of the anti-Semites, it was because of the Jews' own misfortune of being in exile. The Zionists could tearfully argue that the loss of Palestine was the root cause of anti-Semitism and the regaining of Palestine was the only solution to the Jewish question. Everything else could only be palliative or futile.

Walter Laqueur, the doyen of Zionist historians, has asked in his book, *A History of Zionism*, if Zionist insistence on the naturalness of anti-Semitism was not just 'grist to the mill of Nazi propaganda'.[15] It certainly was. Laqueur's question can best be answered with another question: is it difficult to understand the gullible reader of a Nazi newspaper, who concluded that what was said by the Nazis, and agreed to by the Zionists — Jews — had to be right?

There would be worse: any Jewish movement that prattled on about the naturalness of anti-Semitism would, just as 'naturally', seek to come to terms with the Nazis when they came to power.

Notes

1. Marvin Lowenthal (ed.), *The Diaries of Theodor Herzl*, p. 78.

2. Amos Elon, *Herzl*, p. 255.

3. Desmond Stewart, *Theodor Herzl*, p. 322.

4. The WZO is structured by national states, and elections are held on a national basis for the World Zionist Congress; the various ideological tendencies, which are world-wide in their structure, run in the various national elections for delegates.

5. Martin Buber, *On Judaism*, pp. 15–19.

6. Ibid., pp. 75–7.

7. Ignatz Zollschan, *Jewish Questions* (1914), pp. 17–18.

8. Solomon Goldman, *Crisis and Decision* (1938), p. 116.

9. Maurice Samuel, *I, the Jew*, pp. 244–6.

10. 'Our Shomer "Weltanschauung",' *Hashomer Hatzair* (December 1936), p. 26.

11. Ben Frommer, 'The Significance of a Jewish State', *Jewish Call* (Shanghai, May 1935), p. 10.

12. Yehezkel Kaufman, 'Hurban Hanefesh: A Discussion of Zionism and Anti-Semitism', *Issues* (Winter 1967), p. 106.

13. Maurice Samuel, *You Gentiles*, p. 155.

14. Chaim Greenberg, 'The Myth of Jewish Parasitism', *Jewish Frontiers* (March 1942), p. 20.

15. Walter Laqueur, *A History of Zionism*, p. 500.

GERMAN ZIONISM AND THE COLLAPSE OF THE
WEIMAR REPUBLIC

German Jewry was deeply loyal to the Weimar Republic which had put
an end to the discriminations of the Wilhelmine era. Germany's Jews,
(0.9 per cent of the population) were generally prosperous: 60 per cent
were businessmen or professionals; the rest artisans, clerks, students,
with only insubstantial numbers of industrial workers. Most were for
liberal capitalism, with 64 per cent voting for the *Deutsche Demo-
kratische Partei* (DDP). About 28 per cent voted for the moderate
Sozialdemokratische Partei Deutschlands (SPD). Only 4 per cent voted
for the *Kommunistische Partei Deutschlands* (KPD), and the rest were
scattered rightists. Weimar looked safe to all of them as they saw the
Nazi vote drop from 6.5 per cent in 1924 to a mere 2.6 per cent in
1928. None thought horror lay ahead.

Until the late 1920s Hitler had wasted his time trying to recruit the
working class into his National Socialist German Workers' Party, but few
were interested: Hitler had been for the war, they had finally revolted
against it; Hitler was against strikes, they were good trade unionists.
When the Depression finally brought him a mass following it was the
peasants, not the workers, who poured into his movement. Weimar had
changed nothing for them; 27 per cent still tilled less than one hectare
(2.471 acres), another 26 per cent worked less than 5 hectares (12.5
acres). In debt to the banks even before the crisis, these rural Christians
were easily persuaded to focus on the Jews who, for centuries, had been
identified with pawnbroking and usury. The Christian professional
class, already steeped in sabre and beer volkism from their university
days, and the small shopkeepers, resenting the superior competition
from the large Jewish department stores, were the next to break away
from the coalition that had ruled Weimar from its inception and join
the Nazis. From a tiny 2.6 per cent in 1928 the Nazi vote soared to
18.3 per cent in the elections of 14 September 1930.

Religious Jewry turned to its traditional defence organisation, the
Centralverein, the Central Association of German Citizens of the
Jewish Faith; now, for the first time, the department-store owners,
who had become a prime target for the attentions of the Nazi brownshirts, began to contribute to the CV's efforts. The CV's elderly leadership could not understand the collapse of capitalism. They were simply

27

stunned when their party, the DDP, suddenly jack-knifed and turned itself into the moderately anti-Semitic *Staatspartei*. However, younger members of the CV pushed aside the old leadership and were able to get the CV to use the department-store money to subsidise the SPD's anti-Nazi propaganda. After the DDP's betrayal, the SPD picked up approximately 60 per cent of the Jewish vote. Only 8 per cent went Communist, and they received no CV largess for the stated grounds that they were militantly against God; the real concern was that they were equally militant against the CV's financial angles.

Each German Jewish association saw Hitler's ascent through its own special mirror. The young CV functionaries saw that the SPD's working-class base stayed loyal to it and that Jews continued to be integrated into the party at every level. What they did not realise was that the SPD was incapable of defeating Hitler. Before the First World War the SPD had been the largest socialist party in the world, the pride of the Socialist International. But it was no more than reformist and through-out the Weimar Republic it failed to establish the firm socialist base which would have allowed the German working class to resist the Nazis. The onset of the Depression found their own Hermann Muller as Chancellor. Soon their right-wing coalition partners decided the workers would have to bear the weight of the crisis and replaced him with Heinrich Bruning of the Catholic *Zentrumspartei*. The 'hunger chancellor' raised taxes on the lucky ones with jobs to pay ever-smaller benefits to the increasing millions of unemployed. The SPD leaders knew this was suicide but 'tolerated' Bruning, fearing he would bring Hitler into his coalition if they turned away from him. Therefore they did not fight against the cuts in the dole. Bruning had nothing to offer the desperate middle class and more of them put on brown shirts. The SPD's ranks, Jews and non-Jews alike, passively stood by and watched as their party succumbed.

The Communist KPD also defeated itself. Lenin's Bolshevism had degenerated into Stalin's 'Third Period' ultra-leftism, and Rosa Luxem-burg's *Spartakusbund* into Ernst Thaelmann's *Rote Front*. To these sectarians everyone else was a Fascist. The *Sozialdemokraten* were now '*Sozial Faschisten*' and no unity was possible with them.

In 1930 the two working-class parties combined outpolled Hitler 37.6 per cent to 18.3 per cent. He could have been stopped; it was their failure to unite on a militant programme of joint physical defence against the brownshirts and in defence against the government's on-slaught against the standard of living of the masses that let Hitler come to power. Since the Second World War Western scholars have tended to see the KPD 'betraying' the SPD through Stalin's fanaticism. In the Stalinist camp the roles are reversed; the SPD is blamed for leaning on a broken reed like Bruning. But both parties must share the responsibility for the débâcle.

'It is Right, therefore, that They should Fight against Us'

If the SPD and the KPD must bear their full measure of guilt for Hitler's triumph, so too must the *Zionistische Vereinigung für Deutschland* (the Zionist Federation of Germany). Although conventional wisdom has always assumed that the Zionists, with their dire view of anti-Semitism, warned the Jews of the Nazi menace, this is in fact not true. In 1969, Joachim Prinz, the former President of the American Jewish Congress — in his youth a fire-eating Zionist rabbi in Berlin — still insisted that:

Since the assassination of Walther Rathenau in 1922, there was no doubt in our minds that the German development would be toward an anti-Semitic totalitarian regime. When Hitler began to arouse, and as he put it 'awaken' the German nation to racial consciousness and racial superiority, we had no doubt that this man would sooner or later become the leader of the German nation.[1]

Yet a diligent search of the pages of the *Judische Rundschau*, the weekly organ of the ZVfD, will not reveal such prophecies. When a Jew was killed and several hundred Jewish stores looted in a November 1923 hunger riot in Berlin, Kurt Blumenfeld, the Secretary (later President) of the ZVfD, consciously played down the incident:

There would be a very cheap and effective kind of reaction, and we ... decisively reject it. One could incite deep anxiety among German Jewry. One could use the excitement to enlist the vacillating. One could represent Palestine and Zionism as a refuge for the homeless. We do not wish to do that. We do not wish to carry off by demagoguery those who have stood apart from Jewish life out of indifference. But we wish to make clear to them through [our] sincere conviction where the basic error of Jewish *galuth* [exile] existence lies. We wish to awaken their national self-awareness. We wish ... through patient and earnest educational work [to] prepare them to participate in the upbuilding of Palestine.[2]

The historian Stephen Poppel, certainly no enemy of the ZVfD, categorically states in his book, *Zionism in Germany 1897–1933*, that after 1923 the *Rundschau* 'did not begin to take systematic, detailed notice of anti-Jewish agitation and violence until 1931'.[3] Far from warning and defending the Jews, prominent Zionists opposed anti-Nazi activity.

It had been the German Zionists who had most fully elaborated the ideology of the WZO before 1914 and in the 1920s they developed the argument to its logical conclusion: Judaism in the Diaspora was hopeless. There was no possible defence against anti-Semitism and there was no purpose in trying to develop Jewish cultural and community institutions in Germany. The ZVfD turned away from the society in which they lived. There were only two Zionist tasks: instilling nationalist consciousness in as many Jews as would listen and training youths for occupations useful in the economic development of Palestine. Anything else was useless and palliative.

In 1925 the most vehement protagonist of total abstentionism, Jacob Klatzkin, the co-editor of the massive *Encyclopedia Judaica*, laid down the full implications of the Zionist approach to anti-Semitism.

If we do not admit the rightfulness of antisemitism, we deny the rightfulness of our own nationalism. If our people is deserving and willing to live its own national life, then it is an alien body thrust into the nations among whom it lives, an alien body that insists on its own distinctive identity, reducing the domain of their life. It is right, therefore, that they should fight against us for their national integrity . . . Instead of establishing societies for defense against the antisemites, who want to reduce our rights, we should establish societies for defense against our friends who desire to defend our rights.[4]

German Zionism was distinctive in the WZO, in that the ZVfD leaders opposed taking any part in local politics. To Blumenfeld, *grenzuberschreitung* (overstepping the borders) was the dreaded sin. Blumenfeld completely accepted the anti-Semitic line that Germany belonged to the Aryan race and that for a Jew to hold an office in the land of his birth was nothing more than an intrusion into the affairs of another *volk*. In theory the ZVfD insisted that every single one of its members should eventually emigrate to Palestine, but of course this was completely unrealistic. Some 2,000 settlers went from Germany to Palestine between 1897 and 1933, but many of these were Russians stranded there after the revolution. In 1930 the ZVfD had 9,059 paid-up members, but the dues were nominal and in no way a sign of deep commitment. For all Blumenfeld's enthusiasm, Zionism was not an important element in the Weimar Republic.

When the warning signs of the Nazi surge appeared in the June 1930 elections in Saxony, where they obtained 14.4 per cent of the vote, the Berlin Jewish community put pressure on the ZVfD to join a Reichstag Election Committee in conjunction with the CV and other assimilationists. But the ZVfD's adherence was strictly nominal; the assimilationists complained that the Zionists put barely any time or money into it, and it dissolved immediately after the election. A *Rundschau* article by Siegfried Moses, later Blumenfeld's successor as head of the federation, demonstrated the Zionists' indifference to the construction of a strenuous defence:

> We have always believed the defense against anti-Semitism to be a task which concerns all Jews and have clearly stated the methods of which we approve and those which we consider irrelevant or ineffective. But it is true that the defense against anti-Semitism is not our main task, it does not concern us to the same extent and is not of the same importance for us as is the work for Palestine and, in a somewhat different sense, the work of the Jewish communities.[5]

Even after the election in September 1930 the Zionists argued against the notion of creating an effective front against the Nazis. A.W. Rom insisted in the *Rundschau* that *any* defence could only be a waste of time. To him 'The most important lesson we have learned from this election is that it is much more important to strengthen the Jewish community in Germany from within than to conduct . . . an external fight.'[6]

The ZVfD leaders could never effectively unite with the assimilationists on defence work. They were total abstentionists politically, and they were volkists; they did not believe in the CV's fundamental premiss that the Jews were Germans. Their concern was that the Jews should emphasise their Jewishness. They reasoned that if Jews started to consider themselves a separate national minority, and stopped interfering in 'Aryan' affairs, it would be possible to get the anti-Semites to tolerate them on a basis of a 'dignified' coexistence. The assimilationists would have none of this; to them the Zionist position was just an echo of the Nazi line. There is no doubt that the assimilationists were correct. But even if the Zionists had convinced every Jew to support their stance, it would not have helped. Hitler did not care what the Jews thought of themselves; he wanted them out of Germany and, preferably, dead. The Zionist solution was no solution. There was nothing the Jews could have done to mollify anti-Semitism. Only the defeat of Nazism could have helped the Jews, and that could only have happened if they had united with the anti-Nazi working class on a programme of militant resistance. But this was anathema to the ZVfD leadership who, in 1932, when Hitler was gaining strength by the day, chose to organise anti-Communist meetings to warn Jewish youth against 'red assimilation'.[7]

The Zionist Minorities

As Hitler rose to power, minorities within the ZVfD increasingly ignored Blumenfeld's strictures against political action and either worked with the CV or looked to the other political elements for their salvation. Georg Kareski, a banker, had long been in disagreement with Blumenfeld over the ZVfD President's basic indifference to internal Jewish community politics, and in 1919 he had established a *Judische Volkspartei* to run in the Berlin Jewish community elections on a programme with greater emphasis on Jewish schooling. In 1930 Kareski surfaced in the larger German political arena as a candidate for the Reichstag on the Catholic Centre ticket (he lost) and an 'Organisation of Jewish Centre Party Voters' was set up by his co-thinkers. The spectacle amused a Social Democratic wag:

> The homeless Jewish bourgeoisie has in great part sought shelter with the Center Party – Christ and the first Pope were Jews, so why not? Wretched individuals who do violence to their ideas and purposes out of anxiety over 'Socialist expropriation'. What Hitler is to the Christians, the Center Party is to the Jews.[8]

Bismark's *Kulturkampf* against the Catholic Church had made the German Catholic hierarchy very distrustful of anti-Semitism; they feared it would pave the way for further attacks on the Catholic minority as well. In addition, individual bishops, mindful that Jesus was a Jew and that therefore racial anti-Semitism was incompatible with Christianity, had even refused communion to Nazi members. But there had always been anti-Semites among the leaders of the

Centre, and after the 1929 Lateran accord with Mussolini there was growing pressure from the Vatican for a Centre-Nazi accommodation in the name of a fight against Communism. However, Kareski could not see the direction in which class interest was pushing the Catholic upper class, and he completely misjudged Franz von Papen, who took over as a Centre Chancellor after Bruning. Kareski reassured his rich Jewish friends that 'the Papen government has written the protection of the Jews on the flag'.[9] In reality von Papen had always been an anti-Semite and in the end, after he had lost the chancellorship, he was part of the camarilla that convinced President Hindenburg to summon Hitler to power.

On the Zionist left the German branch of the Poale Zion backed the incompetent leadership of the SPD. Before 1914 the SPD refused to associate with Zionism, which it saw as separating the Jews from other workers, and only those elements on the far right of the SPD that supported German imperialism in Africa patronised the Labour Zionists, whom they saw as fellow socialist-colonisers. The Socialist International only established friendly relations with Poale Zion during and after the First World War, when the left-wing anti-colonialist forces joined the Communist International. The Labour Zionists joined the SPD with one central purpose: to gain support for Zionism. As long as the leaders of the SPD had good things to say about Zionism, they, in turn, replied with similar endearments. By 1931 the Labour Zionist leaders in Palestine began to envision a victorious Hitler, but they had no alternative stratagems for the SPD and there is no record of the Poale Zion leaders in Palestine ever publicly quarrelling with their erstwhile comrades in the SPD leadership.

'Germans of the Mosaic Faith are an Undesirable, Demoralizing Phenomena'

The basic Zionist attitude toward the Nazis was that nothing could really be done to stop them, but they felt obliged to do something. The *Encyclopedia of Zionism and Israel* tells us, very vaguely, that the German Zionists tried to persuade Chancellor Bruning to issue a strong declaration against Nazi anti-Semitism by 'stressing the influence of Zionists upon the governments of various nations'. Bruning never replied, 'nor were the Zionists successful in their attempts to obtain governmental support of emigration to Palestine as a constructive outlet for internal pressure'.[10]

Any such statement from Bruning would have been meaningless, unless he had been prepared to crush the Nazis. Any announcement that the government was aiding Jews to leave would have been counter-productive in encouraging the Nazis to increase their efforts in the certainty that the regime was weakening in its defence of Jewish rights. However, Bruning did nothing because the Zionists were bluffing that they had any influence upon 'the governments of various nations', especially Britain.

Weizmann, the prestigious scientist and President of the WZO, who was well connected in London, did next to nothing for German Jewry. He had never liked them, nor did he have any sympathy for their defence efforts against anti-Semitism. As early as 18 March 1912 he had actually been brazen enough to tell a Berlin audience that 'each country can absorb only a limited number of Jews, if she doesn't want disorders in her stomach. Germany already has too many Jews.'[11] In his chat with Balfour, in 1914, he went further, telling him that 'we too are in agreement with the cultural anti-Semites, in so far as we believed that Germans of the Mosaic faith are an undesirable, demoralizing phenomena'.[12] He visited Germany several times in the last years of Weimar. His friends there told him that they did not even want Jews elsewhere to demonstrate on their behalf. Rather, he should get British Conservatives to let it be known that Hitler would discredit himself with them by anti-Semitic actions. Weizmann approached Robert Boothby, a Conservative MP, who told him that quite frankly most Tories saw Hitler as saving Germany from Communism and were far less concerned about his anti-Semitism.[13] By January 1932 Weizmann concluded that emigration of some of Germany's Jews lay ahead. Although he had lost the support of the World Zionist Congress in 1931, had stepped down as President of the organisation and was thus unburdened by office, he did nothing further to mobilise the world or Jewry against Hitler.

In Germany itself the ZVfD never tried to bring the Jews out into the streets, but the *Rundschau* felt free to threaten that the Jews would come out — in New York. In reality, not one demonstration against Hitler was organised in America by the Zionists before he came to power. Rabbi Wise, leader of the American Jewish Congress, did get together with the assimilationists of the American Jewish Committee to ask the leaders of German Jewry how they could help. The German Jewish bourgeoisie merely thanked them for the gesture and assured the Americans that they would be contacted if things got worse. Wise wanted to try for a statement from President Hoover but even that was too radical for the American Jewish Committee, and Wise dropped the matter. Wise and Nahum Goldmann did organise a World Jewish Conference in Geneva in the summer of 1932, but Goldmann, extremely committed, was unwilling to work with assimilationists.[14] Zionism was a minority movement in Jewry at that time; the conference did little more than preach to the converted, and only a minority of the converted at that, since neither Weizmann nor Nahum Sokolow, who had succeeded him as President of the WZO, attended. Nothing came of the meeting and indeed neither Wise nor Goldmann appreciated the full seriousness of the situation. Goldmann, always a believer in the influence of the Great Powers, told the 1932 ZVfD convention that Britain and France, and Russia, would never let Hitler come to power.[15] Stephen Wise retreated even further into that world where perhaps things would not be 'as bad as we dreaded'. On hearing of Hitler's coming to power, he felt the only real danger lay in Hitler's failing to keep his other promises. Then 'he may finally decide that he must yield to his fellow Nazis in the matter of anti-Semitism'.[16]

'Liberalism is the Enemy; It is also the Enemy for Nazism'

Given that the German Zionists agreed with two fundamental elements in Nazi ideology — that the Jews would never be part of the German *volk* and, therefore, they did not belong on German soil — it was inevitable that some Zionists would believe an accommodation possible. If Wise could delude himself that Hitler was the moderate in the Nazis' ranks, why could not others talk themselves into believing that there were elements in the NSDAP who might restrain Hitler? Stephen Poppel has touched on this debate within the ZVfD:

> Some Zionists thought that there might be respectable and moderate elements within the Nazi movement who would serve to restrain it from within . . . These elements might serve as suitable negotiating partners for reaching some kind of German–Jewish accommodation. There was serious division over this possibility, with Weltsch [editor of the *Rundschau*] , for example, arguing in its behalf and Blumenfeld sharply opposing it.[17]

Nor was Robert Weltsch alone. Gustav Krojanker, an editor at the *Judischer Verlag*, the oldest Zionist publishing house in Europe, also saw the two movements' common roots in volkist irrationalism, and drew the conclusion that Zionists should look positively at the nationalist aspects of Nazism. A benign approach toward their fellow volkists, he naively reasoned, would perhaps bring forth an equivalent benevolence toward Zionism on the part of the Nazis.[18] As far as Krojanker and many other Zionists were concerned, democracy's day was over. Harry Sacher, a Briton, one of the leaders of the WZO in the period, explained Krojanker's theories in a review of Krojanker's book, *Zum Problem des Neuen Deutschen Nationalismus*:

> For Zionists, Liberalism is the enemy; it is also the enemy for Nazism; *ergo*, Zionism should have much sympathy and understanding for Nazism, of which anti-Semitism is probably a fleeting accident.[19]

No Zionist wanted Hitler to come to power, no Zionist voted for him and neither Weltsch nor Krojanker collaborated with the Nazis prior to 30 January 1933. Collaboration only emerged later. But these notions were the logical result of decades of Zionist justification for anti-Semitism and failure to resist it. It cannot be argued in their defence that the Zionist leaders did not know what was going to happen when Hitler came to power. He had said more than enough to guarantee that, at the very least, the Jews would be reduced to second-class citizenship. In addition, they knew that Hitler was an admirer of Mussolini and that ten years of Fascism in Italy had meant terror, torture and dictatorship. But in their hostility to liberalism and its commitment to Jewish assimilation, and as opponents of Jews utilising their full democratic rights within the parliamentary system, the Fascist aspect of Nazism never unduly disturbed the leaders of the ZVfD. It never occurred to these sectarians that they had a duty to democracy to mobilise in its defence. The grave implications of another Fascist regime, this time with an avowed anti-Jewish position, in the very heart of Europe, completely eluded them.

Dante has false diviners walking backwards, their faces reversed on their necks, tears pouring from their eyes. For ever. So it is for all who misunderstood Hitler.

Notes

1. Herbert Strauss (ed.), *Gegenwart Im Ruckblick* (Heidelberg, 1970), p. 231.
2. Stephen Poppel, *Zionism in Germany 1897-1933*, p. 119.

3. Ibid.

4. Jacob Agus, *The Meaning of Jewish History*, vol. II, p. 425.

5. Margaret Edelheim-Muehsam, 'Reactions of the Jewish Press to the Nazi Challenge', *Leo Baeck Institute Year Book*, vol. V (1960), p. 312.

6. Ibid., p. 314.

7. Donald Niewyk, *The Jews in Weimar Germany*, p. 30.

8. Donald Niewyk, *Socialist, Anti-Semite and Jew*, p. 213.

9. Leonard Baker, *Days of Sorrow and Pain*, p. 209.

10. Eliazer Livneh, 'Germany: Relations with Zionism and Israel', *Encyclopedia of Zionism and Israel*, vol. I, p. 385.

11. Benyamin Matuvo, 'The Zionist Wish and the Nazi Deed', *Issues* (Winter 1966/7), p. 9.

12. Chaim Weizmann to Ahad Ha'am, in Leonard Stein (ed.), *The Letters and Papers of Chaim Weizmann, Letters*, vol. VII, p. 81.

13. Shlomo Shafir, 'American Jewish Leaders and the Emerging Nazi Threat (1928–1933)', *American Jewish Archives* (November 1979), p. 172.

14. Ibid., p. 175.

15. Walter Laqueur, *History of Zionism*, p. 499.

16. Shafir, 'American Jewish Leaders and the Emerging Nazi Threat', p. 181.

17. Poppel, *Zionism in Germany*, p. 161.

18. Herbert Strauss, *Jewish Reactions to the Rise of Anti-Semitism in Germany*, p. 13.

19. Harry Sacher, review of Gustav Krojanker, *Zum Problem des Neuen Deutschen Nationalismus, Jewish Review* (London, September 1932), p. 104.

The World Zionist Organisation's attitude toward Italian Fascism was determined by one criterion: Italy's position on Zionism. When Mussolini was hostile to them, Weizmann was critical of him; but when he became pro-Zionist, the Zionist leadership enthusiastically supported him. On the day Hitler came to power they were already friends with the first Fascist leader.

As a revolutionary, Mussolini had always worked with Jews in the Italian Socialist Party, and it was not until he abandoned the left that he first began to echo the anti-Semitic ideas of the northern European right-wing. Four days after the Bolsheviks took power, he announced that their victory was a result of a plot between the 'Synagogue', that is, 'Ceorbaum' (Lenin), 'Bronstein' (Trotsky), and the German Army.[1] By 1919 he has Communism explained: the Jewish bankers — 'Rotschild', 'Warnberg', 'Schyff' and 'Guggenheim' — were behind the Communist Jews.[2] But Mussolini was not so anti-Semitic as to exclude Jews from his new party and there were five among the founders of the Fascist movement. Nor was anti-Semitism important to his ideology; in fact it was not well received by his followers.

Anti-Semitism in Italy had always been identified in the public mind with Catholic obscurantism. It was the Church which had forced the Jews into the ghettos and Italian nationalists had always supported the Jews against the Popes, whom they saw as opponents of a united Italy. In 1848 the walls of the Roman ghetto were destroyed by the revolutionary Roman Republic. With their defeat the ghetto was restored, but the final victory of the nationalist Kingdom of Italy in 1870 brought an end to discrimination against the Jews. The Church blamed the Jews for the nationalist victory, and the official Jesuit organ, *Civiltà Cattolica*, continued to insist that they had only been defeated by 'conspiracies with the Jews [that] were formed by Mazzini, Garibaldi, Cavour, Farini and De Pretis'.[3] But this clerical ranting against the heroes of Italian nationalism merely discredited anti-Semitism, particularly among the anti-clerical youth of the nationalist petty bourgeoisie. Since the essence of Fascism was the mobilisation of the middle class against Marxism, Mussolini listened carefully to his followers' objections: what was the point of denouncing Communism as a Jewish conspiracy, if the Jews themselves were not unpopular?

'True Jews have never Fought against You'

As with many another, Mussolini originally combined anti-Semitism with pro-Zionism, and his *Popolo d'Italia* continued to favour Zionism until 1919, when he concluded that Zionism was merely a cat's-paw for the British and he began to refer to the local Zionist movement as 'so-called Italians'.[4] All Italian politicians shared this suspicion of Zionism, including two Foreign Ministers of Jewish descent – Sidney Sonnino and Carlo Schanzar. The Italian line on Palestine was that Protestant Britain had no real standing in the country as there were no native Protestants there. What they wanted in Palestine was an international 'Holy Land'. In agreeing with the position of the pre-Fascist governments on Palestine and Zionism, Mussolini was primarily motivated by imperial rivalry with Britain and by hostility to any political grouping in Italy having a loyalty to an international movement.

Mussolini's March on Rome of October 1922 worried the Italian Zionist Federation. They had no love for the preceding Facta government, given its anti-Zionism, but the *Fascisti* were no better on that score, and Mussolini had made clear his own anti-Semitism. However, their concerns about anti-Semitism were lifted immediately; the new government hastened to inform Angelo Sacerdoti, the chief rabbi of Rome and an active Zionist, that they would not support anti-Semitism either at home or abroad. The Zionists then obtained an audience with Mussolini on 20 December 1922. They assured the *Duce* of their loyalty. Ruth Bondy, a Zionist writer on Italian Jewry, relates: 'The delegation, on its part, argued that Italian Jews would always remain loyal to their native land and could help establish relations with the Levant through the Jewish communities there.'[5]

Mussolini bluntly told them that he still saw Zionism as a tool of the British, but their pledge of loyalty softened his hostility somewhat and he agreed to meet Chaim Weizmann, the President of the WZO, who attended on 3 January 1923. Weizmann's autobiography is deliberately vague, and often misleading, on his relations with the Italian, but fortunately it is possible to learn something of the meeting from the report given at the time to the British Embassy in Rome. This explains how Weizmann tried to deal with the objection that Zionism wore Britain's livery: 'Dr Weizmann, whilst denying that this was in any way the case, said that, even if it were so, Italy stood to gain as much as Great Britain by a weakening of Moslem power.'[6]

This answer cannot have inspired too much confidence in Mussolini, but he was pleased when Weizmann asked permission to name an Italian

Zionist to the commission running their settlement in Palestine. Weizmann knew the Italian public would see this as Fascist toleration for the WZO, which would make it easier for Zionism amongst wary Jews, frightened at the thought of coming into conflict with the new regime. Mussolini saw it the other way around; by such a cheap gesture he would win support both at home and abroad from the Jewish community.

The meeting produced no change in Italian policy toward Zionism or the British, and the Italians continued to obstruct Zionist efforts by harassing tactics on the League of Nations Mandate Commission. Weizmann never, then or later, mobilised opposition to what Mussolini did to Italians, but he had to say something about a regime that actively opposed Zionism. He spoke out, in America, on 26 March 1923:

> Today there is a tremendous political wave, known as Fascism, which is sweeping over Italy. As an Italian movement it is no business of ours — it is the business of the Italian Government. But this wave is now breaking against the little Jewish community, and the little community, which never asserted itself, is today suffering from anti-Semitism.[7]

Italian policy toward Zionism only changed in the mid-1920s, when their consuls in Palestine concluded that Zionism was there to stay and that Britain would only leave the country if and when the Zionists got their own state. Weizmann was invited back to Rome for another conference on 17 September 1926. Mussolini was more than cordial; he offered to help the Zionists build up their economy and the Fascist press began printing favourable articles on Palestinian Zionism.

Zionist leaders began to visit Rome. Nahum Sokolow, then the Chairman of the Zionist Executive and later, in 1931–3, the President of the WZO, appeared on 26 October 1927. Michael Ledeen, a specialist on Fascism and the Jewish question, has described the political outcome of the Sokolow–Mussolini talks:

> With this last meeting Mussolini became lionised by Zionism. Sokolow not only praised the Italian as a human being but announced his firm belief that Fascism was immune from anti-Semitic preconceptions. He went even further: in the past there might have been uncertainty about the true nature of Fascism, but now, 'we begin to understand its true nature ... true Jews have never fought against you'.

These words, tantamount to a Zionist endorsement of the Fascist regime, were echoed in Jewish periodicals all over the world. In this period, which saw a new legal relationship established between the Jewish community and the Fascist state, expressions of loyalty and affection for Fascism poured out of the Jewish centers of Italy.[8]

Not all Zionists were pleased with Sokolow's remarks. The Labour Zionists were loosely affiliated to the underground Italian Socialist Party via the Socialist International and they complained, but the Italian Zionists were overjoyed. Prosperous and extremely religious, these conservatives saw Mussolini as their support against Marxism and its concomitant assimilation. In 1927 rabbi Sacerdoti gave an interview to the journalist Guido Bedarida:

Professor Sacerdoti is persuaded that many of the fundamental principles of the Fascist Doctrine such as: the observance of the laws of the state, respect of traditions, the principle of authority, exaltation of religious values, a desire for the moral and physical cleanliness of family and the individual, the struggle for an increase of production, and therefore a struggle against Malthusianism, are no more or less than Jewish principles.[9]

The ideological leader of Italian Zionism was the lawyer Alfonso Pacifici. An extremely pious man, he ensured that the Italian Zionists were to become the most religious branch of the world movement. In 1932 another interviewer told of how Pacifici also:

expressed to me his conviction that the new conditions would bring about a revival of Italian Jewry. Indeed, he claimed to have evolved a philosophy of Judaism akin to the spiritual *Tendenz* of Fascism long before this had become the rule of life in Italian polity.[10]

Establishment of Relations between Mussolini and Hitler

If the Zionists at least hesitated until Mussolini warmed to them before they responded, Hitler had no such inhibitions. From the beginning of the Fascist take-over, Hitler used Mussolini's example as proof that a terror dictatorship could overthrow a weak bourgeois democracy and then set about smashing the workers' movements. After he came to power he acknowledged his debt to Mussolini in a discussion with the

Italian ambassador in March 1933. 'Your Excellency knows how great an admiration I have for Mussolini, whom I consider the spiritual head of my "movement" as well, since if he had not succeeded in assuming power in Italy, National Socialism would not have had the slightest chance in Germany.'[11]

Hitler had two cavils with Fascism: Mussolini savagely oppressed the Germans in the south Tyrol which the Italians had won at Versailles, and he welcomed Jews into the Fascist Party. But Hitler saw, quite correctly, that what the two of them wanted was so similar that, eventually, they would come together. He insisted that a quarrel with the Italians over the Tyrolians would only serve the Jews; therefore, unlike most German rightists, he was always willing to abandon the Tyrolians.[12] Furthermore, in spite of the fact that he had no knowledge of Mussolini's earlier anti-Semitic remarks, in 1926, in *Mein Kampf*, Hitler declared that in his heart of hearts the Italian was an anti-Semite.

> The struggle that FASCIST ITALY is waging, though perhaps in the last analysis unconsciously (which I personally do not believe), against the three main weapons of the Jews is the best indication that, even though indirectly, the poison fangs of this supra-state power are being torn out. The prohibition on Masonic secret societies, the persecution of the supra-national press, as well as the continued demolition of international Marxism, and, conversely, the steady reinforcement of the Fascist state conception, will in the course of the years cause the Italian government to serve the interests of the Italian people more and more, without regard for the hissing of the Jewish world hydra.[13]

But if Hitler was pro-Mussolini, it did not follow that Mussolini would be pro-Nazi. Throughout the 1920s the *Duce* kept repeating his famous 'Fascism is not an article for export'. Certainly after the failure of the Beer Hall *putsch* and the Nazis' meagre 6.5 per cent in the 1924 elections, Hitler represented nothing. It required the Depression and Hitler's sudden electoral success, before Mussolini began to take serious notice of his German counterpart. Now he began to talk of Europe going Fascist within ten years, and his press began to report favourably about Nazism. But at the same time he repudiated Hitler's Nordic racism and anti-Semitism. Completely disoriented by his philo-Semitism, the Zionists hoped that Mussolini would be a moderating influence on Hitler when he came to power.[14] In October 1932, on the tenth anniversary of the March on Rome, Pacifici rhapsodised about the differences between the real Fascism in Rome and its *ersatz* in Berlin. He saw:

> radical differences between the true and authentic Fascism — Italian Fascism, that is — and the pseudo-Fascist movements in other countries which . . . are often using the most reactionary phobias, and especially the blind, unbridled hatred of the Jews, as a means of diverting the masses from their real problems, from the real causes of their misery, and from the real culprits.[15]

Later, after the Holocaust, in his autobiography *Trial and Error*, Weizmann lamely tried to establish an anti-Fascist record for the Italian Zionists: 'The Zionists, and the Jews generally, though they did not give loud expression to their views on the subject, were known to be anti-Fascist.'[16] Given Mussolini's anti-Zionism in the early years of his Fascist career, as well as his anti-Semitic comments, Zionists hardly favoured him in 1922. But, as we have seen, they pledged their loyalty to the new power once Mussolini assured them that he was not anti-Semitic. In the first years of the regime, the Zionists knew he resented their international affiliations, but that did not bring them to anti-Fascism and, certainly after the statements in 1927 by Sokolow and Sacerdoti, the Zionists could only be thought of as Mussolini's good friends.

Notes

1. Meir Michaelis, *Mussolini and the Jews*, p. 12.

2. Ibid., p. 13.

3. Daniel Carpi, 'The Catholic Church and Italian Jewry under the Fascists', *Yad Vashem Studies*, vol. IV, p. 44n.

4. Michaelis, *Mussolini and the Jews*, p. 14.

5. Ruth Bondy, *The Emissary: A Life of Enzo Sereni*, p. 45.

6. Daniel Carpi, 'Weizmann's Political Activities in Italy from 1923 to 1934', *Zionism* (Tel Aviv, 1975), p. 225.

7. Chaim Weizmann, 'Relief and Reconstruction', *American Addresses* (1923), p. 49.

8. Michael Ledeen, 'Italian Jews and Fascism', *Judaism* (Summer 1969), p. 286.

9. Guido Bedarida, 'The Jews under Mussolini', *Reflex* (October 1927), p. 58.

10. Paul Goodman, 'Judaism under the Fascist Regime', *Views* (April 1932), p. 46.

11. Carpi, 'Weizmann's Political Activities in Italy', p. 238.

12. Adolf Hitler, *Mein Kampf*, p. 628.

13. Ibid., p. 637.
14. Michaelis, *Mussolini and the Jews*, p. 49.
15. Ibid., p. 29.
16. Weizmann, *Trial and Error*, p. 368.

5 GERMAN ZIONISM OFFERS TO COLLABORATE WITH NAZISM

Werner Senator, a leading German Zionist, once remarked that Zionism, for all its world Jewish nationalism, always politically assimilates to the countries within which it operates. No better proof of his remark exists than the political adaptation of the ZVfD to the theories and policies of the new Nazi regime. Believing that the ideological similarities between the two movements – their contempt for liberalism, their common volkish racism and, of course, their mutual conviction that Germany could never be the homeland of its Jews – could induce the Nazis to support them, the ZVfD solicited the patronage of Adolf Hitler, not once but repeatedly, after 1933.

The goal of the ZVfD became an 'orderly retreat', that is, Nazi backing for emigration of at least the younger generation of Jews to Palestine, and they immediately sought contact with elements in the Nazi apparatus whom they thought would be interested in such an arrangement on the basis of a volkish appreciation of Zionism. Kurt Tuchler, a member of the ZVfD Executive, persuaded Baron Leopold Itz Edler von Mildenstein of the SS to write a pro-Zionist piece for the Nazi press. The Baron agreed on the condition that he visited Palestine first, and two months after Hitler came to power the two men and their wives went to Palestine; von Mildenstein stayed there for six months before he returned to write his articles.[1]

Contact with a central figure in the new government came in March 1933, when Hermann Goering summoned the leaders of the major Jewish organisations. In early March, Julius Streicher, the editor of *Der Steurmer*, had declared that, as of 1 April, all Jewish stores and professionals would be boycotted; however, this campaign ran into an immediate snag. Hitler's capitalist backers were extremely worried by the announcement by rabbi Wise of a planned counter-demonstration to be held in New York on 27 March, if the Nazis went ahead with their boycott. Jews were prominent throughout the retail trade both in American and Europe and, fearing retaliation against their own companies, Hitler's wealthy patrons urged him to call off the action. But the Nazis could hardly do that without losing face, and they decided to use German Jewry to head off Wise; thus Hermann Goering called in the Jewish leaders.

German Zionism's influence in Weimar did not merit its leaders' participation, but because they conceived themselves as the only natural negotiating partner with the Nazis, they secured a late invitation. Martin Rosenbluth, a leading Zionist, later told of the incident in his post-war autobiography, *Go Forth and Serve*. Four Jews saw Goering: Julius Brodnitz for the CV, Heinrich Stahl for the Berlin Jewish community, Max Naumann, a pro-Nazi fanatic from the *Verband nationaldeutscher Juden* (VnJ), and Blumenfeld for the Zionists. Goering launched into a tirade: the foreign press was lying about atrocities against Jews; unless the lies stopped, he could not vouch for the safety of German Jewry. Most important, the New York rally had to be called off: 'Dr Wise is one of our most dangerous and unscrupulous enemies.'[2] A delegation was to go to London to contact world Jewry.

The assimilationists declined, claiming that as Germans they had no influence with foreign Jews. This was false, but they hardly wanted to assist in their own destruction. Only Blumenfeld volunteered, but insisted he be allowed to speak truthfully about the Nazi treatment of Jews. Goering did not care what was said to get the rally called off; perhaps a description of the grim situation might make foreign Jews halt for fear of provoking worse. He did not care who went or what arguments were used as long as the deputation agreed to 'report regularly to the German embassy'.[3]

The ZVfD finally sent Martin Rosenbluth and Richard Lichtheim. Fearing exclusive responsibility for the outcome of their strange mission, they prevailed upon the CV to let them take along Dr Ludwig Tietz. Although not a Zionist personally, the wealthy businessman was 'a good friend of ours'.[4] The trio arrived in London on 27 March and immediately met forty Jewish leaders at a meeting chaired by Nahum Sokolow, then President of the WZO. They later met a battery of British officials. The delegates saw two tasks before them: to use the severity of the situation to promote Palestine as 'the logical place of refuge', and to head off all anti-Nazi efforts abroad. They called Wise in New York. Rosenbluth described the incident thus in his memoirs:

> Mindful of Goering's charges . . . we conveyed the message . . . Getting the cryptic rest of our message across to him was somewhat more difficult, since it was necessary to speak in obscure terms in order to confound any possible monitors. Subsequent events proved we had made clear our hidden plea, and that Dr Wise had understood we wanted him to stand firm and under no circumstances

cancel the meeting.[5]

There is no evidence that any effort was made to signal Wise to this effect. Through the research of an Israeli scholar, Shaul Esh, it is now known that the deputation tried to head off demonstrations in New York and Palestine. According to Esh, later that evening they sent cables:

> not in their own name, but in the name of the Zionist Executive in London. The telegrams requested that the recipients immediately dispatch to the Chancellery of the Third Reich declarations to the effect that they do not condone an organised anti-German boycott . . . the Zionist Executive in London learned of this several hours later, they sent another cable to Jerusalem to delay the dispatch of an official declaration to Hitler.[6]

Later, in his own autobiography, *Challenging Years*, Stephen Wise mentioned receiving their cable, but he did not record any cryptic message from the delegation.[7] It is reasonable to assume that he would have recorded it, if he had thought any such attempt was made. In reality, Wise repeatedly raged at the ZVfD in the following years for persistently opposing every attempt by foreign Jews to struggle against the Hitler regime.

The London proceedings were typical of all further ZVfD behaviour. In 1937, after leaving Berlin for America, rabbi Joachim Prinz wrote of his experiences in Germany and alluded to a memorandum which, it is now known, was sent to the Nazi Party by the ZVfD on 21 June 1933. Prinz's article candidly describes the Zionist mood in the first months of 1933:

> Everyone in Germany knew that only the Zionists could responsibly represent the Jews in dealings with the Nazi government. We all felt sure that one day the government would arrange a round table conference with the Jews, at which — after the riots and atrocities of the revolution had passed — the new status of German Jewry could be considered. The government announced very solemnly that there was no country in the world which tried to solve the Jewish problem as seriously as did Germany. Solution of the Jewish question? It was our Zionist dream! We never denied the existence of the Jewish question! Dissimilation? It was our own appeal! . . . In a statement notable for its pride and dignity, we called for a conference.[8]

The document remained buried until 1962, when it was finally printed, in German, in Israel. 'Pride' and 'dignity' are words open to interpretation but, it is safe to say, there was not one word that could be so construed today. This extraordinary memorandum demands extensive quotation. The Nazis were asked, very politely:

> May we therefore be permitted to present our views, which, in our opinion, make possible a solution in keeping with the principles of the new German State of National Awakening and which at the same time might signify for Jews a new ordering of the conditions of their existence . . . Zionism has no illusions about the difficulty of the Jewish condition, which consists above all in an abnormal occupational pattern and in the fault of an intellectual and moral posture not rooted in one's own tradition . . .
>
> . . . an answer to the Jewish question truly satisfying to the national state can be brought about only with the collaboration of the Jewish movement that aims at a social, cultural, and moral renewal of Jewry . . . a rebirth of national life, such as is occurring in German life through adhesion to Christian and national values, must also take place in the Jewish national group. For the Jew, too, origin, religion, community of fate and group consciousness must be of decisive significance in the shaping of his life . . .
>
> On the foundation of the new state, which has established the principle of race, we wish so to fit our community into the total structure so that for us too, in the sphere assigned to us, fruitful activity for the Fatherland is possible . . . Our acknowledgement of Jewish nationality provides for a clear and sincere relationship to the German people and its national and racial realities. Precisely because we do not wish to falsify these fundamentals, because we, too, are against mixed marriage and are for maintaining the purity of the Jewish group . . .
>
> . . . fidelity to their own kind and their own culture gives Jews the inner strength that prevents insult to the respect for the national sentiments and the imponderables of German nationality; and rootedness in one's own spirituality protects the Jew from becoming the rootless critic of the national foundations of German essence. The national distancing which the state desires would thus be brought about easily as the result of an organic development.
>
> Thus, a self-conscious Jewry here described, in whose name we speak, can find a place in the structure of the German state, because it is inwardly unembarrassed, free from the resentment which

assimilated Jews must feel at the determination that they belong to Jewry, to the Jewish race and past. We believe in the possibility of an honest relationship of loyalty between a group-conscious Jewry and the German state . . .

For its practical aims, Zionism hopes to be able to win the collaboration even of a government fundamentally hostile to Jews, because in dealing with the Jewish question no sentimentalities are involved but a real problem whose solution interests all peoples, and at the present moment especially the German people.

The realisation of Zionism could only be hurt by resentment of Jews abroad against the German development. Boycott propaganda — such as is currently being carried on against Germany in many ways — is in essence un-Zionist, because Zionism wants not to do battle but to convince and to build . . . Our observations, presented herewith, rest on the conviction that, in solving the Jewish problem according to its own lights, the German Government will have full understanding for a candid and clear Jewish posture that harmonizes with the interests of the state.[9]

This document, a treason to the Jews of Germany, was written in standard Zionist clichés: 'abnormal occupational pattern', 'rootless intellectuals greatly in need of moral regeneration', etc. In it the German Zionists offered calculated collaboration between Zionism and Nazism, hallowed by the goal of a Jewish state: we shall wage no battle against thee, only against those that would resist thee.

Obsessed with their strange mission, the ZVfD's leaders lost all sense of international Jewish perspective and even tried to get the WZO to call off its World Congress, scheduled for August 1933. They sent their world leadership a letter: 'It will have to express sharp protests', their lives could be at stake at a time when 'our legal existence has enabled us to organise thousands and to transfer large sums of money to Palestine'.[10] The Congress did take place as we shall see, but the ZVfD had nothing to worry about as the Nazis chose to use the occasion to announce that they had made a deal with world Zionism.

'Seeking its own National Idealism in the Nazi Spirit'

The Jewish public knew nothing about von Mildenstein's journey to Palestine in the company of a member of the Zionist Executive, nor about Rosenbluth and Lichtheim's trip to London; nor did they know about the memorandum, nor the request to call off the Zionist Congress. However, they could not miss what was appearing in the *Rundschau*, where assimilationalist German Jewry was roundly attacked. The CV complained bitterly of Zionist '*siegesfanfaren*' as the *Rundschau* rushed to condemn the guilty Jews.[11] The editor, Robert Weltsch, took the occasion of the 1 April boycott to assail the Jews of Germany in an editorial: 'Wear the Yellow Badge with Pride':

> At times of crisis throughout its history, the Jewish people has faced the question of its own guilt. Our most important prayer says, 'We were expelled from our country because of our sins' . . . Jewry bears a great guilt because it failed to heed Theodor Herzl's call . . . Because the Jews did not display their Jewishness with pride, because they wanted to shirk the Jewish question, they must share the blame for the degradation of Jewry.[12]

Even as the Nazis were in the process of throwing the left into concentration camps, Weltsch attacked the left-wing Jewish journalists:

> If today the National Socialist and German patriotic newspapers frequently refer to the type of the Jewish scribbler and the so-called Jewish press . . . it must be pointed out . . . Upright Jews have always been indignant at the raillery and the caricature directed by Jewish buffoons against Jews to the same extent, or even a greater extent, than they aimed them at Germans and others.[13]

Although the left-wing press had been under attack from the day the Nazis came to power, the Jewish newspapers were still legal. Naturally they were censored; if a journal printed something untoward, it would be closed down, temporarily at least. However, the Nazis did not force the Zionists to denounce their fellow Jews.

After the Holocaust Weltsch was quite contrite about the editorial, saying that he should have told the Jews to flee for their lives, but he never claimed that the Nazis made him write the piece. Weltsch was not a Fascist, but he was too much the Zionist sectarian to have really thought through his ideas about the world at large. As were most of the leaders of the ZVfD, he was quite convinced that 'egotistical liberalism' and parliamentary democracy were dead at least in Germany. Internationally, they were still for the British in Palestine, but the *Rundschau*'s correspondent in Italy, Kurt Kornicker, was quite openly pro-Fascist.[14] The ZVfD's leaders became convinced that Fascism was the wave of the future, certainly in Central Europe, and within that framework they counterposed the 'good' Fascism of Mussolini to the 'excesses' of Hitlerism, which they thought would diminish, with their assistance, as time went by.

Racism was now triumphant and the ZVfD ran with the winner. The talk of *blut* began to take hold with a statement by Blumenfeld in April 1933 that the Jews had previously been masking their natural blood-sanctioned apartness from the real Germans, but it reached Wagnerian proportions in the 4 August *Rundschau* with a long essay, '*Rasse als Kulturfaktor*', which pondered on the intellectual implications for Jews of the Nazi victory. It argued that Jews should not merely accept silently the dictates of their new masters; they, too, had to realise that race separation was wholly to the good:

> We who live here as a 'foreign race' have to respect racial consciousness and the racial interest of the German people absolutely. This however does not preclude a peaceful living together of people of different racial membership. The smaller the possibility of an undesirable mixture, so much less is there need for 'racial protection' . . . There are differentiations that in the last analysis have their root in ancestry. Only rationalist newspapers who have lost feeling for the deeper reasons and profundities of the soul, and for the origins of communal consciousness, could put aside ancestry as simply in the realm of 'natural history'.

In the past, the paper continued, it had been hard to get Jews to have an objective evaluation of racism. But now was the time, indeed past time, for a bit of 'quiet evaluation': 'Race is undoubtedly a very important, yes, decisive momentum. Out of "blood and soil" really is determined the being of a people and their achievements.' Jews would have to make good for 'the last generations when Jewish racial consciousness was largely neglected'. The article warned against 'bagatellised' race, and also against the CV, who were beginning to abandon their traditional assimilationist ideology in the wake of the disaster, but 'without changing basically'.

Challenging the racist bona fides of their rivals was not enough. To prove that the 'Jewish Renaissance Movement' had always been racist, the *Rundschau* reprinted two pre-1914 articles under the title 'Voices of the Blood'. '*Das singende Blut*' by Stefan Zweig and '*Lied des Blutes*' by Hugo Salus rhapsodised about how 'the modern Jew . . . recognizes his Jewishness . . . through an inner experience which teaches him the special language of his blood in a mystical manner'.

But although these mimics of the Nazis were confirmed racists, they were not chauvinists. They did not think they were racially superior to the Arabs. The Zionists were even going to uplift their benighted Semitic cousins. Their volkism was only a warped answer to their own 'personality problem', as they put it: it allowed them to reconcile themselves to the existence of anti-Semitism in Germany without fighting it. They hastened to reassure their readers that many modern nations and states were racially mixed and yet the races could live in harmony. Jews were warned: now that they were to become racists, they should not become chauvinists: 'above race is humanity'.[15]

Although racism permeated through the ZVfD's literature, foreign Jewish observers always saw Joachim Prinz as its most strident propagandist. A Social Democratic voter before 1933, Prinz became rabidly volkist in the first years of the Third Reich. Some of the violent hostility towards Jews in his book *Wir Juden* could have been inserted directly into the Nazis' own propaganda. To Prinz the Jew was made up of 'misplacement, of queerness, of exhibitionism, inferiority, arrogance, self-deceit, sophisticated love of truth, hate, sickly, patriotism and rootless cosmopolitanism . . . a psychopathological arsenal of rare abundance'.[16]

Prinz was deeply contemptuous of the rational and liberal traditions which had been the common basis of all progressive thought since the American Revolution. For him the harm that liberalism had done was compensated for only by the fact that it was dying:

> Parliament and democracy are increasingly shattered. The exaggerated harmful emphasis on the value of the individual is recognised to be mistaken; the concept and reality of the nation and the *volk* is gaining, to our happiness, more and more ground.[17]

Prinz believed that an accommodation between Nazis and Jews was possible, but only on the basis of a Zionist–Nazi accord: 'A state which is constructed on the principle of the purity of nation and race can only have respect for those Jews who see themselves in the same way.'[18]

After he came to the United States Prinz realised that nothing he had been saying in Germany sounded rational in a democratic context and he abandoned his bizarre notions, further proof that the German Zionists had simply adapted ideologically to Nazism.[19] But perhaps the best illustration of the Zionists' Nazification was the curious statement by one of the *Rundschau*'s editors, Arnold Zweig, made in his *Insulted and Exiled*, naturally written abroad and published in 1937:

> of all the newspapers published in German, the most independent, the most courageous, and the ablest was the *Judische Rundschau*, the official organ of the Zionist Union of Germany. Although it sometimes went too far in its approval of the Nationalist State (seeking its own national idealism in the Nazi spirit), there, nevertheless, issued from it a stream of energy, tranquility, warmth, and confidence of which the German Jews and Jewry the world over stood in urgent need.[20]

'The Exclusive Control of German Jewish Life'

Not even the Nuremberg Laws of 15 September 1935 challenged the basic German Zionist belief in an ultimate *modus vivendi* with the Nazis. The *HeChalutz* (Pioneer) Centre, in charge of training youth for the kibbutz movement, concluded that the promulgation of laws making mixed marriage a crime was a suitable occasion for a new approach to the regime. The Pioneers came up with a plan for the emigration of the entire Jewish community over a period of 15-25 years. Abraham Margaliot, a scholar at Israel's Yad Vashem Holocaust Institute, has explained the thinking at the Centre in that fateful year:

> The HeChalutz leaders assumed that this underlying goal would prove so alluring to the German authorities that they would agree to extend aid towards further emigration abroad by liberalizing the laws governing the transfer of foreign currency abroad, by providing opportunities for vocational training and by 'political means'.[21]

The *Rundschau* published excerpts from a speech in which Hitler announced that his government still hoped to find a basis for 'a better attitude towards the Jews'.[22] The paper published a statement by A.I. Brandt, the head of the Nazis' press association, which informed a doubtlessly somewhat surprised world that the laws were:

> both beneficial and regenerative for Judaism as well. By giving the Jewish minority an opportunity to lead its own life and assuring governmental support for this independent existence, Germany is

helping Judaism to strengthen its national character and is making a contribution towards improving relations between the two peoples.[23]

The goal of the ZVfD became 'national autonomy'. They wanted Hitler to give Jews the right to an economic existence, protection from attacks on their honour, and training to prepare them for migration. The ZVfD became absorbed in trying to utilise the segregated Jewish institutions to develop a Jewish national spirit. The tighter the Nazis turned the screw on the Jews, the more convinced they became that a deal with the Nazis was possible. After all, they reasoned, the more the Nazis excluded the Jews from every aspect of German life, the more they would have need of Zionism to help them get rid of the Jews. By 15 January 1936 the *Palestine Post* had to make the startling report that: 'A bold demand that the German Zionist Federation be given recognition by the government as the only instrument for the exclusive control of German Jewish life was made by the executive of that body in a proclamation today.'[24]

German Zionist hopes for an arrangement faded only in the face of the ever-mounting intimidation and terror. Even then there was no sign of any attempts at anti-Nazi activity on the part of the ZVfD leaders. Throughout the entire pre-war period there was only a tiny Zionist involvement in the anti-Nazi underground. Although the HeChalutz and Hashomer youth movements talked socialism, the Nazis were not concerned. Yechiel Greenberg of Hashomer admitted in 1938 that 'our socialism was considered merely a philosophy for export'.[25] But almost from the beginning of the dictatorship the underground KPD, always looking for new recruits, sent some of their Jewish cadre into the youth movements and, according to Arnold Paucker — now the editor of London's *Leo Baeck Institute Year Book* — some Zionist youth became involved with the resistance at least to the extent of some illegal postering in the early years of the regime.[26] How much of this was due to the influence of the Communist infiltrators, and how much was spontaneous is impossible to estimate. However, the Zionist bureaucracy vigorously attacked the KPD.[27] As in Italy, so in Germany: the Zionist leadership sought the support of the regime for Zionism and resisted Communism; in neither country could it be thought of as part of the anti-Fascist resistance.

The interrelationship between the ZVfD and the WZO will be described below. Suffice to say for now, that the WZO leaders approved of the general line of their German affiliate. However, within the ranks of the world movement there were many who refused to remain silent while their German branch not only accepted second-class citizenship as no more than the Jews had a right to expect but, even worse, denounced foreign Jews for boycotting Germany. Boris Smolar, the chief European correspondent for the Jewish Telegraphic Agency, the Zionist wire service, spoke for all these when he wrote angrily, in 1935:

> One can understand that a Jewish newspaper which appears in Germany may not be in a position fully to support the demands of World Jewry with regard to the full restoration of Jewish rights. This, however, doesn't justify any official organ to come out and practically agree to the anti-Jewish limitations which exist in Germany. This last is exactly what the *Judische Rundschau* has done.[28]

Prior to the Nazis, German Zionism was no more than an isolated bourgeois political cult. While the leftists were trying to fight the brownshirts in the streets, the Zionists were busy collecting money for trees in Palestine. Suddenly in 1933 this small group conceived of itself as properly anointed by history to negotiate secretly with the Nazis, to oppose the vast mass of world Jewry who wanted to resist Hitler, all in the hope of obtaining the support of the enemy of their people for the building of their state in Palestine. Smolar and their other Zionist critics saw the ZVfD as merely cowardly, but they were quite wrong. Any surrender theory explains nothing of the pre-Hitler evolution of Zionist racism, nor does it go far in explaining the WZO's endorsement of their stance. The truth is sadder than cowardice. The plain fact is that Germany's Zionists did not see themselves as surrendering but, rather, as would-be partners in a most statesmanlike pact. They were wholly deluded. No Jews triumphed over other Jews in Nazi Germany. No *modus vivendi* was ever even remotely possible between Hitler and the Jews. Once Hitler had triumphed inside Germany, the position of the Jews was hopeless; all that was left for them was to go into exile and continue the fight from there. Many did, but the Zionists continued to dream of winning the patronage of Adolf Hitler for themselves. They did not fight Hitler before he came to power, when there was still a chance to beat him, not out of any degree of cowardice, but out of their deepest conviction, which they had inherited from Herzl, that anti-Semitism could not be fought. Given their failure to resist during Weimar, and given their race theories, it was inevitable that they would end up as the ideological jackals of Nazism.

Notes

1. Jacob Boas, 'A Nazi Travels to Palestine', *History Today* (London, January 1980), p. 33.

2. Martin Rosenbluth, *Go Forth and Serve*, p. 253.

3. Ibid., p. 254.

4. Ibid., p. 255.

5. Ibid., p. 258.

6. Yisrael Gutman (in debate), *Jewish Resistance during the Holocaust*, p. 116.

7. Stephen Wise, *Challenging Years*, p. 248.

8. Joachim Prinz, 'Zionism under the Nazi Government', *Young Zionist* (London, November 1937), p. 18.

9. Lucy Dawidowicz (ed.), *A Holocaust Reader*, pp. 150–5.

10. Ruth Bondy, *The Emissary: A Life of Enzo Sereni*, pp. 118–19.

11. Jacob Boas, 'The Jews of Germany: Self-Perception in the Nazi Era as Reflected in the German Jewish Press 1933–1938', PhD thesis, University of California, Riverside (1977), p. 135.

12. Dawidowicz, *A Holocaust Reader*, p. 148.

13. Ibid., p. 149.

14. Meir Michaelis, *Mussolini and the Jews*, p. 122.

15. 'Rasse als Kulturfaktor', *Judische Rundschau* (4 August 1933), p. 392.

16. Koppel Pinson, 'The Jewish Spirit in Nazi Germany', *Menorah Journal* (Autumn 1936), p. 235.

17. Uri Davis, *Israel: Utopia Incorporated*, p. 18.

18. Benyamin Matuvo, 'The Zionist Wish and the Nazi Deed', *Issues* (Winter 1966/7), p. 12.

19. Author's interview with Joachim Prinz (8 February 1981).

20. Arnold Zweig, *Insulted and Exiled* (London, 1937), p. 232.

21. Abraham Margaliot, 'The Reaction of the Jewish Public in Germany to the Nuremberg Laws', *Yad Vashem Studies*, vol. XII, p. 89.

22. Ibid., p. 85.

23. Ibid., p. 86.

24. 'German Zionists Seek Recognition', *Palestine Post* (15 January 1936), p. 1.

25. Yechiel Greenberg, 'Hashomer Hatzair in Europe', *Hashomer Hatzair* (November 1937), p. 13.

26. Author's interview with Arnold Paucker, 28 October 1980.

27. Giora Josephthal, *The Responsible Attitude*, p. 88.

28. Boris Smolar, 'Zionist Overtures to Nazism', *Jewish Daily Bulletin* (8 March 1935), p. 2.

6 THE JEWISH ANTI-NAZI BOYCOTT AND THE ZIONIST-NAZI TRADE AGREEMENT

It was only the incompetence of his foes that allowed Hitler to come to power, and the new Chancellor still had to prove to his capitalist patrons that he could handle the responsibilities of running Germany. His position was by no means completely secure: the workers were still against him, and the industrialists still had to be shown that he could get the economy moving. Abroad the capitalists wavered between relief that he had crushed the Communists and fear that he would eventually start another war. Foreign opinion was now crucial: Germany was dependent on the world market, and Hitler's anti-Semitism became a problem. The Jews were powerful in the emporiums of the world, particularly in two of Germany's biggest markets — Eastern Europe and America. German business interests were by no means certain about their loyalty to the new Chancellor; together with their friends in the army they might have to curb him or even replace him, if they were themselves to suffer losses because the Jews and his other foreign foes united in a boycott of German exports. The regime's own economic experts frankly discussed their grave weakness and were extremely concerned that the New Order might not survive resolute opposition abroad.

The Jews moved very slowly but finally New York's Jewish War Veterans (JWV), after considering the consequences for German Jewry, announced a trade boycott on 19 March 1933 and organised a huge protest parade on the 23rd. The Mayor of New York took part and so did the Communists, whom the ex-servicemen refused to allow into the demonstration until they took down their banners. Spurning the thousands of Communists in New York's Jewish community doomed the tiny veteran group's efforts. Politically extremely naive, the veterans ignored the elementary fact that for a boycott to have even the slightest chance of success, it must have the broadest possible organised unity behind it. Soon after the veterans' failure Abe Coralnik, a Zionist, and Samuel Untermyer, a sympathiser who had donated the money for the new stadium at the Hebrew University in Jerusalem, put together what ultimately became the Non-Sectarian Anti-Nazi League. However, boycott picketing was illegal and Untermyer, a Tammany lawyer, would not break the law. Of course, without mass picketing a boycott cannot be enforced and those in the Jewish community who were determined to impose a boycott turned next to rabbi Wise and the Zionist American Jewish Congress (AJC) to take the lead. At first Wise opposed both demonstrations and a boycott, but by 27 March even he was willing to fill Madison Square Garden for the rally that so disturbed Goering. A large assembly of politicians, churchmen and trade union bureaucrats duly denounced the tyrant in Berlin, but nothing was done to organise mass support. Wise, who had not mobilised the masses before Hitler came to power, was not the one to do it now. On the contrary, he wrote to a friend: 'You cannot imagine what I am doing to resist the masses. They want tremendous street scenes.'[1] He opposed a boycott, hoping that a few demonstrations, alone, would press Roosevelt into intervening. But the State Department saw Hitler as a battering ram against Communism, and the domestic politicians, desperately wanting to end the Depression, craved for Germany as a market. The result was that the Democrats did nothing either against Hitler or for the Jews. As a Democrat himself, Wise continued to hold out against a boycott but, while he was in Europe in August 1933, consulting German Jewish leaders and attending the WZ Congress, the more militant elements in the AJC managed to call a boycott. But the AJC was still a thoroughly bourgeois organisation without experience in mass mobilisation and, like the Anti-Nazi League, it timidly opposed picketing. Its boycott director did nothing more strenuous than issue splendid statistics on how the Nazis' trade was being devastated by the boycott.[2] It was not until its youth group finally rebelled and picketed a department-store chain in the autumn of 1934 that the AJC allowed its affiliates to picket recalcitrant merchants.

Boycotts are almost never successful. Most people think they have done enough if they stop buying the goods, but a boycott can only work if there is a solid organisation prepared to disrupt trade seriously. The blame for the failure to build that movement lay with many: both Jewish and non-Jewish. Certainly the trade union leaders who pledged their opposition to Hitler, but did nothing to mobilise their ranks were to a large measure responsible for the lack of a serious boycott campaign. Certainly those Jewish groups like the JWV, the Anti-Nazi League and the AJC were ineffectual, but there were those in the Jewish community in America and Britain who specifically opposed the very notion of a boycott. The American Jewish Committee, the *B'nai B'rith* (Sons of the Covenant) fraternal order and the Board of Deputies of British Jews refused to back the boycott. They feared that if the Jewish workers, and others as well, took it into their heads to fight

Hitler, perhaps they would stay in motion and come after their own rich closer to home. These worthies confined themselves to charity efforts for German Jewry and its refugees and prayed that Hitlerism would not spread. The *Agudas Yisrael* (Union of Israel), the political arm of the most extreme wing of traditional Orthodoxy, opposed the boycott on religious grounds as well as their social conservativism. They claimed that ever since the ancient Jewish kingdom was destroyed by the Romans, the Talmud had forbidden Jews to revolt against Gentile authority in the Diaspora; they interpreted the boycott as rebellion and therefore forbidden. However, of all of the active Jewish opponents of the boycott idea, the most important was the World Zionist Organisation (WZO). It not only bought German wares; it sold them, and even sought out new customers for Hitler and his industrialist backers.

The Appeal of the Blood Idea

The WZO saw Hitler's victory in much the same way as its German affiliate, the ZVfD: not primarily as a defeat for all Jewry, but as positive proof of the bankruptcy of assimilationism and liberalism. Their own hour was at hand. Zionists began to sound like tent-revivalists: Hitler was history's flail to drive the stiff-necked Jews back to their own kind and their own land. A recent Zionist convert, the then world-famous popular biographer Emil Ludwig, was interviewed by a fellow Zionist on a visit to America and expressed the general attitude of the Zionist movement:

> 'Hitler will be forgotten in a few years, but he will have a beautiful monument in Palestine. You know', and here the biographer-historian seemed to assume the role of a patriarchal Jew – 'the coming of the Nazis was rather a welcome thing. So many of our German Jews were hovering between two coasts; so many of them were riding the treacherous current between the Scylla of assimilation and the Charybdis of a nodding acquaintance with Jewish things. Thousands who seemed to be completely lost to Judaism were brought back to the fold by Hitler, and for that I am personally very grateful to him.'[3]

Ludwig was a newcomer to the movement, but his views were in complete concord with those of such veterans as the celebrated Chaim

Nachman Bialik, thought of then as the poet laureate of Zion. Because of his reputation, his statements were given wide circulation both by the Zionist movement and its left-wing enemies. The poet's concern had long been the breakdown of Jewish unity resulting from the decline of traditional religious faith, and now he could not hide his happiness that Hitler had come just in time to save German Jewry from its own destruction.

> Hitlerism, the poet feels, has rendered at least one service in draw-ing no lines between the faithful Jew and the apostate Jew. Had Hitler excepted the baptized Jews, there would have developed, Bialik contended, the unedifying spectacle of thousands of Jews running to the baptismal fonts. Hitlerism has perhaps saved German Jewry, which was being assimilated into annihilation. At the same time, it has made the world so conscious of the Jewish problem, that they can no longer ignore it.[4]

Bialik, like many other Zionists, thought of the Jews as something of a super race; if only they would finally come to their senses and stop wasting themselves on an ungrateful humanity and started working in their own vineyard.

> Indeed it is quite true that Judaism, by penetrating into all the nations actually did undermine the remnants of that sort of idolatry . . . but perhaps the strongest forces in this process were our 'apo-state' or 'assimilated' Jews of all types, who entered into the very body of Christianity and stirred its very bowels, and went on slowly undermining the remnants of paganism as a result of their Jewish volition and their Jewish blood. I, too, like Hitler, believe in the power of the blood idea. These were the men — although often the names of great non-Jews are called in their stead — who smoothed the roads for the great movements of freedom all over the world: The Renaissance, Liberalism, Democracy, Socialism and Com-munism . . . Anti-Semites sometimes have clear discernment. Jewish influence has indeed been very powerful in this connection; we ought not to deny it.[5]

However, by 1934 Zionism was a movement claiming over a million members world-wide and not all of them accepted the upside-down notion that Hitler really was a boon to the Jews. Some, like the Ameri-can rabbi, Abraham Jacobson, protested against this insane idea, which was still quite widespread even as late as 1936:

> How many times have we heard the impious wish uttered in despair over the apathy of American Jews to Zionism, that a Hitler descend upon them? Then they would realize the need for Palestine![6]

First Dealings with the Nazis

Certainly the WZO was quite prepared to try and use the Nazis for their own purposes. The first overtures to the Nazis were made independently in 1933 by one Sam Cohen, the owner of *Ha Note'a* Ltd, a Tel Aviv citrus export firm. Even under Chancellor Bruning the German government had put a flight tax on capital leaving the country and Cohen had proposed that Zionist *émigrés* be allowed to avoid the tax by purchasing goods in Germany which would later be turned back into cash after sale in Palestine. Bruning had no interest in the idea, but in 1933 Cohen, on his own, presented the plan again. The Nazis were already worried about the effect even the spontaneous and lamentably organised boycott was having on their balance of trade, and Heinrich Wolff, the German Consul in Jerusalem, quickly grasped just how useful Cohen's proposition could be. He wrote to his ministry: 'In this way it might be possible to wage a successful campaign against the Jewish boycott of Germany. It might be possible to make a breach in the wall.'[7]

The Jews, he argued, would be put in a quandary. Further boycott would be seen as imposing problems on emigrants seeking to find new homes for themselves in Palestine or elsewhere. Because of his location, Wolff was one of the first Germans to perceive the growing importance of Palestine in the Jewish equation, and in June he wrote again to Berlin:

> Whereas in April and May the Yishuv was waiting boycott instructions from the United States, it now seems that the situation has been transformed. It is Palestine which now gives the instructions . . . It is important to break the boycott first and foremost in Palestine, and the effect will inevitably be felt on the main front, in the United States.[8]

In early May 1933 the Nazis signed an agreement with Cohen for one million Reichmarks ($400,000) of Jewish wealth to be shipped to

Palestine in the form of farm machinery. At this point the WZO intervened. The Depression had badly affected donations and in March 1933
they had desperately cabled to their followers in America pleading
that if funds were not forthcoming immediately, they were heading for
imminent financial collapse.[9] Now Menachem Ussischkin, head of the
Jewish National Fund, got Cohen to arrange for the release of frozen
JNF monies in Germany via Ha Note'a. The bait for the Nazis was that
the cash was needed to buy land for the Jews whom Hitler would be
pushing out. Cohen also assured Heinrich Wolff that he would operate
'behind the scenes' at a forthcoming Jewish conference in London to
weaken or defeat any boycott resolution.[10] Dr Fritz Reichert, the
Gestapo's agent in Palestine, later wrote to his headquarters reminding
them of the affair:

> The London Boycott Conference was torpedoed from Tel Aviv
> because the head of the Transfer in Palestine, in close contact with
> the consulate in Jerusalem, sent cables to London. Our main func-
> tion here is to prevent, from Palestine, the unification of world
> Jewry on a basis hostile to Germany . . . It is advisable to damage the
> political and economic strength of Jewry by sowing dissension in
> its ranks.[11]

Sam Cohen was soon superseded in these delicate negotiations by
Labour Zionist, Chaim Arlosoroff, the Political Secretary of the Jewish
Agency, the WZO's Palestine centre. Arlosoroff was keenly aware of
the movement's problems. In 1932 he had concluded that they had
failed to attract enough immigrants to overcome the Arabs' numbers
and they were not drawing enough Jewish capital. Hitler in power
would mean war within ten years. To survive in Palestine and solve the
Jewish problem in that period meant swift and vigorous action. Now,
he thought, he had the way for Zionism to solve its difficulties: with
Britain's agreement, they could get both the immigrants and the capital
needed through extending Cohen's project. In an article in the *Rundschau* and elsewhere, he coldly explained that this could only be done
in complete co-operation with Berlin:

> Naturally, Germany cannot expose herself to the risk of upsetting
> her currency and exchange balance in order to meet the Jews, but a
> way out can be found to adjust these different interests . . . It would
> be worth while, leaving all sentimentalities out of the question, to
> reach such an agreement with Germany.

The self-styled Socialist–Zionist then proposed the ultimate alliance, a deal between the Zionists, the Nazis, the Fascists and the British Empire, to organise the evacuation of Jewry from Germany:

> It could also be possible to establish a company, with the participation of the German State and other European, primarily British and Italian interests, which would slowly liquidate the particular properties by issuing letters of credit . . [and creating] . . . A guarantee fund.[12]

He felt his idea was particularly timely because world opinion would support a 'constructive treatment of the Jewish question in Germany'.[13] Knowing the German Jews would not want to put all their money in Hitler's hands, he proposed that the British should choose the fund's manager. His comrade Yitzhak Lufban wrote later that 'Arlosoroff suggested several names, and the Colonial Secretary picked one of them'.[14] In early May 1933, Arlosoroff and the Nazis came to a preliminary understanding to extend Cohen's arrangements. He visited Berlin again in June, and returned to Tel Aviv on 14 June. Two nights later he was assassinated because of his dealings with the Nazis. The killing will be discussed below; it is sufficient to say here that it did not slow down the WZO's accommodation with the Nazis, and a Zionist–Nazi pact was announced by the Nazis in time for the 18th Zionist Congress in August in Prague.

The WZO Justifies the Pact with the Nazis

Hitler's shadow completely dominated the Prague Congress. The WZO's leaders knew that the Nazis were interested in a deal and they determined to avoid offending Germany by limiting discussion of the situation there to the barest minimum.[15] The regime as such was not condemned. The League of Nations was asked to help in the 'fight for the recovery of the rights of the Jews in Germany', but the request was buried in a lengthy discussion of emigration and Palestine.[16] No plan was proposed to put pressure on the world body, nor was any specific action called for on the League's part.

The Zionist–Nazi pact became public the day before a boycott resolution was to be debated, and it may be speculated that the Nazis did this so as to discourage endorsement of the boycott. The leader of the right-wing 'Revisionists', Vladimir Jabotinsky, presented the boycott case, but there was no chance of his proposal getting a serious hearing. The British had arrested several of his Revisionists for Arlosoroff's murder and the prosecutor was putting evidence before the court while the Congress met. As the Revisionists had a history of violence against their Zionist rivals, most delegates were convinced of their complicity in the Arlosoroff affair. Their unsavoury reputation was enhanced when Jabotinsky's own brownshirts accompanied him into the hall in full military formation, compelling the presidium to outlaw the uniforms for fear they would provoke Arlosoroff's Labour comrades into a riot. Jabotinsky's support for the boycott, and his opposition to the pact, was dismissed as the raging of a terrorist opponent of the democratically elected moderate leadership. His resolution was defeated by a vote of 240 to 48.

However, defeating Jabotinsky's resolution did not necessarily mean that the delegates favoured a deal with Hitler and, when the Nazis announced that they had signed an agreement with the Zionists allowing German Jews to ship three million Reichmarks' worth of Jewish wealth to Palestine in the form of German export goods, much of the Congress dismissed the statement as a propaganda stunt. When the truth became clear, pandemonium broke loose. The leadership had completely miscalculated and genuinely expected the pact to be immensely popular. Now, stunned by the hostile opposition, they tried to protect themselves by outright lying; the Labour leader, Berl Locker, brazenly proclaimed: 'the executive of the World Zionist Organisation had nothing to do with the negotiations which led to an agreement with the German government'.[17] No one believed this crude fabrication.

Many delegates, particularly the Americans, were in favour of the boycott and voted against Jabotinsky, primarily because they felt the WZO was too preoccupied with Palestine to take on additional chores. Now Stephen Wise presented the leadership with an ultimatum: explain 'how to prevent German . . . propagandists from utilising the agreement'. His demand 'was heatedly discussed all day . . . by the Political Committee'.[18] In the end the leaders did not dare take official responsibility for the 'Ha'avara' or Transfer Agreement, and pretended that it only bound Germany and the formal signatory, the Anglo-Palestine Bank. But, since the bank was their own bank, they only succeeded in making themselves look ridiculous to friend and foe alike.

The debate over the Zionist–Nazi pact continued angrily until 1935. The Ha'avara rapidly grew to become a substantial banking and trading house with 137 specialists in its Jerusalem office at the height of its activities. The regulations were always changing in response to Nazi pressure, but in essence the agreement was always the same: German Jews could put money into a bank inside Germany, which was then used to buy exports which were sold outside Germany, usually but not exclusively in Palestine. When the *émigrés* finally arrived in Palestine, they would receive payment for the goods that they had previously purchased after they had finally been sold. Fiscal ingenuity extended Ha'avara's operations in many directions, but throughout its operation its attraction to German Jews remained the same: it was the least painful way of shipping Jewish wealth out of Germany. However, the Nazis determined the rules, and they naturally got worse with time; by 1938 the average user was losing at least 30 per cent and even 50 per cent of his money. Nevertheless, this was still three times, and eventually five times, better than the losses endured by Jews whose money went to any other destination.[19]

The top limit through the Ha'avara scheme was 50,000 marks ($20,000 or £4,000) per emigrant, which made the Ha'avara unattractive to the richest Jews. Therefore only $40,419,000 went to Palestine via Ha'avara, whereas $650 million went to the United States, $60 million to the United Kingdom and other substantial sums elsewhere. Yet if, in terms of German Jewry's wealth, Ha'avara was by no means decisive, it was crucial to Zionism. Some 60 per cent of all capital invested in Palestine between August 1933 and September 1939 was channelled through the agreement with the Nazis.[20] In addition, the British set the annual Jewish immigrant quota, using the weak economic absorptive capacity of the country to limit their number; however, 'capitalists' — those bringing in over £1,000 ($5,000) — were allowed in over quota. The 16,529 capitalists were thus an additional source of immigrants as well as an economic harvest for Zionism. Their capital generated a boom, giving Palestine a wholly artificial prosperity in the midst of the world-wide Depression.

At first the WZO tried to defend itself against the charges of boycott-scabbing and outright collaboration by insisting that the Ha'avara transfers did not really break the boycott, since Germany did not receive foreign currency for its goods as they were all purchased inside the country for marks. However, Berlin soon demanded part payment for some of the commodities in foreign currency and soon, too, the WZO started soliciting new customers for Germany in Egypt, Lebanon, Syria and Iraq. Eventually the Zionists began exporting oranges to Belgium and Holland using Nazi ships.[21] By 1936 the WZO began to sell Hitler's goods in Britain.[22]

The WZO was not interested in fighting the Nazis, and every defence of the Ha'avara scheme demonstrated that. Selig Brodetsky, one of the members of the Zionist Executive and later, in 1939, the President of the British Board of Deputies, rebuked the world for scorning them:

> Congress had risen to a level to which few Jewish bodies could have riseñ. It was a very easy thing to use violent words, to organise meetings, to call boycotts, but it was a far more difficult thing to speak calmly and use cool reasoning. It was said that the decisions concerning Germany were too weak. NO! Non-Jews could afford to use strong words, but Jews could not.[23]

It was not the Zionists who were the traitors, it was everyone else that was out of step — or so at least Moshe Beilenson, a leading Labour Zionist, would have had the world believe. This had not been his first effort at collaboration with Fascism. In 1922 he had been one of the delegation that pledged Italian Zionism's loyalty to Mussolini. Now he tried to present a theoretical defence of the Nazi pact:

> after the Ghetto walls had been overthrown, our main weapon for the defense of our lives and our rights was the protest . . . All our protests in the course of decades did not succeed in destroying the reign of persecution not only in the vast empire of the Tsars, but even in the relatively tiny Rumania . . .
>
> The Congress did not 'betray'; it triumphed. It was not 'afraid'; on the contrary, it had the courage to initiate a new Jewish statesmanship . . . Verily, the Eighteenth Congress had the courage to destroy the assimilationist tradition whose chief characteristic is a reliance on others and appeals to others . . . For generations we fought by means of protests. Now we have another weapon in our hand, a strong, trusty and sure weapon: the visa to Palestine.[24]

The great majority of Jews opposed the Ha'avara. It had no defenders outside the WZO, and trading with the Nazis was not popular with many inside its own ranks. Protests started pouring in while the Prague Congress was still in session. The pact was extremely unpopular in Poland, where the Jews feared that if there was no resistance to the anti-Semitism next door, their own Jew-haters would start demanding that the Polish government imitate the Germans. In America and Britain, each with a more or less democratic tradition, many Zionists, including some of the leading names in the movement, opposed it. The prominent Cleveland rabbi, Abba Hillel Silver, was one of the very first to complain, in August 1933:

> Why the very idea of Palestine Jewry negotiating with Hitler about business instead of demanding justice for the persecuted Jews of Germany is unthinkable. One might think that the whole affair was a bankruptcy sale and that the Jews of Palestine were endeavouring to salvage a few bargains for themselves.[25]

Lamentations were heard even at the far corners of the earth. The Melbourne *Jewish Weekly News* protested: 'they will make us a laughing-stock among the Germans, who will be able to declare that when it comes to a conflict between Jewish business and sentiment, business always wins'.[26] Rabbi Wise returned to the subject on innumerable occasions. In September 1933 he referred to Ha'avara as the 'new golden calf − the Golden Orange' and continued: 'I think I speak the mind of Jews everywhere when I say we hold in abhorrence any Jew, whether in or out of Palestine, who undertakes to make any commercial arrangements with the Nazi government for any reason whatever'.[27]

In a speech at a World Jewish Conference at Geneva in 1934, Wise attacked the Labourites who had become the dominant force in Palestinian Zionism:

> One leading Palestinian put it over and over again at Prague: Palestine has primacy. This conference must clearly state, that while Palestine has primacy over all other factors in the equation, its primacy ceases when it comes into conflict with a higher moral law.[28]

Wise had identified the rot in the WZO: the land of Israel had become far more important than the needs of the people Israel. Labour Zionism had become, in the fullest sense, a utopian cult. They saw a new Jew in the old Jewish land as the only way for a Jewish nation to continue to exist. The real Jewish people, the millions of Jews of the Diaspora, were no more than a reservoir from which they would pick young immigrants to build their state. The Diaspora, as such, was doomed: either the Jews would be driven out, as in Germany, or assimilated as in France. With this strange perspective that Jewish survival stood or fell with them in Israel, the Zionists were driven to seek more from the Nazis to make their vision into a reality.

In late 1933 they tried to revive Arlosoroff's full-scale liquidation bank. Weizmann let Cohen propose to the German Foreign Ministry that he, the former President of the movement, now chairman of its Central Bureau for the Settlement of German Jews, should come to Berlin to discuss the liquidation scheme, but the Nazis declined to extend him an invitation.[29] They were always less interested in making a deal with the Zionists than the Zionists were to come to terms with them. The Nazis had achieved what they wanted, the Zionists had broken the boycott and showed no signs of resisting them; for the moment that was enough. But not even that rebuff could throw Weizmann off course. A year and a half later, on 3 July 1935, he wrote to Arthur Ruppin, director of the Colonisation Department in Palestine, and one of the most devoted apostles of further intimacy with the Nazis.

> Dr Moses, as I hear, made contacts with the Reich Ministry for National Economy, and, following a number of talks he had there, submitted a memorandum demanding that eventual additional exports to England, if achieved at the request of our friends in Germany, be used in favor of the £1,000 people.[30]

Weizmann went on to make it clear that the Prague Congress statement about the 'fight' for German Jewish rights was strictly lip-service. He discussed Prague in the context of the forthcoming 1935 Lucerne Congress:

> I know very well that the Congress in Lucerne can by-pass and take no notice of the German Jewish question just as did the Prague Congress . . . I dare to doubt if anyone, especially the German Jews and the German Zionists, will gain advantage from the German Jewish question being treated in all thoroughness, moreover in a special report. It will not achieve a positive useful effect especially today, in view of the readiness in the world to come to terms with Germany. On the other hand, I believe it is very possible that such a report may become dangerous to the only positive thing we have in Germany, the intensified Zionist movement . . . We, being a Zionist Organisation, should concern ourselves with the constructive solution of the German question through the transfer of the Jewish youth from Germany to Palestine, rather than with the question of equal rights of Jews in Germany.[31]

'Constructive', it will be recalled, was always one of Weizmann's

favourite clichés; after the First World War he had assured the capitalists at Versailles that Zionism was constructive, unlike the behaviour of
those Jews who engaged in 'destructive tendencies'. 'Constructive'
thinking with regard to Hitler, so widespread in capitalist circles of the
day, was extraordinary coming from a Jew, but of course High Zionism
was a world away from the ordinary Jewish mentality. Weizmann's
friend, the German-born Ruppin, was a good case in point. A race
improver, it was he who was in charge of turning middle-class youths
into 'constructive' toilers on health-giving Jewish *boden*. In 1934 his
book, *Jews in the Modern World*, openly expressed the accommodationist line of the Zionist movement. In it he told the Jews, again, that
it was their fault that things had occurred in the way they had, and he
admonished them that:

> Such an attempt at a peaceful settlement of the problem would have
> been possible if . . . Jews . . . had recognized that their peculiar posi-
> tion among the Germans was bound to lead to conflicts which had
> their origin in the nature of man, and couldn't be removed by argu-
> ments and reason. Had both sides realized that the present position
> was due not to bad will but to circumstances, which had arisen in-
> dependently of the will of either side, it would have been unnecessary
> to attempt the solution of the Jewish problem in an orgy of un-
> bridled hatred.

His 'misunderstanding' theory developed logically into his concluding:
'Various intermediate and partial solutions will be required to reach a
modus vivendi.'[32]

Lewis Namier, a former Political Secretary of the WZO, and a major
historian of the British aristocracy, had prefaced Ruppin's book.
Knowledgeable Zionists, including Nahum Goldmann, saw Namier as
an intense Jewish anti-Semite.[33] In his devotion to the gentry, he
despised the Jews as the epitome of capitalism, of vulgar 'trade'. As
might be expected, his introduction expressed his 'understanding' of
anti-Semitism — 'not everyone who feels uncomfortable with regard
to us must be called an anti-Semite, nor is there anything necessarily
and inherently wicked in anti-Semitism'.[34] In fact the original draft
was even stronger. Weizmann had read it and had to warn Namier not
to be so open in expressing their mutual toleration of Nazism:

> On p. 6 the lines 'but what has happened etc. . . .' marked in pencil
> seem to me dangerous, although I agree with your conclusion. But

it's a book by Ruppin and a preface by you and it will be quoted in Germany and the 'louts' will say, 'the Jews themselves think that it will be all for the good, etc.' I would omit it if possible.[35]

Such were the minds of the leading figures of the Zionist movement in 1935 as they trooped into their summer Congress at Lucerne. Publicly on record as denying that the Ha'avara had anything to do with them, secretly they were doing all they could to extend it. In every respect their thinking and their policies were at odds with the immense majority of the Jews of the world.

'Trying to Derive the utmost Advantage from it in the Zionist Sense'

The Zionist leadership still had to face one last internal battle over the Ha'avara and their general stance toward the Nazis. Jabotinsky and his Revisionists had split off from the WZO, but a remnant of his followers − now called the *Judenstaat Partei* (Jewish State Party) − had stayed loyal to the WZO and still demanded repudiation of the Transfer. Several journalists described the short but ferocious debate at the 1935 Congress. The *Canadian Zionist* reported that:

A vote was taken and resulted in Mr Grossman's motion [for a debate on whether the Anglo-Palestinian Bank had caused the arrest of picketers who had protested the use of German cement] being defeated. Whereupon there were loud derisive cries of 'Heil Hitler!' on the part of some of Mr Grossman's supporters. This caused pandemonium.[36]

Paul Novick, the editor of the American Communist daily newspaper, the *Morgen Freiheit*, related that the 'Histadrut delegates answered in kind, shouting towards the *Judenstaat* people: "Schuschnigg agents" (meaning agents of Italo-Austrian Fascism).'[37]

The Executive's policy toward Hitler had stout defenders at the Congress. A theoretical defence was presented by Moshe Shertok, who had succeeded Arlosoroff as the organisation's Political Secretary (their equivalent to Foreign Minister). The man who later became the second Prime Minister of Israel sternly told the delegates, and the listening Jewish world, that they just had to realise that:

The Jewish people had no greater hope for success in the struggle for existence than through the upbuilding of Eretz Israel, and they must, therefore, be willing to draw the consequences. They imitated the protests and boycotts practised by other peoples, but forgot that those measures were expressions of the force possessed by those peoples, whereas the Zionist movement had yet to create such a force for itself.[38]

Beyond the Congress some of the most important propagandists of the WZO's strategy were the *shliachim* or emissaries sent out world-wide by the Labour Zionists in Palestine. Enzo Sereni, another graduate of the accommodationist Italian movement, had been the emissary in Germany in 1931-2, but he had done nothing to either mobilise the German Jews or assist the SPD in their fight against the Nazis. Sereni was one of those who saw Hitler as a scourge driving Jewry toward Zionism. He once informed Max Ascoli, an Italian anti-Fascist activist, that 'Hitler's anti-Semitism might yet lead to the salvation of the Jews'.[39] At the Lucerne Congress he was the vigorous exponent of the primacy of Palestine:

We have nothing to be ashamed of in the fact that we used the persecution of the Jews in Germany for the upbuilding of Palestine. That is how our sages and leaders of old have taught us ... to make use of the catastrophes of the Jewish population in the Diaspora for upbuilding.[40]

But by far the best example of the leadership's unwillingness to resist the Nazis was Weizmann's statement:

The only dignified and really effective reply to all that is being inflicted upon the Jews of Germany is the edifice erected by our great and beautiful work in the Land of Israel . . . Something is being created that will transform the woe we all suffer into songs and legends for our grand-children.[41]

The presidium manoeuvred to keep any serious discussion of resistance off the Congress floor, and Wise's name was struck from the speakers' list for fear that he would denounce Hitler. He threatened to walk out of the Congress if he was not allowed to speak and, as the Congress knew they could not afford to have the most famous Zionist in America walk out on such a controversial issue, they finally gave way and let him speak. He duly got up, said that he was opposed to

Hitler — hardly a statement that would have attracted attention in most other company — and sat down. He and Abba Hillel Silver had never really done much more than talk about boycott, and by 1935 there was nothing in America that remotely resembled an effective boycott organisation. In practice, they had no alternative programme for effective resistance; now, primarily focusing on Palestine as a refuge for German Jewry, they capitulated to Weizmann and endorsed the Ha'avara, and after the Lucerne Congress there were no longer any serious differences between them and the international movement. In the end the only official protest against Hitlerism made by the assembly was a half-day cancellation of one of their sessions, a meaningless gesture.

Weizmann had little real difficulty getting the Congress formally to endorse the Ha'avara, but the opposition was able to curb one of its activities. A Ha'avara subsidiary, the Near and Middle East Commercial Corporation (NEMICO), had been set up to solicit new customers for Germany throughout the Middle East. The Egyptian Zionist Federation had threatened to expose the scandal if the world organisation did not put a stop to it, and in the interests of preserving the larger scheme the leadership reluctantly had to sacrifice the NEMICO operation.

The capitulation of the Americans did nothing to quieten Jewish opposition elsewhere. Press criticism was immediate. London's *World Jewry*, then the best Zionist magazine in the English language, excoriated their own World Congress: 'Dr Weizmann went as far as to state that the only dignified reply the Jews could give was a renewed effort for the upbuilding of Palestine. How terrifying the proclamation of the Congress President must have sounded in the ears of Herren Hitler, Streicher and Goebbels!'[42]

The unofficial Zionist press in Britain shared the growing public feeling that war with Hitler was inevitable, and it could not understand the total lack of serious discussion of Nazism at the Congress. The magazine's correspondent described the meeting as strangely depressing: 'We have an agenda more suitable for a board of directors of a limited liability company than for a national conclave with the national destiny in its hands.'[43] Even the *Jewish Chronicle*, always the mouthpiece of the Jewish establishment, complained in the same vein: 'the proceedings were almost as dull as a debate on the Colonial Office in the House of Commons on a Friday morning'.[44] It felt compelled to condemn the decision on the Ha'avara:

The spectacle is puzzling to the world, whose sympathy we bespeak and disheartening to Jews for whom the boycott is one of the few weapons to their hand and who now see themselves deserted by the Movement which they most have a right to claim as an ally in their fight.[45]

In America the opposition to the Ha'avara was particularly intense in the garment industry trade unions, with their hundreds of thousands of Jewish workers. Most of the Jewish labour leaders had always looked upon Zionism with contempt. Many of them were from Russia and knew about the fateful Herzl–Plevhe meeting and how their old enemy Zubatov had backed the Poale Zionists against the Bund. As far as they were concerned the Ha'avara was just Zionism up to its old tricks, and in December 1935 Baruch Charney Vladeck, the Chairman of the Jewish Labor Committee, and himself an ex-Bundist from Poland, debated Berl Locker, the organisational head of the Palestinian Poale Zion, before an overflow crowd in New York.

Locker was compelled to take a defensive position, insisting that the agreement was purely in the interest of the German Jews. Besides, he argued, they would have brought the goods into the country on their own if there were no treaty. Why, if it had not been for the pact, he maintained, the situation would have been far worse in this regard: 'Palestine was presented by a *fait accompli* ... The Transfer agreement prevents the country from being flooded with German merchandise, since goods come in only as there is need of them.'[46]

Vladeck was not to be put off by Locker's obvious subterfuge, and he continued the attack. In New York the local Labour Zionists were simultaneously supporting the boycott in the United States while apologising for the Ha'avara in Palestine, and the old Bundist ridiculed their attempt to run with the fox and hunt with the hounds:

You may argue from now till Doomsday, but this is double book-keeping of the most flagrant sort. That nobody should break the boycott but the Jews of Palestine! And nobody deal with Germany but the Zionist organisation! ... It is my contention that the main purpose of the Transfer is not to rescue the Jews from Germany but to strengthen various institutions in Palestine . . . Palestine thus becomes the official scab-agent against the boycott in the Near East . . . When the news of the Transfer Agreement first came out . . . Berl Locker said: 'Not a single Zionist agency has the slightest connection with the Transfer' . . . From this I can conclude in only one vein: The Transfer Agreement is a blot on the Jews and on the world.[47]

If the majority of Jews did oppose the Ha'avara as treason, there was one at least who was willing to go on record as complaining that Weizmann and his friends were not going far enough. Gustav Krojanker, whose views on the Nazis were discussed in Chapter 3, was now one of the leaders of the *Hitachdut Olei Germania* (the German Immigrants Association in Palestine), and in 1936 the association published his pamphlet, *The Transfer: A Vital Question of the Zionist Movement*. To him Zionism was stark calculation, nothing more, and he was more than willing to draw the logical conclusions already inherent in the Zionist-Nazi pact. He claimed to see Nazism and the opportunities it opened up for Zionism in the authentic Herzlian manner:

His survey of the situation was devoid of any futile grudge-bearing; he perceived two political factors – an organisation of the Jewish people on the one side, and the countries concerned on the other. They were to be partners in a pact.

Krojanker berated the leadership for not having the courage to formally endorse the Ha'avara back in 1933. To him this was merely a capitulation to what he considered the 'Diaspora mentality'. He wanted them to go much further:

The Zionist Movement should have endeavoured . . . to influence the German Government to enter into a statesmanlike treaty, accepting the situation and trying to derive the utmost advantage from it in the Zionist sense.

He insisted that the necessary next step was to help the Nazis break the boycott in Europe itself through an extension of the Ha'avara. Germany 'might even be ready to conclude agreements – if we . . . prepared to extend the "Ha'avara" system to other countries'.[48] But the WZO leadership needed no such coaching from Krojanker. He did not know that, secretly, they had already decided to do just that and now, in March 1936, Siegfried Moses's negotiations had finally created the International Trade and Investment Agency (INTRIA) bank in London to organise sales of German products directly in Britain itself.[49] The Nazis had to content themselves with the satisfaction of the further demoralisation of the boycott forces, as fear of Jewish and general

British hostility to boycott-scabbing made it impossible for INTRIA to go so far as to allow British currency to come directly into German hands. Instead, the goods were bought in Germany for marks and their value was credited to Jewish capitalists needing the £1,000 entry fee required of over-quota immigrants into Palestine. Zionist–Nazi trade relations continued to develop in other spheres as well. In 1937 200,000 crates of the 'Golden Oranges' were shipped to Germany, and 1½ million more to the Low Countries under the swastika flag.[50] Even after *Kristallnacht* — 11 November 1938, the terrible night of the broken glass, when the Nazis finally unleashed the brownshirts to smash Jewish stores — the manager of Ha'avara Ltd, Werner Felchenfeld, continued to offer reduced rates to would-be users of Nazi boats. His only concern was to reassure the squeamish that 'competition with British vessels does not arise, as this transfer arrangement is valid for citrus being shipped to Dutch and Belgian ports, British ports being expressly excluded'.[51]

'What Matters in a Situation of this sort is a People's Moral Stance'

Of course it was the Nazis who were the prime gainers from Ha'avara. Not only did it help them push out a few extra Jews, but it was of immense value abroad, providing the perfect rationale for all those who still wanted to continue trading with the Germans. In Britain, Sir Oswald Mosley's newspaper, the *Blackshirt*, loved it:

> Can you beat that! We are cutting off our nose to spite our face and refuse to trade with Germany in order to defend the poor Jews. The Jews themselves, in their own country, are to continue making profitable dealings with Germany themselves. Fascists can't better counter the malicious propaganda to destroy friendly relations with Germany than by using this fact.[52]

The final evaluation of the WZO's role during the Holocaust cannot be made until the other interrelationships between the Zionists and the Nazis are properly dealt with; however, a preliminary appraisal of Ha'avara can now be safely attempted. All excuses that it saved lives must be strictly excluded from serious consideration. No Zionist in the 1930s thought that Hitler was going to try to exterminate the Jews of either Germany or Europe, and no one tried to defend Ha'avara during its operation in those terms. The excuse was that it saved wealth, not lives. In fact, at the very best, it directly helped a few thousand Jews with money, by allowing them to enter Palestine after the British quotas had been allocated and indirectly it provided an opportunity for others by boosting the Palestinian economy. But every genuine opponent of Nazism understood that once Hitler had taken power and had German Jewry in his claws, the struggle against him could not possibly be curbed by an over-concern for their fate; they were essentially prisoners of war. The battle still had to go on. Naturally no one wished those unfortunates any more grief than necessary, but to have brought the campaign against Nazism to a standstill out of concern for the German Jews would only have accelerated Hitler's further march into Europe. While the WZO was busy saving the property, or, more properly, a piece of the property of the German Jewish bourgeoisie, the '£1,000 people', thousands of Germans – including many Jews – were fighting in Spain, against Hitler's own Condor Legion and Franco's Fascist army. The Ha'avara certainly assisted the Nazis in that it demoralised Jews, some of whom were Zionists, by spreading the illusion that it was possible to come to some sort of *modus vivendi* with Hitler. It also demoralised non-Jews to know that a world-wide Jewish movement was prepared to come to terms with its enemy. Certainly the Ha'avara removed the million-strong Zionist movement from the front line of anti-Nazi resistance. The WZO did not resist Hitler, but sought to collaborate with him and, as can be seen in the proposals of Arlosoroff and Weizmann for a liquidation bank, only Nazi unwillingness to extend their linkage prevented the development of an even greater degree of co-operation. Those Zionists, as with *World Jewry*, who tried to oppose Hitler, must also be severely faulted for their own failure to create an effective Jewish, or even Zionist, boycott machine, but at least they must be credited with some moral stature in that they tried to do something to attack the Nazis. By comparison Weizmann, Shertok and their co-thinkers lose our respect, even if we only set them against their Zionist critics and ignore all other Jewish opinion. At best, it can be said of Weizmann and his ilk that they were the equivalent of Neville Chamberlain; moral and political failures. After the war and the Holocaust, a contrite and remorseful Nahum Goldmann, mortified at his own shameless role during the Hitler epoch, wrote of a dramatic meeting he had with the Czech Foreign Minister, Edvard Beneš, in 1935. Goldmann's vivid account of Beneš's warning to the Jews says all that will ever need to be said on the Ha'avara and the abject failure of the WZO to resist the Nazis:

'Don't you understand', he shouted, 'that by reacting with nothing but half-hearted gestures, by failing to arouse world public opinion and take vigorous action against the Germans, the Jews are endangering their future and their human rights all over the world?' ... I knew Beneš was right ... in this context success was irrelevant. What matters in a situation of this sort is a people's moral stance, its readiness to fight back instead of helplessly allowing itself to be massacred.[53]

Notes

1. Carl Voss, 'Let Stephen Wise Speak for Himself', *Dimensions in American Jewry* (Fall 1968), p. 37.

2. Moshe Gottlieb, 'The Anti-Nazi Boycott Movement in the American Jewish Community, 1933-1941', PhD thesis, Brandeis University 1967, p. 160.

3. Meyer Steinglass, 'Emil Ludwig before the Judge', *American Jewish Times*, (April 1936), p. 35.

4. 'Palestine and the Press', *New Palestine* (11 December 1933), p. 7.

5. Chaim Bialik, 'The Present Hour', *Young Zionist* (London, May 1934), p. 6.

6. Abraham Jacobson, 'The Fundamentals of Jewish Nationalism,' *New Palestine* (3 April 1936), p. 3.

7. David Yisraeli, 'The Third Reich and the Transfer Agreement', *Journal of Contemporary History*, vol. VI (1971), p. 131.

8. Ibid.

9. 'Palestine Drive to Continue', *Israel's Messenger* (Shanghai, 1 May 1933), p. 2.

10. Werner Braatz, 'German Commercial Interests in Palestine: Zionism and the Boycott of German Goods, 1933-1934', *European Studies Review* (October 1979), p. 500.

11. Yisraeli, 'The Third Reich and the Transfer Agreement', p. 132.

12. 'Dr Arlosoroff's Plan', *Jewish Economic Forum* (London, 1 September 1933), p. 9.

13. Chaim Arlosoroff, 'What can Palestine offer to the German Jew?', *Labor Palestine* (June 1933), p. 9.

14. Yitzhak Lufban, 'Arlosoroff's Last Period', *Labor Palestine* (June 1934), p. 6.

15. 'Zionist Congress in Prague', *Zionist Record* (South Africa, 1 September 1933), p. 5.

16. 'The 18th Zionist Congress', *New Judaea* (London, September 1933), p. 193.

17. *Jewish Daily Bulletin* (29 August 1933), p. 4.

18. 'Zionist Congress Votes Inquiry Commission for Palestine Terrorist Groups', *Jewish Daily Bulletin* (1 September 1933), p. 4.

19. Mark Wischnitzer, *To Dwell in Safety*, p. 212.

20. David Rosenthal, 'Chaim Arlosoroff 40 Years Later', *Jewish Frontier* (August 1974), p. 23.

21. 'Reflections', *Palestine Post* (14 November 1938), p. 6.

22. Yehuda Bauer, *My Brother's Keeper*, p. 129.

23. 'Justification of the Zionist Congress', *Zionist Record* (South Africa, 4 October 1933), p. 5.

24. Moshe Beilenson, 'The New Jewish Statesmanship', *Labor Palestine* (February 1934), pp. 8–10.

25. 'Untermyer, Rabbi Silver Denounce Deals Reported Negotiated with Germany', *Jewish Daily Bulletin* (30 August 1933), p. 4.

26. 'The Palestine Orange Agreement', *Jewish Weekly News* (Melbourne, 10 November 1933), p. 5.

27. Clarence Streit, 'League Aid Asked for German Jews', *New York Times* (9 September 1933), p. 5.

28. 'Dr Stephen Wise on Policy of World Jewry', *World Jewry* (London, 24 August 1934), p. 395.

29. Braatz, 'German Commercial Interests in Palestine', p. 504.

30. Chaim Weizmann, 'To Arthur Ruppin', 3 July 1935, in Barnett Litvinoff. (ed.), *The Letters and Papers of Chaim Weizmann, Letters*, vol. XVI, p. 464.

31. Ibid., pp. 465–6.

32. Arthur Ruppin, *The Jews in the Modern World* (1934), pp. 256–7.

33. Nahum Goldmann, *Autobiography*, p. 112.

34. Ruppin, *Jews in the Modern World*, p. xiii.

35. Weizmann, 'To Lewis Namier', 1 October 1933, *Letters*, vol. XVI, p. 54.

36. 'Nineteenth Congress Report', *Canadian Zionist* (September 1935), p. 8.

37. Paul Novick, *Zionism Today* (1936), p. 4.

38. 'Executive Defines its Policies in Reply to Opposition', *New Palestine* (20 September 1935), p. 24.

39. Ruth Bondy, *The Emissary: A Life of Enzo Sereni*, p. 141.

40. Novick, *Zionism Today*, p. 5.

41. Barnett Litvinoff, *Weizmann – Last of the Patriarchs*, p. 182.

42. 'Kiddush Hashem', *World Jewry* (6 September 1935), p. 1.

43. 'Has Congress a Message to Deliver?', *World Jewry*, (30 August 1935), p. 1.

44. 'Reflections on the Zionist Congress', *Jewish Chronicle* (London, 20 September 1935), p. 24.

45. 'Zionists close their Ranks', *Jewish Chronicle* (London, 6 September 1935), p. 9.

46. 'Debating the Issues of the Transfer', *Call of Youth* (January 1936), pp. 3–12.

47. Ibid., pp. 3–6.

48. Gustav Krojanker, *The Transfer: A Vital Question of the Zionist Movement*, pp. 7–10 and 15.

49. Bauer, *My Brother's Keeper*, p. 129.

50. 'Reflections', *Palestine Post* (14 November 1938), p. 6.

51. Werner Felchenfeld, 'Citrus on German Ships', *Palestine Post* (Letters) (17 November 1938), p. 6.

52. 'Blackshirts Peeved at Reich–Zion Trade', *Jewish Daily Bulletin* (6 February 1935), p. 5.

53. Goldmann, *Autobiography*, p. 148.

7 HITLER LOOKS AT ZIONISM

Hitler's view of the Jews and the Jewish problem is sharply expressed in *Mein Kampf*. He goes to great lengths to demonstrate that his Jew-hatred was quite reasonable, that it flowed from experience and the logical inferences to be drawn from clear evidence. He always insisted that his first thoughts towards the Jews were all benign. His father, 'the old gentleman', looked upon anti-Semitism as a left-over religious prejudice and so, we are told, did the enlightened young Adolf. It was only after his mother died, and he moved from provincial Linz to Vienna, that Hitler found occasion to question the glib assumptions of his youth. For there he wandered through the old inner city and encountered a Galician Hasid, 'an apparition in a black caftan and black hair locks. Is this a Jew? was my first thought.' But the more he thought about what he had seen, the more his question assumed a new form: 'Is this a German?'[1] It is in the context of his earliest ruminations on what was, for him, the central question of existence that he introduced Zionism into his opus.

And whatever doubts I may still have nourished were finally dispelled by the attitude of a portion of the Jews themselves. Among them there was a great movement, quite extensive in Vienna, which came out sharply in confirmation of the national character of the Jews: this was the *Zionists*.

It looked, to be sure, as though only a part of the Jews approved this viewpoint, while the majority condemned and inwardly rejected such a formulation. But . . . the so-called liberal Jews did not reject the Zionists as non-Jews, but only as Jews with an impractical, perhaps even dangerous, way of publicly avowing their Jewishness.[2]

There is no better proof of Zionism's classic role as an outrider to anti-Semitism than Hitler's own statement. What more, the reader was to ask, could any reasonable person need? However, before 1914 Hitler had no need to concern himself further with Zionism, as the prospects of a revived Jewish state seemed very remote. It was the Balfour Declaration, Germany's defeat and the Weimar revolution that made him think again about Zionism. Naturally he rolled all three events together. The treacherous Jews showed their true colours in the way in which they welcomed the Balfour Declaration, and it was the Social Democrats, those servants of the Jews, who brought down the Kaiser; but for them Germany would have won. In 1919 Hitler joined the tiny National Socialists and became their inspired beer-hall rabble-rouser, but the dominant ideologist on the finer points of the Jewish question was the Baltic German refugee Alfred Rosenberg, who had developed his theories while still in his native Estonia. By 1919 Rosenberg had already explained Zionism in his book, *Die Spur des Juden im Wandel der Zeiten* (The Trace of the Jews in the Wanderings of Time). It was just another Jewish hustle; the Zionists only wanted to create a hide-out for the international Jewish conspiracy. Jews were, by their racial nature, organically incapable of building a state of their own, but he felt that Zionist ideology served wonderfully as a justification for depriving Germany's Jews of their rights and that, perhaps, there was the possibility of future use of the movement for the promotion of Jewish emigration. Hitler soon began to touch on these themes in his talks, and on 6 July 1920 he proclaimed that Palestine was the proper place for the Jews and that only there could they hope to get their rights. Articles supporting emigration to Palestine began appearing in the party organ, the *Volkischer Beobachter*, after 1920, and periodically party propagandists would return to the point, as did Julius Streicher in a speech given on 20 April 1926 before the Bavarian Landtag.[3] But for Hitler the validity of Zionism only lay in its confirmation that the Jews could never be Germans. In *Mein Kampf*, he wrote:

> For while the Zionists try to make the rest of the world believe that the national consciousness of the Jew finds its satisfaction in the creation of a Palestinian state, the Jews again slyly dupe the dumb goyim. It doesn't even enter their heads to build up a Jewish state for the purpose of living there; all they want is a central organisation for their international world swindle, endowed with its own sovereign rights and removed from the intervention of other states: a haven for convicted scoundrels and a university for budding crooks.[4]

Jews lacked the essential racial character to build a state of their own. They were essentially leeches, lacking in natural idealism, and they hated work. He explained:

For a state formation to have a definite spatial setting always pre-supposes an idealistic attitude on the part of the state-race, and especially a correct interpretation of the concept of work. In the exact measure in which this attitude is lacking, any attempt at forming, even of preserving, a spatially delimited state fails.[5]

In spite of any early musings about Zionism's efficacy in eventually promoting emigration, the Nazis made no effort to establish any relationship with the local Zionists. On the contrary, when the Zionist Congress met in Vienna in 1925, the Nazis were among those who rioted against their presence.[6]

Nazi Patronage of Zionism

Did Hitler always plan to murder the Jews? He set down some early thoughts in *Mein Kampf*:

If in 1914 the German working class in their innermost convictions had still consisted of Marxists, the War would have been over in three weeks. Germany would have collapsed even before the first soldier set foot across the border. No, the fact that the German people was then still fighting proved that the Marxist delusion had not yet been able to gnaw its way into the bottommost depths. But in exact proportion as, in the course of the War, the German worker and the German soldier fell back into the hands of the Marxist leaders, in exactly that proportion he was lost to the fatherland. If at the beginning of the War and during the War twelve or fifteen thousand of these Hebrew corrupters of the people had been held under poison gas, as happened to hundreds of thousands of our very best German workers in the field, the sacrifices of millions at the front would not have been in vain.[7]

However, these thoughts were never the basis of the Nazis' popular agitation prior to the 1933 take-over. Instead, the Nazis primarily focused on denouncing the Jews, rather than explaining what they would do about them after they won. However, for decades 'Kikes to Palestine!' had been the slogan of European anti-Semitism, and the Nazi propagandists used it in their own agitation. In June 1932 the centre-piece for one of their largest anti-Jewish rallies, in Silesian Breslaw, was a huge banner telling the Jews to 'get ready for Palestine!'[8] During the anti-Jewish boycott on 1 April 1933, pickets at the department stores handed out an imitation 'one-way ticket to Palestine' to Jewish-looking passers-by.[9] The official Nazi manifesto proclaiming the anti-Jewish boycott declared that anti-Nazi feeling abroad was due to international Jewry's 'trying to act on the program announced in 1897 by the Zionist Leader Herzl' to stir up foreign states against any country that opposed the Jews.[10] However, none of this was very serious; it was just another expression of rabid anti-Semitism. Until he achieved power, Hitler had not given any serious thought to what he would do with the Jews. Beyond his statement in *Mein Kampf*, there is no evidence to prove that he told even his closest subordinates what he ultimately planned. After all, as he always privately complained, the average SS man was, at bottom, soft — and a blabbermouth. If you talked about killing all the Jews, he was sure to make excuses for his own 'good Jew' and then where were you? Besides, the capitalists had their Jewish business connections abroad, and there were the churches and their scruples about murder. Hitler solved his problem by just ignoring it, leaving every department in the party and government to feel its way to a suitable policy. There were inevitably conflicting schools. Straight terror always had its devotees, but these were more than countered by others who saw the Jews as deeply rooted in the domestic economy as well as having many contacts abroad. Immediate imposition of a ghetto had its partisans, but this was met with the same objections. Emigration was the obvious solution, but where to? Not only would wholesale Jewish emigration make Berlin unpopular among other capitals, but what would happen after the arrival of large numbers of Jews in any of the major cities of the world? They would incite others, and not just Jews, against the Reich and the effect they could have on Germany's trade might well be devastating. It was within this context that the Zionists, Sam Cohen of Ha Note'a and the ZVfD in Germany, first appeared with their proposals.

Ha'avara had several obvious advantages to the Nazis. If Jews went to Palestine, they would only be able to complain to other Jews. In fact, they would even be a moderating influence there, since the fear of worse consequences for their relatives in Germany, if anything were done to make the Nazis cancel the Transfer, would make them reluctant to agitate on a large scale. But the most important use of the Ha'avara agreement was for propaganda. The Nazis now had something to show their foreign detractors who said they were incapable of any policy toward the Jews other than physical brutality. In a speech on 24 October 1933, Hitler crowed that it was he, not his critics, who really was the Jews' benefactor:

> In England people assert that their arms are open to welcome all
> the oppressed, especially the Jews who have left Germany . . . But
> it would be still finer if England did not make her great gesture
> dependent on the possession of £1,000 − England should say:
> 'Anyone may enter' − as we unfortunately have done for 30 years.
> If we too had declared that no one could enter Germany save under
> the condition of bringing with him £1,000 or paying more, then
> today we should have no Jewish question at all. So we wild folk
> have once more proved ourselves better humans − less perhaps in
> external protestations, but at least in our actions! And now we are
> still as generous and give to the Jewish people a far higher percentage
> as their share in possibility for living than we ourselves possess.[11]

Nazi Germany regarded the will of the Fuhrer as having the force of
law, and once Hitler had pronounced, an avowedly pro-Zionist policy
developed. Also in October Hans Frank, then the Bavarian Minister of
Justice, later the Governor-General of Poland, told the Nuremberg
parteitag that the best solution to the Jewish question, for Jews and
Gentiles, alike, was the Palestinian National Home.[12] Still in October,
the Hamburg–South American Shipping Company started a direct
service to Haifa providing 'strictly Kosher food on its ships, under the
supervision of the Hamburg rabbinate'.[13] Jews could still leave for any
country that would have them, but now Palestine became the propagandists' preferred solution to the Jewish question. However, Zionists
were still just Jews, as Gustav Genther of the German Education
School very carefully spelt out:

> Just as we now have friendly relations with Soviet Russia, though
> Russia, as a Communist country, represents a danger to our National
> Socialist State, we shall take the same attitude toward the Jews,
> if they establish themselves as an independent nation, although
> we know they will always remain our enemies.[14]

If this was not enough, a children's game, *Juden Raus!* (Jews Out),
left no illusions as to how the Nazis saw Zionism. The pieces were
little pawns wearing pointed medieval Jewish hats; the players moved
them by rolling dice; the child winning was the one whose Jew first
scurried out, 'off to Palestine!' through the gates of a walled city.[15]
Zionism was despised in Nazi Germany, but the Zionists desperately

needed Nazi patronage if they were to get the capital they required in Palestine and they allowed themselves to believe that the Ha'avara and all the Palestinian talk that followed it would lead to a statesmanlike pact.

'Our Official Good Will Go with Them'

By 1934 the SS had become the most pro-Zionist element in the Nazi Party. Other Nazis were even calling them 'soft' on the Jews. Baron von Mildenstein had returned from his six-month visit to Palestine as an ardent Zionist sympathiser. Now as the head of the Jewish Department of the SS's Security Service, he started studying Hebrew and collecting Hebrew records; when his former companion and guide, Kurt Tuchler, visited his office in 1934, he was greeted by the strains of familiar Jewish folk tunes.[16] There were maps on the walls showing the rapidly increasing strength of Zionism inside Germany.[17] Von Mildenstein was as good as his word: he not only wrote favourably about what he saw in the Zionist colonies in Palestine; he also persuaded Goebbels to run the report as a massive twelve-part series in his own *Der Angriff* (The Assault), the leading Nazi propaganda organ (26 September to 9 October 1934). His stay among the Zionists had shown the SS man 'the way to curing a centuries-long wound on the body of the world: the Jewish question'. It was really amazing how some good Jewish *boden* under his feet could enliven the Jew: 'The soil has reformed him and his kind in a decade. This new Jew will be a new people.'[18] To commemorate the Baron's expedition, Goebbels had a medal struck: on one side the swastika, on the other the Zionist star.[19]

In May 1935 Reinhardt Heydrich, who was then the chief of the SS Security Service, later the infamous 'Protector' of the Czech lands incorporated into the Reich, wrote an article, 'The Visible Enemy', for *Das Schwarze Korps*, the official organ of the SS. In it Heydrich assessed the various tendencies among the Jews, comparing the assimilationists quite invidiously with the Zionists. His partiality towards Zionism could not have been expressed in more unmistakable terms:

> After the Nazi seizure of power our racial laws did in fact curtail considerably the immediate influence of Jews. But . . . the question as he sees it is still: How can we win back our old position . . . We must separate Jewry into two categories . . . the Zionists and those who favor being assimilated. The Zionists adhere to a strict

racial position and by emigrating to Palestine they are helping to build their own Jewish state.

Heydrich wished them a fond farewell: 'The time cannot be far distant when Palestine will again be able to accept its sons who have been lost to it for over a thousand years. Our good wishes together with our official good will go with them.'[20]

'It was a Painful Distinction for Zionism to be Singled out for Favors'

The Nuremberg Laws of September 1935, the finishing touches of Germany's pre-Second World War anti-Jewish legislation, were defended by the Nazis as an expression of their pro-Zionism. They had at least the tacit approval of the wiser heads amongst the Jews themselves. As it happened — and naturally it was more than mere coincidence — every nationwide Jewish organ in Germany was under temporary ban when the laws were promulgated — except the *Rundschau*. It published the codified restrictions with a commentary by Alfred Berndt, the editor-in-chief of the German News Bureau. Berndt recalled that, only two weeks before, all the speakers at the World Zionist Congress in Lucerne had reiterated that the Jews of the world were to be correctly seen as a separate people unto themselves regardless of where they lived. Well then, he explained, all Hitler had done was to meet 'the demands of the International Zionist Congress by making the Jews who live in Germany a national minority'.[21]

One aspect of the laws, now long forgotten but which attracted considerable attention at the time, was the fact that from then on only two flags were to be permitted in the Third Reich, the swastika and the blue-and-white Zionist banner. This, of course, greatly excited the ZVfD, who hoped that this was a sign that Hitler was moving closer to an accommodation with them. But for many foreign Zionists this was a searing humiliation, well-expressed in the anguish of Stephen Wise's own organ, the *Congress Bulletin*:

Hitlerism is Satan's nationalism. The determination to rid the German national body of the Jewish element, however, led Hitlerism to discover its 'kinship' with Zionism, the Jewish nationalism of liberation. Therefore Zionism became the only other party legalized in the Reich, the Zionist flag the only other flag permitted to fly in Nazi-land. It was a painful distinction for Zionism to be singled out for favors and privileges by its Satanic counterpart.[22]

The Nazis were as thorough in their philo-Zionism as in other matters. Now that the Jews were established as a separate people with a separate soil, should they not also have a separate language? In 1936 they added a new *'nach Palastina'* ingredient to their repressive measures. *Jewish Frontier* had to inform its readers distressfully that:

> The attempts to seclude the Jews in the cultural ghetto have reached a new height by the prohibition to rabbis to use the German language in their Chanukah [6 December] sermons. This is in line with the effort made by the Nazis to force the German Jews to use the Hebrew language as their cultural medium. Thus another 'proof' of Nazi-Zionist cooperation is seized eagerly by the Communist opponents of Zionism.[23]

Nazi Leniency towards Zionism

In spring 1934, Heinrich Himmler, Reichsfuhrer of the SS, was presented with a 'Situation Report – Jewish Question' by his staff: the vast majority of Jews still considered themselves Germans and were determined to stay on. Since force could not be used, for fear of potential international repercussions, the way to break down their resistance was to instil a distinctive Jewish identity amongst them by systematically promoting Jewish schools, athletic teams, Hebrew, Jewish art and music, etc. Combined with Zionist occupational retraining centres, this would finally induce the recalcitrant Jews to abandon their homeland. However, this subtle formula was not enough, for whenever pressure against them began to subside the stubborn Jews would start to dig in again. The Nazi policy was therefore to increase support for the Zionists, so that the Jews would plainly see that the way to ward off worse troubles was to join the movement. All Jews, including Zionists, were still to be persecuted as Jews, but within that framework it was always possible to ease the pressure. Accordingly, on 28 January 1935, the Bavarian Gestapo circularised the regular police that henceforward: 'members of the Zionist organisations are, in view of their activities directed towards emigration to Palestine, not to be treated with the same strictness which is necessary towards the members of the German-Jewish organisations [assimilationists].'[24]

The Nazis created complications for themselves with their pro-Zionist line. The WZO needed German-Jewish capital far more than it ever wanted German Jews. It also operated under the immigration quotas set by the British. Its largest following was in Poland, and if it gave out too many certificates to Germans, there would not be enough for its support base in Poland and elsewhere. Therefore the Zionists gave only 22 per cent of the certificates to Germans throughout the 1930s. Furthermore the WZO were not interested in the vast majority of Germany's Jews, since these were not Zionists, did not speak Hebrew, were too old and, of course, did not have the 'right' trades. Either Jewish emigration had to be organised to other countries as well, or Germany would be stuck with the Jews neither it nor the Zionists wanted. Nazi discrimination against anti-Zionists led to problems for those world-based bodies like the American Jewish Joint Distribution Committee, which tried to provide havens for Jews in countries other than Palestine. Yehuda Bauer, one of Israel's most widely known Holocaust scholars, has written of a discussion of the ensuing difficulties between two leading officials of the Joint Distribution Committee:

> [Joseph] Hyman thought that a statement should be made by the German Jews that Palestine was not the sole outlet which of course, frankly speaking, it wasn't. [Bernard] Kahn agreed, but explained that the Nazis supported Zionism because it promised the largest emigration of Jews from Germany; hence German Jewish leadership could not make any public statements about other outlets. Still less could they mention the decision to maintain Jewish institutions in Germany. The Nazis had dissolved one meeting in Germany simply because the speaker had said 'we have to provide for the people who go away and for the Jews who must stay in Germany'.[25]

In practice, the Nazis' concern about where the Jews should go disappeared with the Austrian *anschluss*, which brought so many Jews with it that further attention to their destination would have crippled the expulsion programme. In October 1938 the Nazis discovered that the Poles were about to revoke the citizenship of thousands of their Jewish citizens resident in Germany. They therefore decided to deport the Jews to Poland immediately so that they would not be stuck with thousands of stateless Jews. It was this cold pogrom that led to the massive violence of Kristallnacht in November 1938.

The story was told, many years later, on 25 April 1961, at the trial of Adolf Eichmann. The witness, Zindel Grynszpan, then an old man, was the father of Herszl Grynszpan who, in despair at the deportation of his father back to Poland, had assassinated a German diplomat in Paris and provided the Nazis with the pretext for their terrible night of broken glass. Old Zindel told them of his deportation from his home in Hanover on the night of 27 October 1938: 'Then they took us in police trucks, in prisoners' lorries, about 20 men in each truck, and they took us to the railway station. The streets were full of people shouting: *"Juden raus! Auf nach Palastina!"* '[26]

The significance of Zindel's testimony was utterly lost in the welter of detail in the Eichmann trial. But those Jews were not being sent to Palestine, as the Nazi mob cried; the prosecutor in that courtroom in Jerusalem never thought to ask the elderly Grynszpan a question that we would think to ask: 'What did you think, what did the other Jews think, when they heard that strange cry coming up from the savage mob?' Zindel Grynszpan is long dead, as are most if not all the others who suffered there that hellish night; we have no answer to our query. But what really matters was what was shouted, rather than what was thought about it in that police van. However, we can reasonably suggest that if the ZVfD had resisted Nazism's rise, if the WZO had mobilised Jewry against the New Order, if Palestine had been a bastion of Jewish resistance to Nazism, the Nazis would never have told the Jews, and that mob, that the place for a Jew was in Palestine. Perhaps, then, that Friday night in Hanover the cry would have been 'Jews to Poland', even a straight 'kill the Jews'. The sombre fact is that the mob screamed what had been screamed at them by Hitler's minions: 'Jews to Palestine!'

'The Nazis Asked for a "More Zionist Behaviour" '

That the Nazis preferred the Zionists to all other Jews is a settled point. Even though Joachim Prinz may have winced when he wrote his 1937 article, he was only being honest when he sorrowfully had to admit that:

> It was very difficult for the Zionists to operate. It was morally disturbing to seem to be considered as the favoured children of the Nazi Government, particularly when it dissolved the anti-Zionist youth groups, and seemed in other ways to prefer the Zionists. The Nazis asked for a 'more Zionist behaviour'.[27]

The Zionist movement was always under severe restriction in the

1930s in Germany. The *Rundschau* was banned on at least three occasions between 1933 and November 1938, when the regime finally closed down the ZVfD's headquarters after Kristallnacht. After 1935 the Labour Zionist emissaries were barred from the country, but even then Palestinian Zionist leaders were allowed to enter for specific meetings; for instance Arthur Ruppin was granted permission to enter Germany on 20 March 1938 in order to address a mass indoor rally in Berlin on the effects of the 1936 Arab revolt in Palestine. Certainly, the Zionists had far less trouble than their bourgeois assimilationist rivals at the CV, and it was nothing compared with what the Communists had to face in Dachau at the same time the *Rundschau* was being hawked in the streets of Berlin.

However, the fact that the Zionists became Adolf Hitler's 'favoured children' hardly qualified him as a Jewish nationalist. Even von Mildenstein, for all his Hebrew records, accepted the party line when it turned to outright murder. Throughout the period, the Nazis toyed with the Zionists as a cat would play with a mouse. Hitler never thought he was letting anyone get away from him because he was encouraging Jews to go to Palestine. If the Jews went to far-away America, he might never be able to get at them and they would always remain the foes of the German Empire in Europe. But if they went to Palestine instead? 'There', as a Gestapo agent told a Jewish leader, 'we will catch up with you'.[28]

The Zionists could not even claim that they were duped by Hitler; they conned themselves. Hitler's theories on Zionism, including the Jews' alleged inability to create a state, had all been there, in plain German, since 1926. The Zionists ignored the fact that Hitler hated all Jews, and that he specifically condemned their own ideology. The Zionists were simply reactionaries, who naively chose to emphasise the points of similarity between themselves and Hitler. They convinced themselves that because they, too, were racists, against mixed marriage, and believed that the Jews were aliens in Germany; because they, too, were opposed to the left, that these similarities would be enough to make Adolf Hitler see them as the only 'honest partners' for a diplomatic *détente*.[29]

Notes

1. Adolf Hitler, *Mein Kampf*, p. 56.
2. Ibid.

3. Francis Nicosia, 'Zionism in Nationalist Socialist Jewish Policy in Germany, 1933–9', *Journal of Modern History* (on-demand supplement), (December 1978), pp. D1257–9.

4. Hitler, *Mein Kampf*, pp. 324–5.

5. Ibid., p. 302.

6. F.L. Carsten, *Fascist Movements in Austria*, p. 96.

7. Hitler, *Mein Kampf*, p. 679.

8. Donald Niewyk, *Socialist, Anti-Semite and Jew*, p. 149.

9. Elizabeth Poretsky, *Our Own People*, p. 134.

10. 'No Violence Urged', *Israel's Messenger* (Shanghai, 10 April 1933), p. 19.

11. Norman Baynes (ed.), *Hitler's Speeches, 1922-1939*, vol. I, p. 729.

12. Nicosia, 'Zionism in Nationalist Socialist Jewish Policy', p. D1263.

13. 'Hamburg–Haifa Direct Shipping Line', *Zionist Record* (20 October 1933), p. 15.

14. 'Members of Pro-Palestine Committee in Germany put on Anti-Semitic Blacklist', *Jewish Weekly News* (Melbourne, 30 March 1934), p. 6.

15. *Jewish Central Information Office – The Weiner Library – Its History and Activities 1934-45* (photograph between pp. 212–13).

16. Jacob Boas, 'The Jews of Germany: Self-Perception in the Nazi Era as Reflected in the German Jewish Press 1933–1938', PhD thesis, University of California, Riverside (1977), p. 110.

17. Heinz Hohne, *The Order of the Death's Head*, p. 333.

18. Leopold von Mildenstein (pseudonym von Lim), 'Ein Nazi fahrt nach Palastina', *Der Angriff* (9 October 1934), p. 4.

19. Jacob Boas, 'A Nazi Travels to Palestine', *History Today* (London, January 1980), p. 38.

20. Hohne, *Order of the Death's Head*, p. 333; and Karl Schleunes, *The Twisted Road to Auschwitz*, pp. 193–4.

21. Margaret Edelheim-Muehsam, 'Reactions of the Jewish Press to the Nazi Challenge', *Leo Baeck Institute Year Book*, vol. V (1960), p. 324.

22. 'Baal is not God', *Congress Bulletin* (24 January 1936), p. 2.

23. Abraham Duker, 'Diaspora', *Jewish Frontier* (January 1937), p. 28.

24. Kurt Grossmann, 'Zionists and Non-Zionists under Nazi Rule in the 1930s', *Herzl Yearbook*, vol. VI, p. 340.

25. Yehuda Bauer, *My Brother's Keeper*, p. 136.

26. Hannah Arendt, *Eichmann in Jerusalem*, p. 228.

27. Joachim Prinz, 'Zionism under the Nazi Government', *Young Zionist* (London, November 1937), p. 18.

28. Lucy Dawidowicz, *The War Against the Jews*, p. 115.

29. Boas, *The Jews of Germany*, p. 111.

8 PALESTINE – THE ARABS, ZIONISTS, BRITISH AND NAZIS

It was the Arabs, not the Zionists, who compelled the Nazis to re-examine their pro-Zionist orientation. Between 1933 and 1936, 164,267 Jewish immigrants poured into Palestine; 61,854 came in 1935 alone. The Jewish minority increased from 18 per cent of the population in 1931 to 29.9 per cent in December 1935, and the Zionists saw themselves becoming the majority in the not-too-distant future.

The Arabs reacted first to these statistics. They had never accepted the British Mandate with its declared aim of creating a Jewish National Home in their land. There had been riots in 1920 and 1921; in 1929, after a series of provocations from Zionist chauvinists and Muslim fanatics at the Wailing Wall, the Muslim masses rioted in a wave of atrocious massacres which culminated with 135 Jewish deaths and almost as many Muslims killed, primarily by the British.

Palestinian Arab politics were dominated by a handful of rich clans. The most nationalistic were the Husaynis, led by the Mufti of Jerusalem, al-Hajj Amin al-Husayni. Intensely pious, his response to the Zionist provocations at the Wall was to raise the faithful against the Zionists as infidels rather than as a political enemy. He was suspicious of any social reform and quite unprepared to develop a political programme which could mobilise the largely illiterate Palestinian peasantry. It was this lack of a programme for the peasant majority which guaranteed that he could never create a political force capable of coping with the numerically inferior, but vastly more efficient Zionists. He was compelled to look abroad for a patron to give him some of the strength that his reactionary politics prevented him from generating from within Palestinian society. His choice fell on Italy.

The deal with Rome was completely secret until it was accidentally revealed in April 1935, since it could hardly be justified in the Arab world. Mussolini had used poison gas against the 1931 Senussi uprising in Libya, and was, moreover, openly pro-Zionist. However, Rome was anti-British and was willing to subsidise the Mufti on that account. The first payment was made in 1934, but little was achieved for either the Palestinians or the Italians. Some years later Mussolini's Foreign Minister – his son-in-law, Galeazzo Ciano – had to confess to the German ambassador that:

for years he maintained constant relations with the Grand Mufti of which his secret fund could tell a tale. The return of this gift of millions had not been exactly great and had really been confined to occasional destruction of pipelines, which in most cases could be quickly repaired.[1]

'The Haganah's Goal – A Jewish Majority in Palestine'

Because Hitler did not believe that the Jews could create a state of their own, it did not follow that he would be pro-Palestinian. They too were Semites. In the 1920s many right-wing German political groups began to express sympathy for the oppressed nations of the British Empire as fellow victims of perfidious Albion. However, Hitler would have none of this; the British, after all, were white.

> I as a man of Germanic blood, would, in spite of everything, rather see India under English rule than under any other. Just as lamentable are the hopes in any mythical uprising in Egypt . . . As a volkish man, who appraises the value of men on a racial basis, I am prevented by mere knowledge of the racial inferiority of these so-called 'oppressed nations' from linking the destiny of my own people with theirs.[2]

However, the revolt of the Palestinian Arab masses in 1936 made Berlin re-think the implications of their pro-Zionist policies. Intense unrest had been aroused in October 1935 by the discovery of weapons in a cement cargo bound for Tel Aviv, and the situation became feverish in November when Shaykh Izz al-Din al-Qassam, a popular Muslim preacher, took to the hills with a guerrilla band. British troops soon killed him, but his funeral developed into a passionate demonstration. The crisis dragged on for months before it finally exploded on the night of 15 April 1936, when a remnant of Qassam's band stopped traffic on the Tulkarm road, robbing travellers and killing two Jews. Two Arabs were slain in reprisal the next night. The funeral of the Jews turned into a right-wing Zionist demonstration and the crowd started marching on Arab Jaffa. The police opened fire, four Jews were shot and, again, Arabs were attacked on the streets of Tel Aviv in retaliation. A counter-march soon started for Tel Aviv. The revolt was on. A spontaneous general strike developed and the pressure from below forced the rival cliques within the Arab establishment to unite in an Arab Higher Committee under the leadership of the Mufti. However, the Higher Committee feared that the continuation of the rising would put the peasantry permanently beyond its leaders' control, and finally prevailed upon the strike committees to call off the protest on 12 October, pending the outcome of a British Royal Commission's investigation.

Until the Arab revolt, the Nazis' patronage of Zionism had been warm but scarcely committed, as we have seen. However, with the political turmoil in Palestine and the appointment of the Peel Commission, the WZO saw their chance to persuade the Nazis to make a public commitment to them in Palestine itself. On 8 December 1936 a joint delegation of the Jewish Agency, the highest body of the WZO in Palestine, and the Hitachdut Olei Germania (the German Immigrants Association), went to the Jerusalem office of Doehle, the German Consul-General. The Zionist scholar, David Yisraeli, has related the incident.

> They sought through Doehle to persuade the Nazi government to have its Jerusalem representative appear before the Peel Commission, and declare that Germany was interested in an increased immigration to Palestine because of its eagerness to have the Jews emigrate from Germany. The Consul, however, rejected the proposal on the spot. His official reasons were that considerations of increased immigration from Germany would inevitably bring out the matter of the transfer which was detrimental to British exports to Palestine.[3]

Characteristically, the Zionists were more eager to extend their relationship than the Nazis, but Doehle's rejection of their request did not stop them from further approaches. The outcome of the Peel Commission's expedition was thought crucial to the Zionist endeavour and it was therefore the Haganah, then the military arm of the Jewish Agency (*de facto* the Labour Zionist militia), that obtained Berlin's permission to negotiate directly with the *Sicherheitsdienst* (SD), the Security Service of the SS. A Haganah agent, Feivel Polkes, arrived in Berlin on 26 February 1937 and was assigned Adolf Eichmann as his negotiating partner. Eichmann had been a protégé of the pro-Zionist von Mildenstein and, like his mentor, had studied Hebrew, read Herzl and was the SD's specialist on Zionism. The Eichmann–Polkes conversations were recorded in a report prepared by Eichmann's superior, Franz-Albert Six, which was found in the SS files captured by the American Army at the end of the Second World War:

Polkes is a national-Zionist . . . He is against all Jews who are opposed to the erection of a Jewish state in Palestine. As a Haganah
man he fights against Communism and all aims of Arab–British
friendship . . . He noted that the Haganah's goal is to reach, as soon
as possible, a Jewish majority in Palestine. Therefore he worked, as
this objective required, with or against the British Intelligence
Service, the Sûreté Générale, with England and Italy . . . He declared
himself willing to work for Germany in the form of providing
intelligence as long as this does not oppose his own political goals.
Among other things he would support German foreign policy in the
Near East. He would try to find oil sources for the German Reich
without affecting British spheres of interest if the German monetary
regulations were eased for Jewish emigrants to Palestine.[4]

Six definitely thought that a working alliance with the Haganah
would be in the Nazis' interest. They still needed the latest inside
information on the various Jewish boycott groups and on Jewish plots
against the lives of prominent Nazis. He was eager to allow the SS to
help the Zionists in return.

Pressure can be put on the Reich Representation of Jews in Germany in such a way that those Jews emigrating from Germany go
exclusively to Palestine and not go to other countries. Such measures
lie entirely in the German interest and is already prepared through
measures of the Gestapo. Polkes' plans to create a Jewish majority
in Palestine would be aided at the same time through these measures.[5]

Six's enthusiasm was not shared at the German Foreign Ministry,
which saw Palestine as a British sphere. Berlin's prime interest was in
an understanding with London on the crucial question of the Balkans;
nothing must interfere with that. The officials were also concerned
about how Italy would react to German intervention in Mediterranean
politics. Therefore, on 1 June 1937 the Foreign Minister, Konstantine
von Neurath, sent cables to his diplomats in London, Jerusalem and
Baghdad: neither a Zionist state nor a Zionist political structure under
British rule would be in Germany's interest, as it 'would not absorb
world Jewry but would create an additional position of power under
international law for international Jewry, somewhat like the Vatican
State for political Catholicism or Moscow for the Comintern'. Germany
therefore had 'an interest in strengthening the Arab world', but 'it is
not to be expected, of course, that direct German intervention would

influence essentially the development of the Palestine question'. Under no circumstances were the Palestinians to get more than token support: 'understanding for Arab nationalist aspirations should be expressed more clearly than before, but without making any definite promises'.[6]

Zionist Notions of the Future Israel

British policy towards Palestine at this stage was elegantly expressed in the memoirs of Sir Ronald Storrs, the first military governor of Jerusalem, the Zionist 'enterprise was one that blessed him that gave as well as him that took, by forming for England "a little loyal Jewish Ulster" in a sea of potentially hostile Arabism'.[7] This was the spirit of the Peel Commission's proposal in July 1937 that Palestine be divided into three parts. All of it would stay under British overlordship; Britain would directly retain a strip from Jerusalem to Jaffa, and would hold Haifa for ten years, after which it would be seconded to a Zionist statelet of two pieces with a combined area the size of the English county of Norfolk. The tiny Zionist entity would contain an enormous Arab minority, some of whom the Commission contemplated moving to the Arab state which would get the rest of the country.

Opinion within Zionism was sharply divided. The 'Jewish Ulster' differed from the original in that the Zionists would never see themselves as fulfilled by the partition. Their Eretz Yisrael included all of Abraham's biblical patrimony. In the end the World Zionist Congress's position was a carefully qualified no, meaning a yes: that particular partition was rejected, but the Executive was empowered to haggle further for a better deal.

What kind of state did the Zionist movement envision for itself, and for millions of Jews, in 1937? The Labour Zionists were by far the strongest force in the movement and there was no greater protagonist of acceptance of the partition than its leader, David Ben-Gurion who, in the summer of 1937, solemnly reassured a Zurich session of the World Council of the Poale Zion that they need have no fears in this regard: later they would definitely expand.

> This Jewish state which is now proposed to us, even with all the possible reparations and improvements in our favor, is not the Zionist aim — in this territory one cannot solve the Jewish problem . . . what will happen, in another fifteen (or any other number of) years, when the proposed territorially limited state reaches the point

of saturation of population? . . . Anyone who wants to be frank to himself should not prophesy about what there will be in another fifteen years . . . the adversaries of Partition were right when they claimed that this country was not given for us to partition it – for it constitutes a single unit, not only historically, but also from the natural and economic standpoint.[8]

The Labour Zionists certainly realised now that if a Jewish state was going to be achieved, it would inevitably be against the powerful opposition of the Palestinian people. Although they were basically always Jewish nationalists, they had turned resolutely away from their own past socialist rhetoric, as well as their previous, feeble, efforts to organise Arab workers, and started driving them out of their traditional seasonal jobs in the Jewish orange groves. In general, their thinking had become morbid, and they now consciously looked for their own success to come out of the ruination of the European Jewish middle class. It was to be their flight capital that would build Zion. Enzo Sereni, now an emissary to the USA, was quite correct in assessing the attraction Zionism now held for a portion of the Jewish middle class in Central and Eastern Europe:

Two souls dwell within the breast of the Jewish bourgeoisie, one striving after profits, the other seeking for political power . . . As a political group, the Jewish bourgeoisie cannot really live without the Jewish masses. Only on them can it hope to build its political supremacy. Also, in order to exercise its eventual control over the Arab workers, the Jewish bourgeoisie needs a Jewish proletariat, precisely as the great European powers need a national proletariat for the exercise of their imperial plans.

What separates the Jewish Zionist bourgeoisie from the non-Zionist members of the same class is really only the fact that *the Zionists are clearly aware that they can attain their interest as a class only in the domain of a unified people and no longer as mere individuals, as Jewish assimilationists believed.*[9]

Anti-Semitism was now conceded to be the main force of Zionism but, in addition, there were also positive attractions in the establishment of a Zionist mini-state. Moshe Beilenson, then editor of Labour's daily newspaper, *Davar*, naively expressed these hopes for an Israel as the locus of the future capitalist exploitation of the hinterland:

Great perspectives will open before the 'Greater Zionism' that now only a few among us dare to fight for, a Jewish state in Palestine, leading the East . . . The Jewish state built on such foundations will have the full right, both socially and spiritually, to claim the title of leadership, the title of being the vanguard of the new world in the East . . .

He qualified the realities behind his rhetorical flourish:

Of what value is our closeness of race to the Arab people compared to the great distance between us in ideas, in existence, in our scale of values? In all these matters we are many degrees closer to the Europeans or Americans despite the existing 'racial differences' . . . We want peace with the Arab Yishub . . . with no false philanthropy, and with no make-believe missionaryism. Not for any Revolutionary approach in the Awakening of the East, be it a 'national' East or a 'class' East or a 'religious spiritual' East . . . Not to free others have we come here, but to free ourselves.[10]

These theoreticians were in the process of creating a self-fulfilling prophesy. By talking so determinedly of the inevitable expropriation of European Jewry, to be followed by the exploitation of a Jewish and Arab proletariat, these self-styled socialists were doing nothing to mobilise the Europeans and everything to arouse the wrath of the Palestinians.

Nazi Admiration for Zionist Efforts in Palestine

The Nazis were quite resigned to the partition of Palestine and their main concern became the fate of the 2,000 Germans then living in the country. A few were Catholic monks, a few were mainline Lutherans, but most were Templars, a nineteenth-century sect of pietists who had come to the Holy Land for the shortly expected return of Jesus. They had eventually settled in six prosperous colonies, four of which would be in the Zionist enclave. No matter how much the WZO leadership wanted to avoid antagonising Berlin over the Templars, now almost all good Nazis, the local Nazi party realised that any spontaneous Jewish boycott after partition would make their position totally impossible. The German Foreign Ministry wanted either to have the colonies under direct British control or, more realistically, to have them moved into the Arab territory.

Popular Arab opinion was overwhelmingly opposed to partition, although the Nashishibis — the clan rivals of the dominant Husaynis — would have accepted a smaller Jewish state. They very reluctantly opposed the British proposal and their evident lack of zeal in opposing the partition, coupled with an intense factional hatred for the Husaynis, led to a ferocious civil war within the Arab community. Outside the country the only ruler who dared to hint at acceptance of the scheme was Abdullah of Trans-Jordan, whose emirate was to be merged with the Palestinian statelet. Ibn Saud in Arabia remained silent. Egypt and Iraq's ruling cliques publicly lamented, while privately their only concern was that the partition would arouse their own people and trigger a general movement against them and the British. Understandably, the Germans were completely unconvinced of the Arabs' ability to stave off partition, and when the Mufti finally appeared at their consulate on 15 July 1937, Doehle offered him absolutely nothing. He immediately notified his superiors of the interview: 'The Grand Mufti stressed Arab sympathy for the new Germany and expressed the hope that Germany was sympathetic toward the Arab fight against Jewry and was prepared to support it.' Doehle's response to the proffered alliance was virtually insulting. He told the supplicant that: 'after all, there was no question of our playing the role of an arbiter . . . I added that it was perhaps tactically in the interests of the Arabs if German sympathy for Arab aspirations were not too marked in German statements.'[11]

In October it was the Zionists' turn to court the Nazis. On 2 October 1937, the liner *Romania* arrived in Haifa with two German 'journalists' aboard. Herbert Hagen and his junior colleague, Eichmann, disembarked. They met their agent, Reichert, and later that day Feivel Polkes, who showed them Haifa from Mount Carmel and took them to visit a kibbutz. Years later, when he was in hiding in Argentina, Eichmann taped the story of his experiences and looked back at his brief stay in Palestine with fond nostalgia:

I did see enough to be very impressed by the way the Jewish colonists were building up their land. I admired their desperate will to live, the more so since I was myself an idealist. In the years that followed I often said to Jews with whom I had dealings that, had I been a Jew, I would have been a fanatical Zionist. I could not imagine being anything else. In fact, I would have been the most ardent Zionist imaginable.[12]

But the two SS men had made a mistake in contacting their local agent; the British CID had become aware of Reichert's ring, and two days later they summarily expelled the visitors to Egypt. Polkes followed them there, and further discussions were held on 10 and 11 October at Cairo's Café Groppi. In their report on their expedition Hagen and Eichmann gave a careful rendering of Polkes's words at these meetings. Polkes told the two Nazis:

> The Zionist state must be established by all means and as soon as possible... When the Jewish state is established according to the current proposals laid down in the Peel paper, and in line with England's partial promises, then the borders may be pushed further outwards according to one's wishes.[13]

He went on:

> in Jewish nationalist circles people were very pleased with the radical German policy, since the strength of the Jewish population in Palestine would be so far increased thereby that in the foreseeable future the Jews could reckon upon numerical superiority over the Arabs in Palestine.[14]

During his February visit to Berlin, Polkes had proposed that the Haganah should act as spies for the Nazis, and now he showed their good faith by passing on two pieces of intelligence information. He told Hagen and Eichmann:

> the Pan-Islamic World Congress convening in Berlin is in direct contact with two pro-Soviet Arab leaders: Emir Shekib Arslan and Emir Adil Arslan . . . The illegal Communist broadcasting station whose transmission to Germany is particularly strong, is, according to Polkes' statement, assembled on a lorry that drives along the German–Luxembourg border when transmission is on the air.[15]

Next it was the Mufti's turn to bid again for German patronage. This time he sent his agent, Dr Said Imam, who had studied in Germany and had for a long time been in contact with the German consulate in Beirut, directly to Berlin with an offer. If Germany would 'support the Arab independence movement ideologically and materially', then the Mufti would respond by 'Disseminating National Socialist ideas in the Arab-Islamic world; combatting Communism, which appears to be

spreading gradually, by employing all possible means'. He also proposed
'continuing acts of terrorism in all French colonial and mandated
territories inhabited by Arabs or Mohammedans'. If they won, he
swore 'to utilize only German capital and intellectual resources'. All of
this was in the context of a pledge to keep the Semitic and Aryan races
apart, which task was delicately referred to as 'maintaining and respect-
ing the national convictions of both peoples'.[16]

Palestine was now getting intense scrutiny from every relevant
branch of the German state and party bureaucracy. The pro-Zionists
still had their telling arguments, particularly the economists, who saw
the Ha'avara as helping German industry. The critics of the Nazi-
Zionist relationship were concerned that the proposed Jewish statelet
would be recognised internationally and begin to be seen as a Jewish
Vatican, which could create diplomatic problems for the Germans over
their treatment of the Jews. This was the main argument of Hagen and
Eichmann in their report on their trip.

It was the British who solved the Nazis' dilemma. They had begun
to ponder upon what would follow if they created a Zionist statelet.
The possibility of a world war was evident and the creation of a Zionist
state was guaranteed to drive the Arabs into Hitler's arms. The further
possibility of war with the bellicose Japanese made it crucial to
maintain the ability of moving troops through the Middle East, by land
and via the Suez Canal, without violent native opposition. Peel's partition was therefore hastily buried and the British determined that the
Arab revolt was to be extinguished before the emerging Axis alliance
could profit from it. The revolt was savagely crushed by the British
Army and then Zionist immigration, the cause of the revolt, was
curtailed.

Hitler now no longer had to trouble himself over the possibility of
a Jewish Vatican, but the fact that the British had actually proposed it
made the future possibility of a Jewish state a serious consideration.
Long-term German military calculations now made concern for Arab
opinion a factor in foreign policy. Many German diplomats insisted that
the Ha'avara agreement guaranteed the eventual creation of the state,
and Foreign Office opinion began to turn against it; however, it was
saved by the intervention of Otto von Hentig, a career diplomat who
had dealt with the Zionists under the Kaiser and Weimar. According to
Ernst Marcus, Ha'avara's Berlin representative, von Hentig 'with his
deep love of his nation and its spirit . . . appreciated the driving forces
of Zionism as an element akin to his own feelings'. He therefore worked
with his Zionist associate to try and keep 'preferential treatment of

Palestine' alive.

> He advised me to prepare suitable material in order to prove that the number of Jewish emigrants from Germany to Palestine as well as their financial contribution to the upbuilding of the Jewish home-land were far too small to exert a decisive influence on the development of the country. Accordingly, I compiled a memorandum which emphasised the share of Polish Jews in the work of reconstruction in all its important phases, described the financial contribution of American Jewry and contrasted it with the small effort made by the Jews of Germany.[17]

Von Hentig knew that the task of persuading Hitler to help Zionism had to be done in person and at the 'favourable moment', when he was laughing and jolly and full of his customary goodwill toward Jews. One day in early 1938, von Hentig called with the good news: 'The Fuehrer had made an affirmative decision and that all obstacles in the way of emigration to Palestine had now been removed.'[18]

At first the Nazis had tried to stay neutral during the Arab revolt. On Coronation Day in 1937 all the Templar colonies flew the swastika in sympathy with Britain and they were under strict orders not to solicit the British troops nor to have anything to do with the Mosley-ites.[19] But Berlin kept the pressure on and, while Jewish money and emigrants were still pushed towards Palestine, in 1938 Admiral Wilhelm Canaris, the head of the *Abwehr* Intelligence Division, put the Mufti on his payroll. However, the Mufti showed no signs of political or military competence and the money, which was always irregular, finally stopped.[20] Further military non-involvement in the Arab revolt re-mained strict policy until the Munich Conference in September 1938, and arms shipments were prepared only in late 1938. Even then the desire not to antagonise London with threats to the British Empire led to the sudden cancellation of the first shipment via Saudi Arabia when the Germans became convinced that the Saudi Foreign Minister was a British agent.[21] With the aborting of the arms shipment, German concern for the Arab revolt ceased.

The Failure of the Mufti's Collaboration with the Dictators

The Mufti gained nothing, then or later, from his collaboration with either Rome or Berlin, nor could the Palestinian interest ever have been served by the two dictators. When the Mufti approached the Nazis, they were encouraging Jews to emigrate to Palestine; yet not once in all of his pre-war dealings with the Nazis did he suggest that they stop the very emigration which was the source of Zionism's new strength. Later, during the Second World War, his Jew-hatred and his anti-Communism persuaded him to go to Berlin and to oppose any release of Jews from the camps for fear that they would end up in Palestine. He eventually organised Muslim SS troops against the Soviets and the Yugoslav partisans.

The Mufti was an incompetent reactionary who was driven into his anti-Semitism by the Zionists. It was Zionism itself, in its blatant attempt to turn Palestine from an Arab land into a Jewish state, and then use it for the yet further exploitation of the Arab nation, that generated Palestinian Jew-hatred. Rabbi Yitzhak Hutner of Aguda Yisrael gave a perceptive explanation for the Palestinian's career.

It should be manifest, however, that until the great public pressures for the establishment of a Jewish state, the Mufti had no interest in the Jews of Warsaw, Budapest or Vilna. Once the Jews of Europe became a threat to the Mufti because of their imminent influx into the Holy Land, the Mufti in turn became for them the *Malekh Hamoves* — the incarnation of the Angel of Death. Years ago, it was still easy to find old residents of *Yerushalayim* who remembered the cordial relations they had maintained with the Mufti in the years before the impending creation of a Jewish State. Once the looming reality of the State of Israel was before him, the Mufti spared no effort at influencing Hitler to murder as many Jews as possible in the shortest amount of time. This shameful episode, where the founders and early leaders of the State were clearly a factor in the destruction of many Jews, has been completely suppressed and expunged from the record.[22]

If the Mufti's collaboration with the dictators cannot be justified, it becomes absolutely impossible to rationalise the Haganah's offers to spy for the Nazis. Given the outcry against the Ha'avara and the servile posture of the ZVfD, it seems certain that, at the very least, a significant minority of the WZO would have voted with their feet had they known of the Haganah's subterranean betrayal.

Notes

1. 'Hitler's Friends in the Middle East', *Weiner Library Bulletin*, vol. XV (1961), p. 35.

2. Adolf Hitler, *Mein Kampf*, pp. 658–9.

3. David Yisraeli, 'Germany and Zionism', *Germany and the Middle East, 1835–1939* (1975), p. 158.

4. David Yisraeli, *The Palestine Problem in German Politics 1889–1945* (Hebrew), Bar-Ilan University, Appendix (German): 'Geheime Kommandosache Bericht', pp. 301–2.

5. Ibid., p. 304.

6. *Documents on German Foreign Policy*, Series D, vol. V, (Washington, 1953), pp. 746–7.

7. Ronald Storrs, *Orientations*, p. 405.

8. *The Voices of Zionism* (Shahak reprint), p. 18.

9. Enzo Sereni, 'Towards a New Orientation', *Jews and Arabs in Palestine*, pp. 282–3.

10. Moshe Beilenson, 'Problems of a Jewish–Arab Rapprochement', *Jews and Arabs in Palestine*, pp. 193–5.

11. *Documents on German Foreign Policy*, pp. 755–6.

12. Adolf Eichmann, 'Eichmann Tells His Own Damning Story', *Life* (28 November 1960), p. 22.

13. Klaus Polkehn, 'The Secret Contacts: Zionism and Nazi Germany 1933–41', *Journal of Palestine Studies* (Spring 1976), p. 74.

14. Heinz Hohne, *The Order of the Death's Head*, p. 337.

15. Polkehn, 'The Secret Contacts', p. 75.

16. *Documents on German Foreign Policy*, p. 779.

17. Ernst Marcus, 'The German Foreign Office and the Palestine Question in the Period 1933–39', *Yad Vashem Studies*, vol. II, pp. 187–8, 191.

18. Ibid., pp. 192–3.

19. H.D. Schmidt, 'The Nazi Party in Palestine and the Levant 1932–9', *International Affairs* (London, October 1952), p. 466.

20. Yisraeli, 'The Third Reich and Palestine', *Middle East Studies* (May 1971), p. 349.

21. *Documents on German Foreign Policy*, p. 811.

22. Yitzhak Hutner, 'Holocaust', *Jewish Observer* (October 1977), p. 8.

THE WORLD JEWISH CONGRESS

Although the WZO permitted the ZVfD to seek collaboration with Nazism, and its leaders were eager to sell Hitler's wares abroad and even spy for him, they did not want the menace to spread. Even the Zionist movement in Palestine realised that fund-raising from a universally ruined Jewry would hardly be the same as collecting for the victims in Germany alone. Not willing to fight Hitler themselves, for fear that he would abrogate the Ha'avara agreement and outlaw the ZVfD if they gave him any trouble, Sokolow and Weizmann dreamt of a great power alliance that would hold Hitler back, but this was always an empty fantasy. Those in the WZO led by Goldmann and Wise, who wanted to struggle, invariably found the two presidents either indifferent or opposed, but Hitler's growing strength compelled the more militant faction to establish a World Jewish Congress (WJC) as a Jewish defence organisation.

Both Goldmann and Wise were themselves deeply committed to Zionism; Goldmann had even opposed inviting any assimilationists — that is to say, the majority of Jewry — to their preliminary conference in 1932.[1] Furthermore, they did not think to challenge Weizmann's right to retake the WZO presidency in 1935. Nevertheless, the WZO was determinedly opposed to the new initiative, for fear that it would deflect energy away from Palestine back toward world Jewry. In February 1934, a year after Hitler came to power, Sokolow, who was then still the WZO President, was reported speaking against the World Jewish Congress:

Doubt as to the wisdom of convening the World Jewish Congress tentatively scheduled for this summer was expressed by Nahum Sokolow, President of the World Zionist Organization . . . the Zionist veteran regards the fact that, at the Geneva Jewish Conference last summer where the World Jewish Congress was discussed, some question was raised as to whether or not Palestine should be included in the program of the World Jewish Congress, to be an indication of the disagreements and party battles which might take place in calling the parley . . . Mr Sokolow presents an alternative plan, according to which all shades of Jewry would be called upon to construct a Jewish body for Jewish self-defense, the execution of well considered, carefully formulated plans of such a body, which would include all Jewish groups with the exception of the avowed assimilationists, would bring much good, Mr Sokolow believes.[2]

Sokolow was also stalling because he was afraid of the attacks on the Ha'avara agreement that were sure to be made at a broad World Jewish Congress. Stephen Wise returned fire:

> We were given warnings that support would be alienated for the World Jewish Congress if the [Geneva] Conference adopts a resolution against the Palestine–German transfer agreement. I do not fear this threat. The Jewish people are prepared to accept the guidance of Eretz Israel, but not commands or threats, when they conflict with the interests of all Jews.[3]

The conflict was painful to Wise; he had once thought along similar lines to Sokolow, but although he still thought of Palestine as the most positive side of Jewish life, he simply could not put Zionism so far ahead of the danger that threatened European Jewry:

> I know very well some Zionist will say: only Eretz Israel interests me. Palestine has the primary place. I was the one who first used the word 'primary' some years ago; I had to withdraw the word 'primary' when I had the courage to say that though Palestine has the primary place in Jewish hopes, I cannot, as a Jew, be indifferent to the Galuth . . . if I had to choose between Eretz Israel and its upbuilding and the defense of the Galuth, I would say that then the Galuth must perish. But after all, the more you save the Galuth, the more you will ultimately do for Eretz Israel.[4]

The WJC movement continued to gain strength in spite of Sokolow's opposition; the Nazi pressure was too great, the ranks wanted their movement to do something, and when Wise reluctantly endorsed the Ha'avara at the 1935 World Zionist Congress, the idea of the WJC finally received formal sanction from the WZO. However, there was never much enthusiasm for the WJC within the WZO. Chicago's *Jewish Chronicle*, itself an opponent of the WJC movement, accurately described the lack of serious interest in the idea of a defence organisation, even as late as May 1936, almost three and a half years into the Third Reich:

individual leaders of the Mizrachi and the Jewish State Party have no faith or interest in the Congress . . . Hadassah is not roused on the matter, and the poll of the members of the Executive Committee of the Zionist Organization of America revealed . . . the majority is overwhelmingly opposed to the Congress.[5]

Despite the hostility of the right wing, the WJC had to come. This was now the period of the Popular Front; the Social Democrats and the Stalinists had finally learned the necessity for unity against Fascism in the wake of disaster, and the Zionists had to come up with a 'Jewish' equivalent or lose their small following among the Jewish workers, particularly in Poland, who were influenced by Popular Front notions. Labour Zionist support for Wise and Goldmann was enough to overcome the right wing, but the paradox was that the WJC was doomed to fail precisely when it suddenly threatened to turn into a genuine Popular Front.

'Centers about the Anti-Fascist Struggle Alone'

The American Communist Party (CPUSA) decided to back the World Jewish Congress as their leaders believed that once inside the movement they would not have any problem getting the honest Zionist ranks to focus their primary attention on the Nazi menace rather than Palestine. But admitting the pro-Arab CPUSA was out of the question for Wise. The fight against Hitler was important, but Palestine and Zionism were ultimately more important. His *Congress Bulletin* came out flatly against letting the Communist Party in:

Although the struggle against anti-Semitism and Fascism will, of necessity, be one of the chief issues on the agenda of the Congress . . . the problems with which the World Jewish Congress will deal . . . will also include the upbuilding of Palestine and the struggle for religious and cultural freedom for Jews in all countries . . . The instructions under which the American Jewish Communists are trying to find their way into all coordinated Jewish efforts, centers about the anti-Fascist struggle alone . . . the *'Morning Freiheit'* could easily spare itself the trouble of even considering the question of the participation of the Jewish Communists.[6]

The World Jewish Congress finally held its foundation congress in

Geneva in August 1936. A pro-Communist American delegation attended, in the hope that they would win last minute admittance in a floor fight, but it was to no avail. The meeting passed a boycott resolution against the Nazis, but there was never any serious effort to establish it. Weizmann's loyal lieutenant in the USA, Louis Lipsky, the President of the Zionist Organisation of America, had only reluctantly agreed to the idea of holding the Congress; taking real action against Hitler was far more than he and his cohorts were prepared to accept. A correspondent for *World Jewry* described Lipsky's scuttling of the one anti-Nazi action that the Congress thought to take:

> The general boycott resolution . . . was adopted unanimously . . . but when it came to the question of giving practical effect to the resolution, then it was that the opposition made itself felt. The Commission had drawn up a resolution demanding the creation of a special department for boycott work . . . To this certain American delegates, led by Louis Lipsky, strongly objected . . . it is clear that the responsible authorities are not enamoured of the proposal and I am inclined to doubt if they really intend to give it practical effect.

The observer went on to describe the Congress as 'confused as to its means and lacking just that touch of inspired leadership that might have made its advent a turning point in Jewish history'.[7]

The magazine's gloomy description was fully justified. This was a conclave primarily of professional Zionist leaders; these were not the people to build a serious boycott or do anything else to fight Hitler. Without unity with the assimilationalist Jews, including the Communists, as well as Gentile anti-Nazis, they could never begin to harm the Nazis either through the boycott or any other way. Their refusal to work with the Stalinists was not because of hostility to the regime in the Soviet Union. Zionism was banned there, the Hebrew language was seen as alien to the real lives of the Jewish masses, but none of them saw the Soviet Union as anti-Semitic; on the contrary. When Stephen Wise was asked to join John Dewey's commission to investigate Stalin's charges that Trotsky was a Nazi agent, he declined. Trotsky had called Stalin an anti-Semite and that, Wise insisted, was so obviously untrue that it made everything else he said equally suspect. There is no doubt that Wise and his associates thought there would be war and they wanted to see the United States, Britain and the Soviets united against Hitler; they had no confidence in the masses stopping Nazism and, consistent with their reliance on the ruling classes to solve the Jewish question, they saw an alliance of the Great Powers as the only possible weapon against Hitler. Despite their enthusiasm for an alliance between their ruling-class patrons and Stalin, the members of the American Jewish Congress were not economic radicals and had no desire to involve themselves with their own local Communist party. That and the pro-Arab Communist line ruled out any association with the CPUSA. The lack of political realism in the World Jewish Congress flowed out of the marginal nature of Zionism in the real life of world Jewry. The more the Zionists worked for remote Palestine, the less they involved themselves in the real struggles of the Jewish masses. When a mass street movement became imperative, the WJC had neither the desire nor the experience to run such a struggle nor the willingness to learn.

Between the 1936 World Jewish Congress and the Stalin–Hitler pact, the CPUSA membership increased to 90,000 and had a union following of over a million. It became politically much more important than Wise's American Jewish Congress or the American Zionist movement. Certainly the Communists and the Zionists had great differences. Each had severe limitations, and clearly much more than a boycott was required to beat Hitler, but there can be no doubt that an alliance between the two forces would have galvanised the Jewish community in America, and many non-Jewish anti-Nazis would have moved together with them. Whether such a coalition would have been effective is another matter, but the WJC's refusal to take in the Communist Party was a tremendous blow to the Jewish struggle against Hitler. The desperately needed united Jewish front became another tragic sacrifice to Zionism.

Notes

1. Shlomo Shafir, 'American Jewish Leaders and the Emerging Nazi Threat (1928–1933)', *American Jewish Archives* (November 1979), p. 175.
2. 'Doubt Wisdom of Convening World Congress', *Jewish Daily Bulletin* (11 February 1934), pp. 1, 12.
3. 'Jewish World Conference', *South African Ivri* (September 1934), p. 1.
4. 'Rabbi Wise', *New Palestine* (14 February 1934), pp. 5–7.
5. 'Foredoomed to Fail', *Chicago Jewish Chronicle* (1 May 1936), p. 8.
6. 'Communists Take Note', *Congress Bulletin* (13 March 1936), p. 2.
7. 'Was the Congress Worthwhile?', *World Jewry* (21 August 1936), p. 67.

10 ZIONIST-REVISIONISM AND ITALIAN FASCISM

Menachem Begin's surprising rise to power in 1977, after a lifetime of opposition within the Zionist movement, quite naturally created considerable interest in his personal career. However, Begin himself, for all his present fame and power, would still refer to himself as nothing more than a disciple of Vladimir Jabotinsky, the founder of his tendency and the man he considers the greatest Jew since Herzl.

The creator of the Jewish Legion and the founder of the Haganah (Defence), Jabotinsky is the Revisionists' acclaimed hero. Yet at his death in New York's Catskills in August 1940, he was the most despised ideological thinker in the Jewish political world. Typical of the style of the man was the extraordinary Ukrainian pact he engineered in a hotel room in Prague in August 1921. He had travelled to Prague for a World Zionist Congress, and he had a visitor there, an old friend, Maxim Slavinsky, Simon Petliura's ambassador. The regime in the Ukraine had collapsed. Petliura, caught between Polish imperialism and Bolshevism, had let Poland take Ukrainian lands in return for arms against the Red Army, but the aid was to no avail and the remnants of his army had to flee into Polish-occupied Galicia. Slavinsky told Jabotinsky of the latest plan: the 15,000 remaining troops would attack the Soviet Ukraine in 1922. The ambassador of the notorious pogromist Petliura government and the organiser of the Haganah worked out a secret agreement. Jabotinsky, on his own, without reference to the WZO, pledged to work within his movement to organise Zionist police to accompany Petliura's troops in their raid. They were not to fight the Red Army, but would guard the Jews of the towns captured by the very soldiers that would bring them into the region.

The pact was disclosed by the Ukrainians to prove that they had changed their ways. The WZO was aghast, and Jabotinsky had to defend himself against all Jewish opinion, which could not stomach any association with the discredited murderer. In the end the incursion never came off; France withdrew its subsidy, and the nationalist force disintegrated. Jewry divided between those who regarded Jabotinsky as a fool or a villain; everywhere the Communists used the pact to discredit Zionism among Jews, but Jabotinsky was unrepentant. He would have done the same for the Leninists, if only they had asked:

A Jewish gendarmerie with the White Army, a Jewish gendarmerie with the Red Army, a Jewish gendarmerie with the Lilac and Pea-green Army, if any; let them settle their quarrels, we shall police the towns and see to it that the Jewish population should not be molested.[1]

The Poale Zionists demanded an investigation, as they claimed the agreement had endangered the legality of their own barely tolerated organisation in the Soviet Union, but Jabotinsky had travelled to the United States on a seven-month lecturing tour and the investigating panel could not be scheduled until 18 January 1923. In the end the hearing was never held, as Jabotinsky suddenly resigned from the WZO the night before he was to testify. He always claimed that his resignation had nothing to do with the pending inquiry, and insisted that he resigned due to a running dispute concerning relations with Britain, but few believed him. He re-entered the ranks shortly after, but his opponents saw no further point in officially pursuing the matter as he no longer had any position within the movement. When he began to organise his new tendency the attacks resumed, and for the rest of his life he had to defend his escapade. But throughout his career Jabotinsky was noted for his imperious contempt for his critics; he simply told the hostile world that 'When I die you can write as my epitaph − "This was the man who made the pact with Petliura".'[2]

'We Want a Jewish Empire'

Jabotinsky returned to the now wary WZO in 1923 as the far-right opponent of the leadership, determined to 'revise' their stance; he denounced Weizmann for not demanding the reconstitution of the Jewish Legion. He had also seen Churchill separate Trans-Jordan from the Jewish 'National Home' in Palestine, and when the WZO reluctantly accepted Churchill's decision he had only gone along out of a sense of discipline but thenceforward the claim that Jordan was eternally Jewish became the *idée fixe* of his new programme: 'One side of the Jordan is ours − and so is the other'. So goes *Shtei Gadot*, the song still most commonly identified with the Revisionist movement.

Jabotinsky never shared the naive illusion that the Palestinians would some day welcome foreign domination of their country. At a time when Ben-Gurion and his friends still thought they could convince the Palestinian masses to accept Zionism as in their own interest,

Jabotinsky developed his own blunt thesis in an article, *The Iron Wall (We and the Arabs)*, written in 1923:

> Zionist colonisation must be either terminated or carried out against the wishes of the native population. This colonisation can, therefore, be continued and make progress only under the protection of a power independent of the native population — an iron wall, which will be in a position to resist the pressure to the native population. This is, *in toto*, our policy towards the Arabs . . . A voluntary reconciliation with the Arabs is out of the question either now or in the near future.[3]

He had nothing but ridicule for the Zionist leaders who mouthed peace while demanding that the British Army protect them; or their hope of an Arab ruler (the favoured candidate was Faisal of Iraq) who would deal with them over the heads of the Palestinians and impose them on the natives with an Arab bayonet. He repeated over and over that there could be only one way to a Zionist state:

> If you wish to colonise a land in which people are already living, you must provide a garrison for the land, or find some 'rich man' or benefactor who will provide a garrison on your behalf. Or else — or else, give up your colonisation, for without an armed force which will render physically impossible any attempt to destroy or prevent this colonisation, colonisation is impossible, not 'difficult', not 'dangerous', but IMPOSSIBLE! . . . Zionism is a colonising adventure and therefore it stands or falls by the question of armed force. It is important . . . to speak Hebrew, but, unfortunately, it is even more important to be able to shoot — or else I am through with playing at colonisation.[4]

Jabotinsky understood that, for the moment, the Zionists were too weak to hold off the Arabs without the backing of the British, and Revisionism became loudly Empire loyalist. In 1930 Abba Achimeir, the ideologue of their Palestinian branch, proclaimed their interest lay 'in expanding the British empire even further than intended by the British themselves'.[5] However, they had no intention of hiding behind the British any longer than necessary. In 1935 a Jewish Communist journalist encountered Jabotinsky on board an ocean liner on his way to the United States and obtained an interview with him. Robert Gessner's article in the *New Masses* became the talk of Jewish America.

He announced he would speak frankly, so that Revisionism would be made clear . . . 'Revisionism', he began, 'is naive, brutal and primitive. It is savage. You go out into the street and pick any man − a Chinaman − and ask him what he wants and he will say one hundred per cent of everything. That's us. We want a Jewish Empire. Just like there is the Italian or French on the Mediterranean, we want a Jewish Empire.'[6]

'He had Caught a Glimpse of the Great Secret of Politically Minded Peoples'

Despite its members' enthusiasm for the British Empire, eventually Revisionism had to look elsewhere for a new imperial protector. Britain was not willing to do more than guard the Zionists, and not too effectively at that, and the Zionists had to buy land inch by inch. Nor could anyone seriously believe that Britain would ever give Trans-Jordan to the Zionists. The Revisionists therefore began to look for a new Mandatory firmly committed to a more ruthless policy towards the Arabs and therefore willing to back the construction of a Zionist garrison-state. Italy seemed the obvious answer, not because of any sympathy for Fascism, but because of Italy's own imperial aspirations. Jabotinsky had been a student in Italy and he loved the old liberal-aristocratic order. In his own mind he was the Jewish Mazzini, Cavour and Garibaldi all rolled into one, and he could not see anything wrong with the liberal traditions that Mussolini so thoroughly repudiated. In fact he sneered at Fascism. In 1926 he wrote:

> There is today a country where 'programs' have been replaced by the word of one man . . . Italy; the system is called Fascism: to give their prophet a title, they had to coin a new term − *'Duce'* − which is a translation of that most absurd of all English words − 'leader'. Buffaloes follow a leader. Civilized men have no leaders.[7]

Yet, despite Jabotinsky's broad-mindedness, his own style came to mimic the militarism of Mussolini and Hitler. His novel *Samson*, published in 1926, remains one of the classics of totalitarian literature.

> One day, he was present at a festival at the temple of Gaza. Outside in the square a multitude of young men and girls were gathered for the festive dances . . . A beardless priest led the dances. He stood on

the topmost step of the temple, holding an ivory baton in his hand. When the music began the vast concourse stood immobile . . . The beardless priest turned pale and seemed to submerge his eyes in those of the dancers, which were fixed responsively on his. He grew paler and paler; all the repressed fervor of the crowd seemed to concentrate within his breast till it threatened to choke him. Samson felt the blood stream to his heart; he himself would have choked if the suspense had lasted a few moments longer. Suddenly, with a rapid, almost inconspicuous movement, the priest raised his baton, and all the white figures in the square sank down on the left knee and threw the right arm towards heaven − a single movement, a single, abrupt, murmurous harmony. The tens of thousands of onlookers gave utterance to a moaning sigh. Samson staggered; there was blood on his lips, so tightly had he pressed them together . . . Samson left the place profoundly thoughtful. He could not have given words to his thought, but he had a feeling that here, in this spectacle of thousands obeying a single will, he had caught a glimpse of the great secret of politically minded peoples.[8]

The wish for a more determined Mandatory easily overcame Jabotinsky's distaste for Italy's internal regime, and many of his recruits had never had any difficulties with Fascism's domestic style. By the mid-1920s he had attracted several ex-Labour Zionists who turned savagely on their former comrades and Mussolini became their hero. In August 1932, at the Fifth Revisionist World Conference, Abba Achimeir and Wolfgang von Weisl, the leaders of Palestine's Revisionists, proposed Jabotinsky as *Duce* of their one faction of the WZO. He flatly refused, but any contradiction between himself and the increasingly pro-Fascist ranks was resolved by his moving closer to them. Without abandoning his previous liberal rhetoric, he incorporated Mussolini's concepts into his own ideology and rarely publicly criticised his own followers for Fascist-style assaults, defending them against the Labour Zionists and the British.

The argument has been made that Revisionism as such was not Fascist because there were legitimate differences within the ranks and that ultimately decisions were made by vote at conventions or by means of the plebiscite. In reality, it is difficult to think of how much more undemocratic the movement could have been without it formally becoming a proper Fascist grouping. By 1932−3 Jabotinsky had decided that it was time for them to withdraw from the WZO, but most of the Executive of their world union were opposed as they saw nothing to be gained by splitting. He suddenly cut the debate off by arbitrarily taking personal control over the movement and letting the ranks choose between him and the superseded Executive in a plebiscite. A letter written in December 1932 demonstrates that he knew full well in what direction he was leading the organisation: 'The time has apparently come when there must be a single, principal controller in the movement, a "leader", though I still hate the word. All right, if there must be one, there will be one.'[9]

Jabotinsky knew he could not lose the vote; to the tens of thousands of youthful Betar brownshirts he represented the militarism they wanted against an Executive of the same genteel bourgeoisie as the Weizmann clique. It was always the Betar youth group that was the central component of Diaspora Revisionism. The semi-official *History of the Revisionist Movement* declares that, after a discussion of whether to set up on a democratic basis, the decision was taken for a 'hierarchic structure of a military type'.[10] In its classic form the Betar chose its *Rosh Betar* (High Betar), always Jabotinsky, by a 75 per cent majority vote, he picked the leaders of the national units; they, in turn, selected the next lower leaders. Opposition was allowed, but after the purge of the moderates in the early 1930s the only serious internal critics were sundry 'maximalists', extremists who would complain, at various times, that Jabotinsky was not a Fascist, or was too pro-British or was insufficiently anti-Arab. When the average Betari put on his brownshirt he could be forgiven if he thought he was a member of a Fascist movement, and that Jabotinsky was his *Duce*.

The Jewish Bourgeoisie – the Only Source of our Constructive Capital

From the beginning the Revisionists saw the middle class as their clientele and they had a long hatred of the left. In 1933 a youth wrote to Jabotinsky asking why he had become so vehemently anti-Marxist; Jabotinsky wrote a remarkable article, 'Zionism and Communism', explaining their total incompatibility. In terms of Jewry, 'Communism strives to annihilate the only source of our constructive capital – the Jewish bourgeoisie – because their foundation is our root, and its principle is the class struggle against the bourgeoisie.' In Palestine Marxism, by definition, meant the sharpest opposition to Zionism:

the essence of Communism consists in that it agitates and must incite the Eastern Nations against European dominance. This dominance in its eyes is 'imperialistic' and exploitative. I believe otherwise and think that European dominance makes them civilized, but that is an incidental question and does not belong to the matter. One thing is clear: Communism incites and must incite the Eastern Nations and this it can do only in the name of national freedom. It tells them and must tell them: your lands belong to you and not to any strangers. This is how it must speak to the Arabs and the Arabs of Palestine . . . For our Zionist lungs, Communism is suffocating gas and this is how you must deal with it.[11]

Typically for him, he jumped from a correct premiss to an incorrect conclusion. In logic, Zionism and Marxism are indeed incompatible, but it did not follow in life that those who did try to mix the two were really in the enemy camp. In practice, the Socialist-Zionist sacrifices socialism to Zionism, not the other way around, but Jabotinsky maintained that there was no substantive difference between the Communists and the Poale Zionists:

I do not believe that there is any difference between Communism and other forms of Socialism based on class views . . . The only difference between these two camps is one of temperament – the one rushes ahead, the other is slightly slower: such a difference is not worth the value of the ink-drop necessary to describe it in writing.[12]

Jabotinsky's mind always ran to the linear. The capitalist class was the main force of Zionism; it followed, logically, that strikes repelled investment in Palestine. They might be acceptable in advanced industrial countries, their economies could take them, but not where the foundations of Zion were still being laid brick by brick. In exact imitation of the Italian Fascists, the Revisionists opposed 'both' strikes and lock-outs, with strikes being seen as the highest of crimes:

And by 'obligatory' arbitration we mean this: after the election of such a permanent board, recourse to it should be proclaimed as the only legitimate way of settling industrial conflicts, its verdicts should be final, and both strike and lockout (as well as boycott of Jewish labor) should be declared treasonable to the interest of Zionism and repressed by every legal and moral means at the nation's disposal.[13]

The Revisionists were not about to wait until they took state power to break their Labour rivals. Achimeir, their leader in Palestine (Jabotinsky had been barred from Palestine by the High Commissioner after Revisionist provocations had triggered the 1929 Arab explosion) flagrantly ran his *Yomen shel Fascisti* (Diary of a Fascist) in their paper. He had his equivalent of the Italian *squadristi*, the *Brith Ha-Biryonim* (Union of Terrorists), so styled after the ancient *Sicarii* — the dagger-wielding Zealot assassins active during the Judaean revolt against Rome — and he whipped up the Revisionist youth for a final showdown with the Labour Zionists:

> We must create groups for action; to exterminate the Histadrut physically; they are worse than Arabs . . . You're no students; you're just so much molasses . . . There isn't one among you capable of committing murder after the fashion of those German students who murdered Rathenau. You are not possessed of the nationalist spirit that dominated the Germans . . . Not one of you is capable of murder after the manner in which Karl Liebknecht and Rosa Luxemburg were murdered.[14]

Palestine now witnessed the Zionists, in the shape of the Histadrut, driving thousands of Arabs out of their seasonal jobs in the Jewish orange groves and the Revisionist Fascists descending upon the Histadrut. But although the Arab workers still lacked the leadership to defend themselves the Histadrut was well organised. After a series of sharp clashes, including a decisive battle in Haifa, on 17 October 1934, when 1,500 Labour Zionists stormed the Revisionist headquarters and injured dozens of the Fascists, the Revisionist campaign withered away. The Histadrut ranks were quite willing to respond to the Fascist onslaught by carrying the fight to the enemy and crushing them, but the Labour Zionist leadership was as unwilling to fight Fascism in Palestine as anywhere else and let them escape their defeat out of fear that a serious battle would alienate Diaspora Zionism's middle-class following.

The Revisionists' Relations with the Italian Fascists

In the early 1930s Jabotinsky decided to set up a party school in Italy and the local Revisionists, who openly identified themselves as Fascists, lobbied Rome. He knew well enough that picking Italy as the locale for a party school would only confirm their Fascist image, but he had moved so far to the right that he had lost all concern for what his 'enemies' might think and he even emphasised to one of his Italian followers that they could set up their proposed school elsewhere but 'we . . . prefer to have it established in Italy'.[15] By 1934 the Italians had decided that, for all their friendliness to them, Sokolow and Weizmann and the WZO leadership had not the least thought of breaking with London. Nor were the Italians pleased at the growing ascendancy within the WZO of the Social Democratic Labour Zionists who were affiliated, however distantly, to their own underground socialist enemies. They were therefore quite willing to show support for the Revisionists who were evidently the Fascists of Zion. In November 1934 Mussolini allowed the Betar to set up a squadron at the maritime academy at Civitavecchia run by the Blackshirts.

Even after the Arlosoroff assassination in 1933 and the strike-breaking campaign organised by Achimeir against the Histadrut, Ben-Gurion still worked out a peace agreement with Jabotinsky in October 1934, but the Histadrut ranks rejected it and the Revisionists finally set up their own New Zionist Organisation (NZO). Jabotinsky asked his Italian supporters to arrange to have the first NZO world congress in Trieste in 1935, flaunting the fact that he did not care what people would think of his movement holding its foundation congress in Fascist Italy.[16] In the end the event was held in Vienna, but Jabotinsky visited the Civitavecchia academy after the Congress. Curiously, he never met Mussolini — perhaps he was concerned to prove he still was not just another 'head buffalo'.

Although there is not one statement by Jabotinsky in which he called himself a Fascist, and innumerable proclamations of his Gladstonian credentials, every other major political tendency saw the Revisionists as Zionism's Fascists. Weizmann privately attributed Arlosoroff's murder to their Fascist style; Ben-Gurion routinely referred to 'Vladimir Hitler' and even went so far as to call the Nazis the 'German Revisionists'.[17] Von Mildenstein told his readers of his encounter on board a ship with *'ein judischer Faschist'*, a Betari; he described the youths as 'the Fascist group among the Jews. Radical Nationalists, they are adverse to any kind of compromise on the questions of Jewish nationalism. Their political party is the Revisionists.'[18]

The highest such accolade was from Mussolini who, in 1935, told David Prato, later to become chief rabbi of Rome, that: 'For Zionism to succeed you need to have a Jewish state, with a Jewish flag and a Jewish language. The person who really understands that is your fascist, Jabotinsky.'[19]

The majority of the movement thought of themselves as opponents of democracy and as Fascists or near sympathisers. Jacob de Haas, an intimate of Herzl's, had converted to Revisionism in the mid-1930s and, to show that they were not 'just Jabotinsky', he had presided at the Vienna NZO Congress. When he returned to America he gave his impressions of the gathering in his column in Chicago's *Jewish Chronicle*. After hastily reassuring his readers that he really was not defending Fascism, he told them they had to:

> realize that democracy is a dead issue in most of Europe. Its chief exhibition in the common mind is the bluster and contrivance of endless parties and subparties . . . The delegates were not fascists, but having lost all faith in democracy they were not anti-fascist. They were however very anti-Communistic.[20]

If de Haas, in America, had to ease his sceptical readers into awareness that the majority of his movement had nothing but contempt for democracy, Wolfgang von Weisl, the financial director of the Revisionists, had no such hesitation about telling a diplomatic newspaper in Bucharest that 'although opinions among the Revisionists varied, in general they sympathized with Fascism'. He was positively eager to let the world know that 'He personally was a supporter of Fascism, and he rejoiced at the victory of Fascist Italy in Abyssinia as a triumph of the White races against the Black.'[21] In 1980 Shmuel Merlin described his own feelings toward Mussolini in the mid-1930s, when he was the young Secretary-General of the New Zionist Organisation.

> I admired him but I was not a fascist. He idealized war. I felt war was necessary, but to me it was always a tragedy . . . I did regret that Achimeir titled his column 'Diary of a Fascist', it just gave an excuse for our enemies to attack us, but it certainly did not break up our friendship.[22]

Whatever Jabotinsky might have thought he was leading, there can be no doubt that these three prominent members of the Revisionist movement were talking about a Fascist grouping. Von Weisl's evaluation seems quite reasonable; the Fascist component within the leadership was massive and it was they, not Jabotinsky, who ran the movement in Palestine, Poland, Italy, Germany, Austria, Latvia and Manchuria, at least. At the very best Jabotinsky must be thought of as a liberal-imperialist head on a Fascist body. Present-day Revisionists do not deny the presence of avowed Fascists in their movement in the 1930s; instead they overemphasise the distinctions between Jabotinsky and the Fascists. The academy at Civitavecchia, they allege, was but mere Mazzinism. Nationalists are allowed, they claim, to seek the aid of an imperialist rival of their own oppressor; surely, they insist, that does not therefore imply endorsement of the internal regime of their patron. They then point to Jabotinsky's admonition to the Betarim at Civitavecchia:

> Do not intervene in any party discussions concerning Italy. Do not express any opinions about Italian politics. Do not criticize the present regime in Italy — nor the former regime. If you are asked about your political and social beliefs answer: I am a Zionist. My greatest desire is the Jewish state, and in our country I oppose class warfare. This is the whole of my creed.[23]

This most diplomatic formula was calculated to please the Italian Fascists without antagonising any conservative supporters of the old regime whom a Betari might chance to encounter. Opposition to the class struggle was the litmus test for Mussolini, who was never particularly concerned whether his foreign admirers specifically thought of themselves as pure Fascists. However, Jabotinsky's letter to the Betarim was not the end of the story. His apologists omit the actual situation at the school where his strictures were ignored. The March 1936 issue of *L'Idea Sionistica*, the magazine of the Revisionists' Italian branch, described the ceremonies attendant to the inauguration of the Betar squad's new headquarters:

> The order — 'Attention!' A triple chant ordered by the squad's commanding officer — 'Viva L'Italia! Viva Il Re! Viva Il Duce!' resounded, followed by the benediction which rabbi Aldo Lattes invoked in Italian and in Hebrew for God, for the king and for Il Duce . . . *'Giovinezza'* [the Fascist Party's anthem] was sung with much enthusiasm by the Betarim.[24]

We may be sure that the same chants were cried when Mussolini himself reviewed the Betarim in 1936.[25] Jabotinsky knew that his Italian followers were admirers of Mussolini, but when he was sent a copy of Mussolini's *Dottrina del fascismo* all he could say in rebuke was a mild: 'I am permitted to hope that we have the capacity to create a doctrine of *our own*, without copying others.'[26] And, for all his personal reservations about Fascism, he definitely wanted Mussolini as the Mandatory for Palestine, writing to a friend in 1936 that his choices ran to:

> Italy or some condominium of less anti-Semitic states interested in Jewish immigration, or a direct Geneva [League of Nations] Mandate . . . Before June 30 – July 15 I sounded alternative no. 1. Result: not yet ripe, not by a long shot.[27]

Jabotinsky became Mussolini's defence attorney within the Jewish world. While he was visiting America in 1935 on a lecture tour he wrote a series of articles for New York's *Jewish Daily Bulletin*, a short-lived English-language Zionist paper devoted exclusively to Jewish affairs. In the 1930s, most Jews followed the common usage and referred to the fight against Hitler as part of the 'anti-Fascist struggle'; Jabotinsky was determined to put a stop to that, since he understood too well that as long as the Jews saw Hitler as another Fascist, they would never approve of the Revisionist orientation towards Mussolini. His brief for the Italian Fascist regime shows us exactly how he put his personal objections to the politics of a 'buffalo herd' far behind his growing commitment to his hoped-for Italian Mandatory:

> Whatever any few think of Fascism's other points, there is no doubt that the Italian brand of Fascist ideology is at least an ideology of racial equality. Let us not be so humble as to pretend that this does not matter – that racial equality is too insignificant an idea to out-balance the absence of civic freedom. For it is not true. I am a journalist who would choke without freedom of the press, but I affirm it is simply blasphemous to say that in the scale of civic rights, even the freedom of the press comes before the equality of all men. Equality comes first, always first, super first; and Jews should remember it, and hold that a regime maintaining that principle in a world turned cannibal does, partly, but considerably, atone for its other short-comings: it may be criticized, it should not be kicked at. There are enough other terms for cussing use – Nazism, Hitlerism, Polizeistadt, etc. – but the word 'fascismo' is Italy's copy right and should therefore be reserved only for the correct kind of discussion, not for exercises in Billingsgate. Especially as it may yet prove very harmful. That government of the copy right is a very powerful factor, whose sympathy may yet ward off many a blow, for instance in the League of Nations councils. Incidentally, the Permanent Mandate

Commission which supervises Palestinian affairs has an Italian chairman. In short — though I don't expect street-urchins (irrespective of age) to follow advise of caution — responsible leaders ought to take care.[28]

The Revisionists Rationalise their Links with the Fascists

The orientation towards Mussolini ended in total débâcle. Blindly groping for a hammer against their Arab, British and Jewish foes, the Revisionists were the only ones who did not see what was coming. A photostat of a letter from Emir Shekib Arslan to the Mufti, concerning the spreading of pro-Italian propaganda, had appeared in the Palestine press in 1935 and by 1936 Radio Bari was blaring anti-British broadcasts at the Arabs. By then the Revisionists were so used to defending Mussolini that they simply would not acknowledge his collaboration with the Mufti and the Palestinian cause. As late as 1938 William Ziff, an advertising executive who headed American Revisionism, tried to play down the Italian involvement with the Mufti in his book, *The Rape of Palestine*.

> In beautifully chosen words which inferred an anti-Jewish as well as an anti-British plot, the British Foreign Secretary pinned the whole blame on the Italians. The entire liberal press rose to the bait so dexterously flicked upon the water. Like a pack of dogs hot after game, the Marxist press aggressively took up the cry.[29]

Despite the fact that the Revisionists had clearly backed the wrong horse he continued:

> There can be no doubt that Mussolini, a hard-fisted realist, would have considered it good business if he could have disengaged the Jews from the British orbit. A powerful independent Zion with which he was on a friendly footing would have suited him perfectly. The Jews themselves eliminated this prospect by their persistent Anglophilism, and Mussolini had come to regard Zionism as merely a mask for the creation of another zone of English political and economic expansion in the Mediterranean. It hence looms in the Italian mind as an anti-Italian force. Nevertheless, not a shred of real evidence has ever been offered to substantiate the charge that

Italian intervention was a factor in the recent Arab revolt in Pales-tine.[30]

Eventually it was Spain, not Palestine, that persuaded Mussolini to support Hitler. Mussolini grasped that he and Hitler now had to stay united to ward off revolution elsewhere, and that it was only through an alliance with the German power that he could hope to expand his empire. But he also knew that it was impossible to be Hitler's ally and have Jews in his own party. He therefore concocted a Latinised Aryan-ism, expelled the Jews from the party and the economy, and geared up for war. The Revisionists declared that they were wrong for the right reasons.

> For years we have warned the Jews not to insult the fascist regime in Italy. Let us be frank before we accuse others of the recent anti-Jewish laws in Italy; why not first accuse our own radical groups who are responsible for what happened.[31]

With Mussolini's turn toward Hitler, the Revisionists' own Fascism became an impossible liability in the Jewish world and when Jabotinsky died in New York in August 1940 they hastily dropped the title of Rosh Betar, which had become redolent of Fascism. They would not admit that they had been Fascist themselves, merely that no one could possibly fill Jabotinsky's shoes. Recent Revisionist choniclers naturally tend to avoid or play down the role of their internal Fascists, such as Achimeir, and Civitavecchia is usually passed over with little more than an exonerating 'the founders of the Israeli navy were trained there'.

'Among the most Disturbing Political Phenomena of our Time'

It is impossible to end a discussion of Revisionism and Fascism without mentioning briefly Begin's role during these events. His post-war books, *The Revolt* and *White Nights*, omit his own activities in the 1930s, and Jabotinsky is portrayed as a misunderstood exponent of military defence. But at the age of 22 Begin was prominent enough in the Polish Betar to sit with Jabotinsky on the presidium of the 1935 Polish Revisionist conference in Warsaw. By 1938 he was the dominant figure at the Betar's Warsaw world conference, and by 1939 he had been appointed head of Polish Betar. But, despite the fact that he has been called a Fascist by innumerable opponents, no specifically pro-Mussolini writings by him are ever cited and, by now, it must be presumed that none exist. However, if it is true that he never openly expounded Fascism, Yehuda Benari, director of the Jabotinsky Institute, and the author of the article on Begin in the *Encyclopedia of Zionism and Israel*, categorically states that in 1939 'he joined the radical wing of the Revisionist movement, which was ideologically linked with the B'rit HaBiryonim'.[32] Begin was a personal friend of Achimeir, who had been deported to Poland in 1935, as well as von Weisl, who frequently came to Warsaw to negotiate with the Polish government on behalf of the NZO. He was an intimate friend of Nathan Yalin-Mor and at that time an admirer of Avraham Stern, both committed totalitarians. Even after the Second World War, as the leader of the *Herut* Party in the new Israeli state, Begin had both Achimeir and von Weisl writing for their daily newspaper.

In December 1948, on the occasion of his first visit to the United States, Albert Einstein, Hannah Arendt, Sidney Hook and others sent a letter to the *New York Times* exposing Begin's politics. Given the record of his movement and his intimate associations with the openly Fascist elements of pre-war Revisionism, their evaluation of Begin's ideological commitment bears quotation:

> Among the most disturbing political phenomena of our time is the emergence in the newly created state of Israel of the 'Freedom Party' (*Tnuat HaHerut*), a political party closely akin in its organization, methods, political philosophy and social appeal to the Nazi and Fascist parties . . . They have preached an admixture of ultra-nationalism, religious mysticism and racial superiority . . . they have proposed corporate unions on the Italian Fascist model . . . In the light of the forgoing considerations, it is imperative that the truth about Mr Begin and his movement be made known in this country. It is all the more tragic that the top leadership of American Zionism has refused to campaign against Begin's efforts.[33]

Notes

1. Joseph Schechtman, 'The Jabotinsky–Slavinsky Agreement', *Jewish Social Studies* (October 1955), p. 297.

2. Ibid., p. 306.

3. Marie Syrkin, 'Labor Zionism Replies', *Menorah Journal* (Spring 1935), p. 72.

4. Vladimir Jabotinsky, 'The Iron Law', *Selected Writings* (South Africa, 1962), p. 26.

5. Yaacov Shavit, 'The Attitudes of the Revisionists to the Arab Nationalist Movement', *Forum on the Jewish People, Zionism and Israel* (Spring 1978), p. 102.

6. Robert Gessner, 'Brown Shirts in Zion', *New Masses* (19 February 1935), p. 11.

7. Vladimir Jabotinsky, 'Jewish Fascism', *The Zionist* (London, 25 June 1926), p. 26.

8. Vladimir Jabotinsky, *Samson* (American edn, entitled *Prelude to Delilah*), pp. 200–1.

9. Joseph Schechtman, *Fighter and Prophet*, p. 165.

10. Yehuda Benari and Joseph Schechtman, *History of the Revisionist Movement*, vol. I, p. 338.

11. Vladimir Jabotinsky, 'Zionism and Communism', *Hadar* (February 1941), p. 33.

12. Shlomo Avineri, 'Political Thought of Vladimir Jabotinsky', *Jerusalem Quarterly* (Summer 1980), p. 17.

13. Vladimir Jabotinsky, *State Zionism*, p. 10.

14. Syrkin, 'Labor Zionism Replies', p. 79.

15. Jabotinsky, letter to Leone Carpi, 7 October 1931, in D. Carpi, A. Milano and A. Rofe (eds.), *Scritti in Memoria Di Leone Carpi*, p. 42.

16. Ibid., 21 May 1935, pp. 54–5.

17. Michael Bar-Zohar, *Ben-Gurion* (American edn), p. 67.

18. Leopold van Mildenstein, 'Ein Nazi fahrt nach Palastina', *Der Angriff*, (Berlin, 27 September 1934), pp. 3–4.

19. Bar-Zohar, *Ben-Gurion – The Armed Prophet*, p. 46.

20. Jacob de Haas, 'New Struggles in an Old World', *Chicago Jewish Chronicle* (18 October 1935), p. 9.

21. 'Dr von Weisl Believes in Fascism', *World Jewry* (London, 12 June 1936), p. 12.

22. Author's interview with Shmuel Merlin, 16 September 1980.

23. Vladimir Jabotinsky, 'Letter to Plugat Civitavecchia', *Selected Writings* (USA).

24. 'Supplemento al no. 8 di *L'Idea Sionistica*' (March 1936), p. 2.

25. *Mussolini, My Husband* (Italian film documentary).

26. Jabotinsky, 29 January 1934, *Scritti*, p. 52.

27. Schechtman, *Fighter and Prophet*, p. 304.

28. Jabotinsky, 'Jews and Fascism – Some Remarks – and a Warning', *Jewish Daily Bulletin* (11 April 1935), p. 3.

29. William Ziff, *The Rape of Palestine* (1938), p. 428.

30. Ibid., p. 429.

31. Paul Novick, *Solution for Palestine* (1939), p. 18.

32. Yehuda Benari, 'M'Nahum Begin', *Encyclopedia of Zionism and Israel*, vol. I, p. 116.

33. 'New Palestine Party', *New York Times* (4 December 1948) (Letters), p. 12.

11 REVISIONISM AND NAZISM

Early in 1932, Norman Bentwich, the former Attorney-General of Palestine, and a Zionist, was honoured by the Hebrew University with a chair in International Law and Peace. As he started his inauguration lecture, shouts suddenly came out of the audience: 'Go talk peace to the Mufti, not to us'. He began again, but this time he was bombarded with a shower of stink bombs and leaflets announcing that the Revisionist students were opposed to both him and his topic, and the hall had to be cleared by the police.[1] At the very time that Hitler's brownshirts were breaking up meetings, it was inevitable that Jerusalem's Jewish public should see the brownshirted Betarim as their own Nazis. By 1926, Abba Achimeir had already written about the necessity of murdering their opponents, and when the students came up for trial, their barrister, a prominent Revisionist, cheerfully took on their characterisation of Jewish Nazism.

> Yes, we Revisionists have a great admiration for Hitler. Hitler has saved Germany. Otherwise it would have perished within four years. And if he had given up his anti-Semitism we would go with him.[2]

Certainly many of the Revisionist ranks throughout the world originally looked upon the Nazis as akin to themselves: nationalists and Fascists. In 1931 their American magazine, the *Betar Monthly*, had openly declared their contempt for those who called them Nazis.

> When provincial leaders of the left-wing of petty Zionism like Berl Locker call us Revisionists and Betarim — Hitlerites, we are not at all disturbed . . . the Lockers and their friends aim to create in Palestine a colony of Moscow with an Arab instead of a Jewish majority, with a red flag instead of the White and Blue, with the 'Internationale' instead of the 'Hatikvah' . . . If Herzl was a Fascist and Hitlerite, if a Jewish majority on both sides of the Jordan, if a Jewish State in Palestine which will solve the economic, political, and cultural problems of the Jewish nation be Hitlerism, then we are Hitlerites.[3]

The Revisionists were Zionists and as such shared their movement's fundamental agreement with the Nazis that the Jews could never be real Germans. Nazism was inevitable and understandable. This view was well expressed by Ben Frommer, an American Revisionist in 1935. To Frommer, the Jew:

> No matter what country he inhabits . . . is not of the tribal origins . . . Consequently the Jew's attempt at complete identity with his country sounds spurious; his patriotism despite his vociferousness, hollow even to himself; and therefore his demand for complete equality with those who are of the essence of the nation naturally creates friction. This explains the intolerance of the Germans, Austrians, Poles and the increasing tide of antagonism in most European countries . . . It is presumptuous on the part of a Jew to demand that he be treated as lovingly as say a Teuton in a Teutonic country or a Pole in a Polish country. He must jealously guard his life and liberty, but he must candidly recognize that he does not 'belong'. The liberal fiction of perfect equality is doomed because it was unnatural.[4]

Revisionist Flirtation with the Nazis

Like the other German Zionists, the Revisionists were exclusively concerned with Palestine, and during Weimar they made no effort to organise Jewish resistance to Hitler. When the Nazis finally came to power, the Revisionists interpreted the victory as a defeat for their own Jewish ideological rivals and a vindication of their own ideas, both Zionist and Fascist. They went one stage further than the rest of the ZVfD and the *Rundschau* and imitated the Nazis' style. The banker Georg Kareski, seeing his rich Catholic associates in the Centre Party working with or joining the triumphant Nazis, decided to show Hitler there were Zionists who shared the Nazis' ethos. He joined the Revisionists and quickly became a leader of the German movement and attempted a *putsch* at the Berlin Jewish community centre in May 1933. This has been described by Richard Lichtheim in his history of German Zionism. Kareski:

> thought the Zionists had missed the opportunity to place themselves at the head of German Judaism through a revolutionary act. With the aid of a number of young people from 'Betar' . . . he 'occupied' the building of the Jewish community in 1933. He was quickly

forced to clear out, however, since the members of the community refused to go along with this. The result of this foolish action was his expulsion from the ZVfD. At the outset Kareski probably believed that the spirit of the times demanded such an act and that the outmoded conceptions of the bourgeois-liberal Jews had to be altered in favor of national-Zionist views in this violent fashion. In the following years he fell into a rather questionable relationship of dependency on the Gestapo, to whom he sought to recommend himself and his Betar group as the real representatives of the radical Zionist point of view corresponding to National Socialism.[5]

This was too much for Jabotinsky. He had not paid much attention to Germany in the final Weimar years. Throughout the 1929–33 period his prime concern was dealing with the British proposals on Palestine which were a response to the brief but bloody massacres of 1929, largely triggered by Revisionist provocations at the Wailing Wall. As with many right-wingers, Jabotinsky did not think that Hitler in power would be quite as anti-Semitic as he seemed in opposition. Shmuel Merlin, Secretary-General of the NZO, has explained that: 'He was not panicky, he thought that Hitler would either reform or yield to the pressure of the Junkers and Big Business.'[6] However, by March 1933 Jabotinsky grasped that Germany was now the implacable foe of Jewry and he was appalled at the antics of Kareski.[7] He hastily wrote to Hans Block, Kareski's predecessor as Chairman of the German Revisionists:

I do not know exactly what happened, but any flirting with the Government or its representatives and ideas I would consider simply criminal. I understand that one can silently bear schweinerie; but to adapt oneself to schweinerie is verboten, and Hitlerism remains schweinerie in spite of the enthusiasm of millions which impresses our youth so much in a manner similar to that in which Communist enthusiasm impresses other Jews.[8]

'The Triple Alliance of Stalin–Ben-Gurion–Hitler'

Jabotinsky also had to deal with the problem of Achimeir's Fascism in Palestine. Flirting with Mussolini had been acceptable, but a pro-Nazi line was an outrage. He wrote to Achimeir in the strongest terms in 1933,

The articles and notices on Hitler and the Hitlerite movement appearing in *Hazit Ha'am* are to me, and to all of us, like a knife thrust in our backs. I demand an unconditional stop to this outrage. To find in Hitlerism some feature of a 'national liberation' movement is sheer ignorance. Moreover, under present circumstances, all this babbling is discrediting and paralyzing my work . . . I demand that the paper join, unconditionally and absolutely, not merely our campaign against Hitler Germany, but also our hunting down of Hitlerism, in the fullest sense of the term.[9]

Jabotinsky had supported the anti-Nazi boycott from the beginning, and his denunciation of his followers in Palestine brought them into line; soon they, who had been praising Hitler for saving Germany, began to denounce the WZO for its refusal to take part in the boycott. The prime target of their attacks was Chaim Arlosoroff, the Political Secretary of the Jewish Agency, who was known to be negotiating with the Nazis. On 14 June 1933, Arlosoroff returned from Europe. On 15 June, *Hazit Ha'am* ran a furious attack on him by Yochanan Pogrebinski, *The Alliance of Stalin-Ben-Gurion-Hitler*. The curious title interconnects two of the central themes of the Revisionist line: the Labour Zionists were really plotting to set up a pro-Communist Arab regime and, at the same time, sell out the Jews to the Nazis. It is necessary to quote Pogrebinski's article at length, as it illuminates all subsequent events:

We have read . . . an interview with Mr Arlosoroff . . . Among other meaningless words and stupidities in which this red mountbank excels, we find that the Jewish problem in Germany can be solved only by means of a compromise with Hitler and his regime. These men . . . have now decided to sell for money the honor of the Jewish People, its rights, its security and standing in the whole great world, to Hitler and the Nazis. Apparently these red charlatans were disturbed by the success of the boycott against German goods which was proclaimed by the great leader of the Jews in our generation, V. Jabotinsky, and which was supported by the Jews of the whole world . . .

The cowardice to which the Palestine Labor Party has stooped in selling itself for money to the biggest Jew-hater, has now reached its lowest point, and has no parallel in all Jewish history . . . Jewry will welcome the triple alliance of 'Stalin-Ben-Gurion-Hitler' only with repulsion and detestation . . . The Jewish people has always known how to deal with those who have sold the honor of their nation and its Torah, and it will know today also how to react to this shameful deed, committed in the full light of the sun, and before the eyes of the whole world.[10]

On the evening of 16 June, Arlosoroff and his wife took a stroll along Tel Aviv's beach. Two young men passed them twice. Mrs Arlosoroff became worried and her husband tried to calm her: 'they are Jewish, since when are you afraid of Jews?' Shortly afterwards they appeared again. ' "What time is it?" – one of them asked. A flashlight blinded us, and I saw a pistol pointed at us.'[11] A shot rang out and Arlosoroff fell dead.

The British police had little difficulty with the crime. The murder took place on a beach; bedouin trackers were soon set to work. Two days later Avraham Stavsky and Zvi Rosenblatt, both Revisionists, were brought in for an identity parade. Mrs Arlosoroff nearly fainted when she recognised Stavsky who, she claimed, held the flashlight. The police raided Abba Achimeir and found his diary. One of his notes told of a party held in his home immediately after the killing to celebrate a 'great victory'. This prompted the police to arrest him as the mastermind behind the assassination.[12]

The prosecution case was so strong that the defence was forced to resort to desperate measures. While the trio were in jail awaiting trial, an Arab, Abdul Majid, jailed for an unconnected murder, suddenly confessed the slaying, by claiming that he and a friend had wanted to rape Mrs Arlosoroff. He soon recanted his confession, made it again and retracted it for a second time; he claimed that Stavsky and Rosenblatt had bribed him to make his statement. The case came to trial on 23 April 1934. Achimeir was acquitted without having to present a defence; the diary was not enough to prove prior conspiracy. After hearing Rosenblatt's defence, the court cleared him. Then, by 2 to 1, Stavsky was found guity, and on 8 June was sentenced to be hanged. On 19 July the Palestine Court of Appeal acquitted him on a combination of technicalities. There had been procedural errors pertaining to the tracking. Once that evidence was thrown out, there was no longer any material corroboration to support Mrs Arlosoroff's accusation. Palestine law, unlike British law, demanded such verification to corroborate the testimony of a single witness in a capital offence. The Chief Justice was plainly displeased; 'in England . . . the conviction would have to stand', and he denounced the defence for the bogus confession,

> The whole interposition of Abdul Majid in this case leaves in my
> mind a grave suspicion of a conspiracy to defeat the end of justice
> by the suborning of Abdul Majid to commit perjury in the interests
> of the defence.[13]

It was not until 1944 that new evidence turned up, but this was not
made public until 1973. When Lord Moyne, the British High Commissioner for the Middle East, was assassinated in Cairo in 1944 by two
members of the 'Stern Gang', a Revisionist splinter group, a Palestinian
ballistics expert, F.W. Bird, examined the murder weapon and found it
had been used in no less than seven previous political slayings: two
Arabs, four British police and the Chaim Arlosoroff murder. Bird
explained, in 1973, that he: 'did not give evidence of the Arlosoroff
connection at the time of the trial of the two murderers of Lord Moyne
as the chain of evidence of the Arlosoroff exhibits had been broken
during the eleven year gap'.[14]

The entire Revisionist movement, including Jabotinsky, categorically
denied that any Revisionists were involved in the crime, but the Labour
Zionists never doubted their guilt and when the Court of Appeal
released Stavsky, a riot broke out between the two factions in the Great
Synagogue of Tel Aviv which Stavsky attended. Throughout the Holocaust period the Arlosoroff murder was one of the Labour Zionists'
principal reasons for denouncing the Revisionists. As Arlosoroff was a
prime mover in establishing the Ha'avara agreement, the foundation
of WZO policy towards the Nazis, responsibility for the murder has
important implications in considering relations between the Nazis and
the Zionists. From the evidence in the case there seems little doubt that
Stavsky and Rosenblatt did assassinate Arlosoroff, although in 1955
Yehuda Arazi-Tennenbaum, a former Labour Zionist, and a former
Mandatory policeman who had worked on the case, announced that
Stavsky was innocent and that the Arab was pressured to recant his
confession. However, this testimony was extremely suspect, not least
for the fact that it had taken him 22 years to come forth with it.[15] It
is much less clear whether Achimeir plotted the murder. Certainly there
is not the slightest evidence that Jabotinsky knew about the crime in
advance. He claimed to believe in Abdul Majid's inherently improbable
confession, but it is highly significant that in 1935 he insisted on insert-
ing a clause into Betar's fundamental principles: 'I shall prepare my arm
to defend my people and shall not carry my arm but for its defence.'

Jabotinsky's Efforts to Maintain the Boycott

The immediate impact of the murder was to make a nonsense of Jabotinsky's efforts to sustain the anti-Nazi boycott at the August World Zionist Congress held in Prague. During the Congress, Jewish Telegraphic Agency despatches reported the police discovery of his letter to Achimeir, which threatened to expel him if he continued to praise Hitler.[16] This episode and the fact that he appeared in the Congress hall with a squad of brownshirt Betarim discredited Jabotinsky as some kind of Jewish Nazi. The Congress's decision to reject the boycott was moulded by several factors but, in general, the delegates felt whatever was wrong with Weizmann, Revisionist opposition to the WZO's German policy was deeply suspect and tarnished by their raving about the 'Stalin–Ben-Gurion' cabal to turn Palestine into an Arab Communist state.

However, Jabotinsky spoke for many besides his own narrow following when he argued for a struggle against Hitler. He knew there was never the remotest possibility of a *modus vivendi* between the Jews and Adolf Hitler. Jabotinsky understood that the German Jews were prisoners in Hitler's war against world Jewry. 'If Hitler's regime is destined to stay, world Jewry is doomed'; German Jewry was 'but a minor detail', he wrote.[17]

After the congress defeated his resolution, 240 to 48, Jabotinsky held a press conference to denounce the Ha'avara and to announce the Revisionist Party as a temporary central body to run a world-wide anti-Nazi campaign. He expressed his willingness to work with the Non-Sectarian Anti-Nazi League and other boycott forces, but he never contemplated any sort of mass mobilisation. He opposed what he called a 'negative' boycott. His would be positive, emphasising 'buying . . . from more acceptable origins'. His office would give out 'exact descriptions of all articles recommended . . . addresses and telephone numbers of the shops where these articles are to be found'.[18] The Revisionists dutifully set up a 'Department of Economic Defence' in their Paris headquarters, but by 6 February 1934 Jabotinsky was already lamenting that he had to do all the work himself as:

the executive committee members shrank from saddling themselves with a job which could not be done without a fattish budget . . . all the work has been done by an unpaid secretary plus a half time typist lad.

Until he got some cash there would be no 'big public gestures (which would be very easy): the Jewish world has had enough of big appeals of this kind, unfollowed by systematic action'.[19] On 13 September 1935, at the New Zionist Organisation's founding congress, Jabotinsky was still talking about a boycott, but in the future tense: 'a Jewish Boycott Organisation, headed by himself is to be created'.[20] Jabotinsky's 'commercial advertising agency' could never inspire anyone as, at best, it would have produced a paper mountain. However, the Revisionists did do boycott work all over the world, but as classic sectarians they held their own anti-Nazi rallies in their stronghold in Eastern Europe. Alone they could accomplish nothing and inevitably they turned to more congenial activities directly pertaining to Palestine.

'There will be no War'

For all his subjective anti-Nazism, Germany was never Jabotinsky's prime focus. According to Shmuel Merlin, 'Jabotinsky did not feel that the Hitler regime was permanent or stable.'[21] There is a legend that he warned Jews of the coming Holocaust, and some of his statements do have a prophetic ring until closely scrutinised: '*if* Hitler's regime is destined to stay, world Jewry is doomed'; but he thought the regime was unstable and was certain to collapse if it ever went to war.[22] His admirers quoted his constant theme: 'Liquidate the Diaspora or the Diaspora will liquidate you.' For all its oracular quality, he did not mean that Germany would conquer Europe or massacre the Jews. Merlin is accurate: ' "Liquidate the Diaspora" did not refer to Hitler at all. Our main focus was always Poland and Eastern Europe.'[23] The slogan referred to the destruction of the economic position of the Jewish middle class in Poland, where it was being squeezed out by the spreading peasant co-operatives and driven out by pogroms organised by the Christian nationalist middle class.

In the 1930s, Jabotinsky never understood that Nazism was produced by an age of war and revolution, and had to go down in war and revolution. He convinced himself that the capitalists would never allow themselves to be dragged to their destruction in another war, and in 1939 he wrote to his sister: 'There will be no war; the German insolence will soon subside; Italy will make friends with the British . . . and in five years we will have a Jewish state.'[24] He was living in Pont d'Avon in France in the summer of 1939, and in the last week of August he still was writing: 'There is not the remotest chance of war

. . . The world looks a peaceful place from Pont d'Avon, and I think Pont d'Avon is right.'[25]

The Revisionist response to the Nazi take-over of Austria and Czechoslovakia had been feverish. At the Warsaw Betar World Congress in September 1938, 25-year-old Menachem Begin demanded the immediate conquest of Palestine. Jabotinsky knew this was impossible; they could never beat the British, the Arabs or even the Labour Zionists, and he ridiculed his over-zealous disciple, comparing his words to the 'useless screeching of a door'.[26] But by August 1939, reflecting the same desperation as the ranks, Jabotinsky concluded that, if the Revisionists could not immediately save the Jews in Europe, at least they could go down nobly and perhaps inspire the Jews by their gesture; thus he decided to invade Palestine, landing an armed boatload of Betarim on the beach at Tel Aviv. His underground force there, the Irgun (the organisation, from *Irgun Zvei Leumi*, National Military Organisation), would rise and seize Government House in Jerusalem, and hold it for 24 hours, while a provisional Jewish government was proclaimed in Europe and New York. After his own capture or death, it would operate as a government-in-exile.[27] The adventure's model was the 1916 Easter Monday rising in Ireland. There the leaders were executed after capture, but ultimately the rising triggered a British withdrawal from the southern part of the country. However, it is impossible to see how Jabotinsky's invasion could have convinced the Jewish population in Palestine, the majority of whom were his enemies, to rise up after his defeat. The sheer fantasy of the plan was revealed on the night of 31 August/1 September 1939. The British CID arrested the entire command of the Irgun while they sat debating whether to take part in the scheme and, within hours, Hitler's armies marched into Poland, starting the war that Jabotinsky had just insisted would never happen.[28]

Notes

1. Norman and Helen Bentwich, *Mandate Memories, 1918-1948*, p. 150.
2. Elis Lubrany, 'Hitler in Jerusalem', *Weltbuhne* (Berlin, 31 May 1932), p. 835.
3. 'Jerusalem or Moscow – Herzl or Lenin', *Betar Monthly* (15 August 1931), pp. 2, 5-6.
4. Ben Frommer, 'The Significance of a Jewish State', *Jewish Call* (Shanghai, May 1935), pp. 10-11.
5. Richard Lichtheim, *Die Geschichte des Deutschen Zionismus*, pp. 258-9.
6. Author's interview with Shmuel Merlin 16 September 1980.

7. Ibid.

8. Joseph Schechtman, *Fighter and Prophet*, p. 217.

9. Ibid., p. 216.

10. Eliazer Liebenstein, *The Truth About Revisionism* (1935), pp. 51–3.

11. Sraya Shapiro, 'Arlosoroff Planned Revolt in 1932', *Jerusalem Post* (11 June 1958), p. 4.

12. 'Revisionists in Palestine seek to explain away Incriminating Testimony', *Jewish Daily Bulletin* (29 August 1933), p. 4.

13. 'Stavsky Appeal Allowed', *Palestine Post* (22 July 1934), p. 8.

14. 'Trace 1933 Murder Weapon to Stern Group Death Squad', *Jewish Journal* (10 August 1973).

15. 'Stavsky was Framed', *Jewish Herald* (South Africa, 24 February 1955), p. 3.

16. *Jewish Daily Bulletin* (24 August 1933), p. 1.

17. Schechtman, *Fighter and Prophet*, p. 214.

18. Ibid., pp. 218–19.

19. Ibid., pp. 219–20.

20. 'New Zionists Vigorous Policy', *World Jewry* (London, 13 September 1935), p. 13.

21. Interview with Merlin.

22. Jacob Katz, 'Was the Holocaust Predictable?', *Commentary* (May 1975), p. 42.

23. Interview with Merlin.

24. Schechtman, *Fighter and Prophet*, p. 366.

25. Ibid.

26. Daniel Levine, 'David Raziel, The Man and his Times', PhD Thesis, Yeshiva University, 1969, pp. 80, 240–1.

27. Schechtman, *Fighter and Prophet*, pp. 482–3.

28. Nathan Yalin-Mor, 'Memories of Yair and Etzel', *Jewish Spectator* (Summer 1980), p. 36.

12 GEORG KARESKI, HITLER'S ZIONIST QUISLING BEFORE QUISLING

The fact that Jabotinsky opposed Hitler, and was able to convince Abba Achimeir to stop praising him, did not mean that all Revisionists accepted this position. Some Revisionists were still convinced that collaboration was the way forward for Zionism. The most notorious of these was Georg Kareski, whom (as we have seen) Jabotinsky tried to curb in 1933.

By 1919-20 Kareski had already disregarded the ZVfD's preoccupation with Palestine work and concentrated on Jewish community politics. In an age of declining faith, when many German Jews were opting for mixed marriages and atheism, those who clung to the sectarian Jewish community became even more inward-looking. In 1926 Kareski's introverted Zionist *Judische Volkspartei*, in alliance with other religious isolationists, was able to upset the reformed 'Liberal' German-nationalist leadership, and in January 1929, he became Chairman of the Berlin Jewish community. But his success was short-lived, and the liberals defeated him in November 1930. Kareski had entered German politics in the September 1930 Reichstag elections as a candidate of the Catholic *Centre*, which was attractive to him both for its concern for religious education and its social conservatism. With Hitler's coming to power, Kareski joined the Revisionists, which he now saw as the potential Jewish equivalent of the successful Nazis. They had been an insignificant faction within the ZVfD, gaining only 1,189 of the 8,494 votes in the delegate election for the 1931 World Zionist Congress. By 1933 the Revisionists were reduced to further futility by their division into rival cliques. Kareski, with his prestige as a notable member of the community, had no difficulty in becoming the leader of these dispirited forces and merging them into a new *Staatzionistische Organisation*.

In May 1933 he attempted his ludicrous *putsch* at the Berlin Jewish community centre and was expelled from the ZVfD. His career and his association with the Nazis developed further after the Revisionist split from the WZO, following the defeat of the anti-Nazi boycott at the Prague Congress. As the Revisionists were no longer *de facto* a part of the WZO, the Palestine Office in Berlin was ordered to exclude Betarim from consideration for immigration certificates. The Revisionists responded by starting brawls at ZVfD meetings, shouting: 'You Marxist swine! You are all sympathizers of the Histadrut which belongs to the Second International!'[1] As a result of this the ZVfD headquarters were temporarily closed in June 1934. By 6 August, one of the State Zionist leaders, Dr Friedrich Stern, sent the Nazis a letter explaining that the growth of their anti-Marxist youth group, the *Nationale Jugend Herzlia*, was stunted by their exclusion from emigration by the Palestine Office staffed by allegedly pro-Marxist Histadrut supporters from the ZVfD. Stern proposed that the Palestine Office be turned over to them. The ZVfD found out about the plot through Hechalutz spies in the Herzlia and through their own contacts in the regime and hence the scheme failed.[2] The Nazis quickly realised that if they gave the Palestine Office to the State Zionists the WZO would not give out any certificates in Germany. As long as the Nazis needed the WZO and the Jewish charities to organise the emigration, they could not impose a collaborator on the Jewish community. Kareski's campaign put Jabotinsky in an impossible position: while he was denouncing the WZO for the Ha'avara, his own movement in Germany was working for the Nazis, and he soon had to announce that from then on 'the wing of Zionism who share our Herzlian views also know that "Marxist" is a word never to be used in polemics'.[3]

The Nazis had decided on a general policy of favouring Zionists over non-Zionist Jews, and within that line they decided that open encouragement of the State Zionists rather than suppression of the 'Marxists' of the ZVfD would have to be their strategy. On 13 April 1935, the Gestapo notified the regular police that, henceforward, the State Zionists would receive:

> exceptionally and always revocably, permission to let its members belonging to the '*National Youth Herzlia*' and '*Brith Hashomrim*' wear uniforms indoors . . . because the State Zionists have proven to be the organisation which had tried in any way, even illegally, to bring its members to Palestine, and which, by its sincere activity directed towards emigration, meets half-way the intention of the Reich Government to remove the Jews from Germany. The permission to wear a uniform should spur members of the German-Jewish organisations to join the State Zionist youth groups where they will be more effectively urged to emigrate to Palestine.[4]

Despite the relationship between the State Zionists and the Gestapo, Kareski was still welcome at the NZO Congress in Vienna in 1935.

When the Revisionists had decided to support the anti-Nazi boycott, they had formally disaffiliated their German unit in an effort to protect it; thus it was obvious that Kareski was there with the encouragement of the Gestapo to lobby against the boycott. The uneasy ranks wished to distance themselves from the State Zionists and they compelled a resolution that, under the circumstances, there was not and could not be a Revisionist movement in Germany.[5] Kareski made the mistake of travelling to the following Betar Congress in Cracow in the company of a known Jewish Gestapo agent, and some German Betarim reported them to Jabotinsky.[6] He was asked to leave, and Jabotinsky was compelled to call on him to defend himself publicly and deny any connection to the Nazis.[7] However, later, in 1936, he used Kareski as his go-between with the German publishing house holding the copyright to one of his books. Jabotinsky assumed no further responsibility for Kareski after Cracow, but as long as he remained in Germany Kareski was in contact with the minority within the world Revisionist movement, notably those around von Weisl in Vienna, who continued to agree with his pro-Nazi line.

'The Zionists as the "Racial Jews" have at least Given us a Formal Guarantee'

Kareski's repeated failure to get the German Jews to accept his approach never discouraged the Nazis from trying to impose him on the community. In late 1935, they forced him on the *Reichsverband judischer Kulturbunde*. These Culture Leagues had been set up to provide jobs for Jewish musicians, writers and artists who had been thrown out of their positions, and the Gestapo had decided that a genuine Zionist spirit would do the Leagues some good.[8] Benno Cohen of the ZVfD had been appointed assistant to their director, conductor Kurt Singer, but that was not enough: the performers were still really cultural assimilationists, and in October 1935 Kareski, who had nothing to do with the arts, was appointed to a more senior position than Singer, and Cohen was dismissed. The conductor told the Nazis that he would resign rather than work with Kareski, and the Leagues were closed down in an attempt to force them to accept Kareski. The refusal of the Jews to concur with Nazi policy gained attention in the Nazi press, and Hans Hinkel, the bureaucrat in charge of the Leagues, publicly explained his choice of a new director.

I have consciously allowed the Zionist movement to exert the strongest influence upon the cultural and spiritual activities of the Kulturbund because the Zionists as the 'Racial Jews' have at least given us formal guarantees of cooperation in acceptable form.[9]

The Zionists to whom Hinkel referred were the State Zionists, even less popular at that time than in 1931; realistically they did not number much more than a few score adult party members and 500 youth.[10] However, the Nazis made much of Kareski in their propaganda. As the former head of the Berlin Jewish community, the head of the State Zionists, and now the head of the Culture Leagues, he sounded a very impressive figure. *Der Angriff* interviewed him on 23 December:

I have for many years regarded a complete separation between the cultural activities of the two peoples as a condition for a peaceful collaboration . . . provided it is founded on the respect for the alien nationality . . . The Nuremberg Laws . . . seem to me, apart from their legal provisions, entirely to conform with this desire for a separate life based on mutual respect. This is especially so when one takes into account the order for separate school systems which has been issued previously. The Jewish schools fill an old political demand of my friends, because they consider that the education of the Jew in accordance with his traditions and his mode of life is absolutely essential.[11]

However, the Culture Leagues were too important to the Nazis as a model of cultural separatism to be abandoned because of Kareski, and eventually the Nazis allowed them to be reorganised without him. By 1937 Kareski and the Gestapo were ready for another manoeuvre. This time their target was the *Reichsvertretung der deutschen Juden* (the Reich Representation of German Jews). Kareski formed an alliance with discontented conservative assimilationists within the Berlin community, and they proposed a programme whereby the State Zionists would take over the political work of the organisation and the religious congregations would run the charitable functions. Max Nussbaum, rabbi of the Great Jewish Congregation of Berlin, later told of the Nazi pressure for the Revisionist line. The Gestapo's *Judenkommissar*, Kuchmann, took it into his head to become an expert on the Jewish question, reading every available book on modern Jewry. Now determined to do the right thing by his charges, he summoned Nussbaum.

As a result of his diligence, he suddenly fell in love with Revisionism, asserting to each of us who had the misfortune to be summoned to his office, that this was the only solution of the Palestine problem and constantly blaming official Zionism for being 'red' and 'left'. One day in the Spring of 1937, he called me to his office and told me bluntly that I had to take over the leadership of the Revisionist group, to make Revisionism more popular with German Jewry, to drop my propaganda for the 'Meineckestrasse-Zionism' [ZVfD] . . . When I refused . . . he 'punished' me by a speaking and writing prohibition for one year.[12]

Again the attempt failed; foreign Jews could not be made to subsidise a German Jewish central organisation run by a traitor, and the Nazis backed down. As a consolation prize the Nazis, in spring 1937, made the *Staatzionistische Organisation* the only authorised Jewish representative for dealing with the German public-relief agencies.[13]

Kareski's usefulness to the Nazis came to an end in July 1937, when a scandal was uncovered in his *Iwria* bank. He had been making illegal loans to members of its board and his personal friends, and he tried to cover himself with a cheque on the account of the Berlin Jewish community, making one of his clerks accept it with only his signature in violation of the requirement that it be countersigned. The cashier took the cheque under protest and notified the Berlin congregation. There is no evidence that Kareski personally profited from his manipulations — he used the loans as chits to gain allies within the Jewish community — but in the end the bank failed and Kareski decided to visit Palestine.[14]

His visit was not a success. On 6 October 1937, the German Jewish community in Haifa discovered that he was there and a large mob turned out to greet him, chasing him through the streets. He finally had to barricade himself into a house until he was rescued by the police.[15] The German Immigrants Association (the HOG) publicly accused him of seeking to be appointed leader of German Jewry with the aid of the Nazis, of trying to incite the murder of the ZVfD's chairman, of trying to destroy the Zionist organisation, and of corruption in his bank. Kareski made the mistake of denying the charges and insisting on a trial in the rabbinical courts. In June 1938 the court, headed by the chief rabbi, found the HOG's charges to be fully borne out by the evidence.[16] The decision effectively ended his active political career.

'A Jewish Legion to Protect the Jews in Palestine from Attack'

Despite Jabotinsky's disowning him, Kareski always had his apologists within the Revisionist movement. There had always been those who disagreed with Jabotinsky's anti-Nazism. If it was permissible for Jabotinsky to try to deal with Simon Petliura in the Slavinsky agreement when the Ukrainian Army had already butchered 30,000 Jews, why was a deal with Hitler unacceptable? Prior to Kristallnacht Hitler had killed no Jews as Jews. These Revisionists were convinced that Hitler's victory foretold a Fascist age and that the Jews simply had to understand that and come to terms with it. The circle around von Weisl, who was Jabotinsky's negotiator with the other authoritarian dictatorships in Eastern Europe, agreed with Kareski's approach. In 1936, von Weisl, apparently acting on his own, contacted the British Fascists and proposed a fantastic wartime alliance between Britain, Japan, Poland and Germany, together with a future Revisionist state, against the Soviets and the Arab and Asian colonial revolutions.[17]

It would be pleasant to report that the rabbinical court's decision finally ended Kareski's career, and that he died alone and hated, but on 2 August 1947, the 68-year-old Kareski was the chairman of a Revisionist health fund in Palestine. Some friends even tried to have a street named after him in Ramat Gan.[18] He even has his latter-day apologists who suggest that, given what we know of the abandonment of the Jews by the rest of the world, as soon as Hitler took over rapid emigration was the only solution.

Kareski, a classic Revisionist, albeit of an extreme brand, was a traitor to the German Jewish community. His vision ran to nothing more prophetic than a Revisionist state stretching from the Mediterranean to the Euphrates with Mussolini as its Mandatory protector.[19] He certainly did not foresee the Holocaust. In 1935 he was proposing a 25-year evacuation plan from Germany with 20,000 emigrants per year. His concern was to use the Jugend Herzlia as 'a Jewish Legion to protect the Jews *in Palestine* from attack' (my emphasis).[20]

It is not surprising that the Nazis used Kareski as their collaborator in Germany. His rival amongst the assimilationists, Max Naumann, was totally unacceptable for his insistence on full Jewish participation in the Third Reich. Kareski appeared before the Nazis as if sent by central casting: the caricature of the stage Jew, a crooked usurer, as zealous as any medieval rabbi to keep the Jews apart from unbelieving humankind, and at the head of a brownshirted emigrationist movement.

Notes

1. 'Revisionists Cause Crisis in German Zionism', *Palestine Post* (25 June 1934), p. 1.

2. Herbert Levine, 'A Jewish Collaborator in Nazi Germany: The Strange Career of Georg Kareski, 1933–37', *Central European History* (September 1975), p. 262.

3. Vladimir Jabotinsky, 'Jews and Fascism', *Jewish Daily Bulletin* (11 April 1935), p. 2.

4. Kurt Grossmann, 'Zionists and non-Zionists under Nazi Rule in the 1930s', *Herzl Yearbook*, vol. IV (1961–2), pp. 341–2.

5. Author's interview with Shmuel Merlin, 16 September 1980.

6. Author's interview with Paul Riebenfeld, 17 January 1978.

7. 'See Kareski's Hand in Leader's Ousting', *Congress Bulletin* (24 January 1936), p. 4.

8. Levine, 'Jewish Collaborator in Nazi Germany', pp. 266–7.

9. 'Kareski Again', *American Hebrew* (21 February 1936), p. 406.

10. Solomon Colodner, *Jewish Education under the Nazis*, p. 111.

11. 'Georg Kareski Approves of Ghetto Laws – Interview in Dr Goebbel's "*Angriff*"', *Jewish Chronicle* (London, 3 January 1936), p. 16.

12. Max Nussbaum, 'Zionism under Hitler', *Congress Weekly* (11 September 1942), p. 13.

13. A.M.H., 'The Jewish Year in the Diaspora', *Palestine Post* (5 September 1937), p. 5.

14. Leonard Baker, *Days of Sorrow and Pain*, p. 213.

15. 'Mr Kareski Abused by Haifa Crowd', *Palestine Post* (7 October 1937), p. 3.

16. 'Kareski's Charge Dismissed', *Palestine Post* (10 June 1938), p. 8.

17. Levine, 'Jewish Collaboration in Nazi Germany', p. 272.

18. Ibid., p. 253.

19. Ibid., p. 272.

20. Jacob de Haas, 'The Sharp End of the Axe', *Chicago Jewish Chronicle* (15 November 1935), p. 9.

13 CHOOSING THE CHOSEN PEOPLE – THE DOCTRINE OF 'ZIONIST CRUELTY'

The statistics on Jewish emigration from Germany vary to some degree, depending on the authority, but broadly speaking they tally. Herbert Strauss, for one, estimates that there were 270,000–300,000 *émigrés* in all, of whom 30,000 perished in their presumed countries of refuge.[1] Yehuda Bauer reckons there were 44,537 legal emigrants to Palestine from Germany and Austria from 1933 to 1938 – 'about 20 per cent' of all Jewish immigrants.[2] The *Encyclopedia Judaica* reckons 55,000 went to Palestine by 1939.[3] Fawzi Abu-Diab lists only 39,131 German immigrants from 1919 to 1945, but his low German listing is qualified by Mandate and Jewish Agency categories of 'authorised travellers', 'stateless' and 'unspecified', many of whom were German domiciled in those years.[4] In comparison the *Encyclopedia Judaica* estimates 63,000 emigrants went to the United States, 40,000 to the United Kingdom, 30,000 to France, 25,000 to Belgium and 25,000 to Argentina.[5] The International Settlement in Shanghai took in about 16,000 from 1938 to 1941, and South Africa let in 5,000.[6]

It was the British, not the Zionists, who determined the immigration policy for Palestine, using a combination of political considerations – for example, an evaluation of the reaction of the Arabs, and relatively objective computations related to the absorptive capacity of the Jewish economy. Each year a quota would be set and the precious immigration certificates were given to the WZO. There were always political criteria for would-be immigrants. Communists were always barred and 6 per cent of the certificates had to be given to the anti-Zionist Agudaists but, on the other hand, £1,000 capitalists were always allowed entry over the quota. Until the 1936 Arab revolt compelled the Mandatory to drastically lower immigration, the Jewish Agency never seriously challenged London over the proposed figures or the economic rationales behind them.

The WZO's own immigration policy had slowly evolved. Before the First World War, most immigrants came from Russia, but the Bolshevik revolution eventually closed that source; in the post-war era it was Poland that provided the largest contingent of settlers. The anti-Semitic line of the Polish *Endek* government encouraged thousands of artisans and lower-middle-class Jews to consider emigration. Refused entry to

America because of its new immigration restrictions, they turned to Palestine, and their capital influx soon produced a land boom as Tel Aviv lots were hawked in the market-places of Warsaw. The Jewish National Fund, which organised the agricultural colonies of the WZO, was also compelled to pay exorbitant prices for its own land requirements. Tel Aviv did expand as a result of the new immigration, but primarily as independent Polish artisans moved in: the old patriarch with his extended family working a few handlooms. The Poles were solving their own problems, but their tiny establishments could never become the basis of a Zionist economy, an absolute essential if they were ever to wrest the country from the Arabs. Eventually the land boom collapsed, leading to the ruin of many of the little shopkeepers and large unemployment in the building trades; although the fall in prices suited the JNF, they now had to cope with the needs of the unemployed.

The experience produced drastic policy changes, and it was determined that they could not afford the social costs of petty-bourgeois immigration. As early as 1924 Weizmann began to denounce the new settlers, whom he saw as carrying with them 'the atmosphere of the ghetto', and he warned that 'we are not building our National Home on the model of Djika and Nalevki . . . here we have reached home and are building for eternity'.[7]

It was the policy of 'no Nalevki' — the great ghetto of Warsaw — that turned Zionism away from the mass of ordinary Jews, who were not Zionist for the most part, and even from the ranks of the Diaspora Zionist movement. They lacked the skills and resources needed in Palestine, and henceforward Zionism would no longer serve them; immigrants would be selected strictly to the advantage of Zion. In Palestine itself the WZO decided that the unemployed should be encouraged to re-emigrate so as to save the outlay on unemployment benefits.[8] Strong preference began to be shown for the collectivist kibbutzim of the Labour Zionist tendencies as an alliance developed between Weizmann's circle, who, though bourgeois themselves, were desperately looking to cut the costs of colonisation, and the leftists who had a vision of a generation of 'healthy' Jews, no longer in 'Diaspora' occupations, building a socialist nation on its own land. Their youthful pioneers had turned their backs on the values of their middle-class families and would endure great economic privations for the good of the cause. Zionism became a tough-minded utopia which helped the image of the Jew, but did not attempt to solve any of the problems of the Jewish masses in Europe.

'The Cruel Criteria of Zionism'

The week of terror unleashed against the Jews by the Nazis' victory in the elections of March 1933 had brought thousands on to the streets outside the Palestine Office in Berlin, but there was still no desire to turn Palestine into a genuine refuge. Emigration had to continue to serve the needs of Zionism. Only young, healthy, qualified and committed Zionists were wanted. The German HaChalutz Pioneers declared unrestricted emigration to Palestine to be a 'Zionist crime'.[9] Enzo Sereni, then the Labour Zionist emissary in Germany, laid down their criteria:

> Even in this difficult hour we must allot most of the 1,000 immigration certificates to pioneers. This may seem cruel, but even if the British were to grant 10,000 certificates instead of the 1,000 they are giving us now, we would still say: Let the young people go, for even if they suffer less than the older ones, they are better fitted for the task in Palestine. Children can later bring their parents, but not the other way around.[10]

Weizmann had overall charge of emigration from Germany between 1933 and his re-election to the presidency in 1935. His report in January 1934 listed some of the standards used for choosing prospective immigrants. Those who were 'over 30, and possess no capital and no special qualifications cannot be absorbed in Palestine unless specific openings for the work they did in Germany are found'.[11] On 26 April he specifically excluded several important groupings from serious consideration as immigrants: 'former businessmen, commercial travellers, artists, and musicians will this time hardly be eligible for certificates'.[12] Most German Jews were simply not wanted in Palestine, they were either too old, or their occupation did not fit the country's needs, or they spoke no Hebrew and were not committed ideologically. Among themselves the Zionist leadership was quite frank about what they were doing. In 1933 Berl Katznelson, then editing the Histadrut's daily newspaper, *Davar*, reflected their mentality: 'we know that we are not able to transfer all of German Jewry and will have to choose on the basis of the cruel criteria of Zionism'. In 1935 Moshe Sharett (Shertok) again declared that circumstances obliged them to treat Diaspora Jewry with a degree of cruelty.[13] The Israeli scholar Abraham Margaliot has written about a speech given by Weizmann before the Zionist Executive in 1935:

he declared that the Zionist movement would have to choose between the immediate rescue of Jews and the establishment of a
national project which would ensure lasting redemption for the
Jewish people. Under such circumstances, the movement, according
to Weizmann, must choose the latter course.[14]

The British — reacting to Arab pressures against all immigration, and
diplomatic interventions from Poland, Romania and other anti-Semitic
regimes in Eastern Europe in favour of increased quotas, as well as the
economic needs of the country — determined just how many and what
economic categories of Jews could enter in any given year. However,
the British never required anyone to know Hebrew, nor did they care
if a would-be immigrant was a non-Zionist. Nor did they concern
themselves with where the immigrants came from; London would have
been pleased if the WZO had chosen fewer Americans and more
Germans. Given the political realities of the Mandate, Zionist emigration could never have been the way out for the entire German Jewry
but, within the strictures imposed by the British, Zion did not ever
want to be the salvation of German Jewry.

Who, then, were given certificates by the fourteen Palestine Offices
around the world? According to Abu-Diab's statistics, 27,289 Jews
entered Palestine as legal immigrants in 1933; 36,619 in 1934; and
55,407 in 1935, making a total of 119,315 for the three-year period.
Of these 18,206 were listed as German.[15] Additional immigrants who
had been domiciled in Germany came in as Poles and other nationalities. There were 1,979 of these in 1935.[16] During those three years the
largest national component of Jewish immigration was Polish, 42.56
per cent in 1934 and 44.12 per cent in 1935.[17] Polish anti-Semitism
was chronic during those years, and the decision to give Poles more
certificates than Germans can be rationalised; but during those same
years no less than 3,743 immigrants came from the United States and
an additional 579 from the rest of the western hemisphere. British
Jewry's contingent was 513 and Africa sent 213 immigrants.[18] Turkey
provided 1,259 in 1934–5. The combined figure for Britain, the western
hemisphere, Africa and Turkey during those years was 6,307. Even if
the Polish statistics can be defended, these cannot. Not one of these
Jews required rescue and, indeed, no one pretended that rescue played
any part in their selection. They were picked because they were
Zionists, and primarily because of their youth and training. During
those same three years, two-thirds of all German Jews who applied for
certificates were turned down.[19]

'No Jewish Organisation would . . . Sponsor a Bill'

Since they did not want the bulk of German Jewry in Palestine, it might be assumed that the Zionist movement, at least in America, tried to find other havens for their brethren, but this is not so. Throughout the world, the Jewish bourgeoisie acted timidly out of fear that 'too many' refugees in any country would unleash local anti-Semitism. Sending the refugees to Palestine seemed to be the perfect answer and the American Jewish press condemned the British quotas in Palestine, although it maintained a discreet silence about America's own tight restrictions.

It was the Austrian *anschluss* in March 1938 that finally unleashed Nazi violence against the Jews. Two Democratic congressmen, Dickstein and Celler of New York, each proposed bills slightly liberalising the US immigration laws, but they were both dropped, without a hearing, in April 1938, after the Jewish, Christian and non-sectarian refugee agencies decided that the right wing would use the occasion to propose yet worse restrictions. The word went out to politicians: if hearings are held we might have to testify against reform.[20] A Communist Party front, the Jewish People's Committee, obtained a copy of one of Stephen Wise's epistles on behalf of the Jewish refugee groups, through the office of Brooklyn Democrat, Donald O'Toole. The Communists published the document in a pamphlet, *Jews in Action*, in an attempt to discredit their pro-British Zionist rivals at the time of the Hitler-Stalin pact. However, there is no doubt that the letter is genuine and it gives a clear indication of the mood of the Zionist movement.

I wish I thought that it were possible for this measure to be passed without repercussions upon the Jewish community in this country. I have every reason to believe, unfortunately, that any effort that is made at this time to waive the immigration laws, however humanitarian the purpose, will result in serious accentuation of what we know to be a rising wave of anti-Semitic feelings in the country . . . It may interest you to know that some weeks ago the representatives of all the leading Jewish organisations met in conference to discuss the President's proposal and other proposals which have been made to waive the immigration barrier. It was the consensus of opinion that such bills at this moment in the light of present unemployment in this country and in the light of the inspired propaganda directed against the Jewish people, and circulated throughout the country, would be injurious to the purposes which all of us would like to serve. For that reason it was decided that no Jewish organisation would at this time, sponsor a bill which would in any way alter the present immigration laws.[21]

Could the American Zionist movement have done more to try to obtain refuge for the German Jews? The answer is clearly yes. The immigration laws had been passed in 1921-4, during a wave of xenophobia, and were designed to exclude practically everyone apart from the old settler stock: the British, Irish and Germans. That actually meant a relatively high German quota, but reactionaries in the State Department and the Democratic Party deliberately misinterpreted the regulations to create barriers to Jews fully utilising the allotment. Had any kind of resolute effort been made to mobilise the Jewish masses, and the larger liberal community, there can be no doubt that Roosevelt could not have withstood that pressure. The Jews and the liberals were simply too important in his party to be refused, if they had seriously demanded proper enforcement of the regulations. However, the Zionists never launched a national campaign and only worked on individual injustices; no Zionist organisation ever did more than call for the smallest amendments to the immigration laws. Only the left, notably the Trotskyists and the Stalinists, ever demanded that the gates be thrown wide open to the Jews.

There were several reasons for the American Zionists' response to the refugee problem. In the early 1920s they had never thought of organising the Jews, together with the other ethnic communities that were discriminated against in the proposed restrictions, for a struggle against the quotas. They knew that as long as America was open to immigrants, the Jews would continue to turn their backs on poverty-stricken Palestine. In the 1930s many American Zionists still saw sanctuary in any other country but Palestine as offering little more than a '*nachtasylum*' – a palliative at best, a danger at worst, since they believed that the Jewish immigrant always brought anti-Semitism in his wake and they feared for themselves. Anti-Semitism was quite widespread in America at that time, although, of course, the Zionist movement never sought to organise any kind of defence against physical assaults. However, it must be emphasised that American anti-Semitism was never out of control and the Jewish community as such was never in danger. No Jew was ever killed in anti-Semitic incidents at a time when the lynching of Blacks was not uncommon in the American South. Additionally, the vast majority of Zionists, and most other Jews as well, supported Roosevelt's domestic reforms and feared that raising the refugee and immigration questions would work against the Democratic Party. Assisting some of the German Jews to settle in Palestine became a convenient substitute for a genuine effort to combat anti-Semitism within the capitalist establishment in America.

'We Are Risking the Existence of Zionism'

Could Palestine ever have been the solution to the plight of the refugees? With the report of the Peel Commission in July 1937, London had seriously considered creating a Jewish statelet, but even if the British had carried this through, it would not have resolved the desperate situation, nor did the WZO pretend it would. Weizmann testified before the Commission, telling them that he was a scientist; he knew Palestine with its backward economy could not possibly sustain all of Central and Eastern Europe's Jews. He wanted two million youth, and he later told the Zionist Congress in 1937 of his testimony before the Commission:

> The old ones will pass; they will bear their fate, or they will not. They were dust, economic and moral dust, in a cruel world . . . Two millions, and perhaps less; *'Scheerith Hapleta'* − only a branch will survive. They had to accept it. The rest they must leave to the future − to their youth. If they feel and suffer, they will find the way, *'Beacharith Hajamin'* [at the end of times] .[22]

With the abandonment of the Peel proposals, Zionism ceased to have any real relevance for the Jews of Europe. The British had cut immigration in an effort to placate the Arabs, and only 61,302 Jews were allowed entry to Palestine from 1936 to 1939; the WZO allowed entry to only 17,421 from Germany. However, not even the terrible danger to the Jews of Central Europe, nor their own abandonment by their imperial patron could shake the determination of the leaders of the WZO: under no circumstances was Zionism to be shunted aside in the now frantic scramble to find havens for the desperate Jews. When, after Kristallnacht, the British, in the hope of easing the pressure for increased immigration into Palestine, proposed that thousands of children be admitted directly into Britain, Ben-Gurion was absolutely against the plan, telling a meeting of Labour Zionist leaders on 7 December 1938:

If I knew that it would be possible to save all the children in Germany by bringing them over to England, and only half of them by transporting them to Eretz Yisrael, then I would opt for the second alternative. For we must weigh not only the life of these children, but also the history of the People of Israel.[23]

Britain's policy was firmly fixed; there was not the slightest chance of London suddenly allowing any mass immigration into Palestine, yet Ben-Gurion persisted, refusing to contemplate other sanctuaries. On 17 December 1938 he warned the Zionist Executive:

If Jews will have to choose between the refugees, saving Jews from concentration camps, and assisting a national museum in Palestine, mercy will have the upper hand and the whole energy of the people will be channelled into saving Jews from various countries. Zionism will be struck off the agenda not only in world public opinion, in Britain and the United States, but elsewhere in Jewish public opinion. If we allow a separation between the refugee problem and the Palestinian problem, we are risking the existence of Zionism.[24]

Weizmann's immediate response to Kristallnacht was to propose a plan to the British Colonial Secretary that Iraq allow in 300,000 Jews for £20 million or £30 million or, better, take in 100,000 Palestinians 'whose land would then pass to Jewish immigrants'.[25] To use his own words on Herzl's famous negotiations with von Plevhe in 1903: 'unreality could go no further': that Iraq should let in 300,000 Jews at the behest of the Zionists and the British, or take in Palestinians so that they could be displaced by Jews! Britain had sanctioned Zionism in the Balfour Declaration for its imperial purposes; those interests had shifted, and Zionism was impotent and totally unwilling to look for alternatives for the Jewish masses in their hour of destruction.

It is in the nature of things that Zionists today should put the blame on the British, and through them the Arabs, for the low number of refugees admitted into Palestine during the 1930s. But this is a self-serving argument; if the Zionists were never interested in turning Palestine into a genuine refuge, why should such a sanctuary have been any concern of either the British or the Arabs? The Palestinian attitude toward Jewish immigration into their country is easily understood. Although Britain must be condemned for abandoning the Jews of Europe, it is not for the Zionists to do it. They knew full well that imperial interest had always been behind London's patronage of their movement. They were warned repeatedly by the left that the interests of the Jewish masses and the British Empire could never be reconciled. The WZO must be held responsible for its own betrayal of German Jewry: it turned its back on them in the cause of what has been so perfectly described as their 'Tiffany's window for glittering Jews'.[26]

Notes

1. Herbert Strauss, 'Jewish Emigration from Germany – Nazi Policies and Jewish Responses', *Leo Baeck Institute Year Book*, vol. XXV, p. 327.

2. Yehuda Bauer, *My Brother's Keeper*, pp. 156–63.

3. 'Germany', *Encyclopedia Judaica*, vol. 7, col. 491.

4. Fawzi Abu-Diab, *Immigration to Israel*, p. 6.

5. *Encyclopedia Judaica*, vol. 7, col. 491.

6. David Kranzler, 'The Jewish Refugee Community of Shanghai, 1938–45', *Weiner Library Bulletin*, vol. XXVI, nos. 3–4 (1972-3), p. 28.

7. Chaim Weizmann, *Trial and Error*, p. 301.

8. Walter Laqueur, *History of Zionism*, p. 317.

9. Abraham Margaliot, 'The Problem of the Rescue of German Jewry during the Years 1933–1939; the Reasons for the delay in the Emigration from the Third Reich', *Rescue Attempts During the Holocaust* (Israel), p. 249.

10. Ruth Bondy, *The Emissary*, p. 116.

11. 'Weizmann makes first Report on German-Jewish Settlement in Palestine', *New Palestine* (31 January 1934), p. 6.

12. Chaim Weizmann, in Barnett Litvinoff (ed.), *The Letters and Papers of Chaim Weizmann, Letters*, vol. XVI, p. 279.

13. Margaliot, 'Problem of the Rescue of German Jewry', p. 255.

14. Ibid.

15. Abu-Diab, *Immigration to Israel*, p. 6.

16. *American Jewish Yearbook, 1936-37*, p. 585.

17. Ibid.

18. Abu-Diab, *Immigration to Israel*, p. 6.

19. Margaliot, 'Problem of the Rescue of German Jewry', p. 253.

20. David Wyman, *Paper Walls: America and the Refugee Crisis 1938-41*, pp. 67–8.

21. *Jews in Action – Five Years of the Jewish People's Committee* (undated), p. 7.

22. 'Dr Weizmann's Political Address – 20th Zionist Congress', *New Judaea* (London, August 1937), p. 215.

23. Yoav Gelber, 'Zionist Policy and the Fate of European Jewry (1939–42)', *Yad Vashem Studies*, vol. XII, p. 199.

24. Ari Bober (ed.), *The Other Israel*, p. 171.

25. Martin Gilbert, 'British Government Policy toward Jewish Refugees (November 1938–September 1939)', *Yad Vashem Studies*, vol. XIII, p. 130.

26. Ben Hecht, *Perfidy*, p. 19.

In 1933 Mussolini was well regarded by conservatives. He was thought to be the only one to have the ear of his wild disciple in Berlin, and the Zionists hoped that he would advise Hitler that to antagonise the Jews unduly could only cause needless problems. They also believed that Mussolini might be prevailed upon to join London and Paris in guaranteeing Vienna against a Nazi take-over.

Nahum Sokolow, then President of the WZO, saw Mussolini on 16 February 1933. Sokolow was not a strong figure; he had only been elected in 1931 on Weizmann's resignation after losing a vote of confidence on his policy of accommodation to the British, and he made no requests of Mussolini. However, Mussolini spoke of his 'cordial sympathy' for the Jews. When the Nazis announced their anti-Jewish boycott for 1 April, Mussolini sent his ambassador to see Hitler on 31 March, urging him to call it off. At this meeting the Führer heaped praise upon the *Duce*, but Adolf Hitler was the world's greatest expert on the Jews and needed no lecture on how to deal with them. Was it his fault that the leading Marxists were Jews? And what excesses had he perpetrated on the Jews that his name should be so maligned abroad, he retorted. No, his admirers might thank him if he called off the boycott, but his many enemies would all take it as a sign of weakness. Hitler asked that the next time the ambassador saw Signor Mussolini:

Add this: That I do not know whether in two or three hundred years my name will be venerated in Germany for what I so ardently hope to be able to do for my people, but of one thing I am absolutely certain: that five or six hundred years from now, the name of Hitler will be glorified everywhere as the name of the man who once and for all rid the world of the plague of Judaism.[1]

The Italians, who were concerned about Germany's designs on Austria, were on relatively good terms with the British as a result and gave London a report on the Hitler interview, but there is no reason to believe that Mussolini ever passed on these ominous words to the Zionists, nor is there evidence that the WZO ever presumed to request that the Italians pass them such information on Hitler's intentions. The WZO's interest lay in getting Mussolini to support them on Palestine, ally with the British on Austria, and lobby on behalf of German Jewry within the Nazis' parameters. There was an old tradition in the Jewish communities of Eastern Europe of the *shtadlin* (the interceder), the rich Jew who would go to the resident Haman and bribe him to call off the mob. But Hitler was not the ordinary Jew-hating king, or even a Petliura, and no Jew was allowed in his presence. Although Zionism had to fight the traditional *shtadlinim* for power within the Jewish communities and made much of the timidity of these people, the WZO looked to Mussolini to be their proxy intercessor with Hitler. Getting Mussolini to whisper into Hitler's ear was but the latest form of *shtadlinut*.

'My Third and Last Interview with Mussolini'

Though his prophesy to Mussolini's ambassador was awesome, Hitler was acutely aware of his weakness in early 1933. The opposition to stepping up the persecution of the Jews, as witness both Mussolini's intervention and the pleas of the German bourgeoisie, who were concerned for their export markets in the United States, compelled him to restrict the boycott to a one-day warning to the Jews. But Mussolini took this caution to mean that some form of *modus vivendi* was possible. He had tried to help the Jews; now he had to do likewise for Hitler. He asked Angelo Sacerdoti, the chief rabbi of Rome, to put him in contact with the heads of Jewry, suggesting that Hitler could scarcely be expected to stop his activities, if he did not have prior guarantees from world Jewry that they would call off their own demonstrations against him. Weizmann was already scheduled to visit Rome on 26 April 1933, and the rabbi suggested him as the logical contact; thus the third Weizmann–Mussolini meeting was quickly arranged.

Their discussion is shrouded in obscurity. Nahum Goldmann, Weizmann's long-standing associate, has remarked that anything unpleasant 'simply put his memory out of action'.[2] The record in Weizmann's autobiography, *Trial and Error*, is inconsistent. He wrote of 'My third and last interview with Mussolini', and then discussed their fourth conference.[3] Was it ever possible to forget a meeting in Mussolini's famous office? The reception at the Palazzo Venezia was meant to be memorable: a bell opened a window and an officer loudly announced that *dottore* Weizmann was there to see *Il Duce*; a row of soldiers ushered him to the next floor, where he was again heralded; this was repeated four times. After a wait in a splendid Renaissance drawing-room, Weizmann was announced by a final footman and he stepped into the fabled chamber. It was huge, at least 40–50 paces long; at the far end of the almost empty hall was Mussolini, sitting alone, the only light coming from a lamp on his small desk.

Other Italian and Zionist documents reveal some of the content of their conversation. Mussolini made his proposition that the heads of Jewry should declare that they were willing to call off their demonstrations and negotiate with Hitler. He had his own anti-Semitic notion of Jewry as a collective body, and Weizmann had to explain that he had no control over the non-Zionists and anti-Zionists, nor even over his own movement which had compelled his own retirement from active office. He was now organising the immigration of German Jews into Palestine and would not take on further assignments; later, he said that he told Mussolini he did not negotiate with 'wild beasts'.[4] The curtain over the meeting prevents us from hearing more of their dialogue, but 26 April was still prior to Sam Cohen's deal with the Nazis in May; even if Weizmann had had knowledge of Cohen's discussions in Berlin, he could hardly have raised this still vague project. But by 17 June, when he wrote to Mussolini asking for another meeting in July, Arlosoroff had returned home from his own parleys with the Nazis over the terms of the extended Ha'avara and it is reasonable to think that Weizmann wanted to discuss the proposed Fascist participation in the Political Secretary's liquidation bank. Weizmann could now prove to the Italians that the WZO was willing to come to terms with Hitler, even if that organisation could not order all Jewry to stop demonstrating. Although there is no evidence that the April conversation resulted in Weizmann's trying to get the pledge out of the world's Jewish leaders, rabbi Sacerdoti did attempt to carry out Mussolini's urgings. On 10 July he reported to the *Duce* that he had met five Jewish leaders, the chief rabbi of France, the President of the *Alliance Israélite Universelle*, Neville Laski, head of the Board of Deputies of British Jews, and Norman Bentwich and Victor Jacobson of the WZO. They had all agreed to call off demonstrations, if Hitler would restore the Jews' rights.[5]

'I shall be Able to Place at your Disposal a whole Team of Chemists'

Although Weizmann wanted a quicker meeting, his fourth conversation with Mussolini could not be arranged until 17 February 1934. Through the reports he gave at the time to the British and the report of Victor Jacobson of the Zionist Executive, in addition to Italian documents, the record of the fourth meeting is fairly complete. Mussolini asked if he had tried to deal with Hitler; Weizmann, who, through his friend Sam Cohen, had just asked to be invited to Berlin to discuss the liquidation bank proposal, told him, again, that he did not negotiate with wild beasts.[6] They changed the subject and went directly to the topic of Palestine; Mussolini supported Weizmann's idea of partition and an independent Zionist mini-state with the proviso that it should be independent of Britain. Mussolini also told him that he would help the Zionists establish their new merchant marine, although it is doubtful if Weizmann knew anything about the Revisionists' planned school at Civitavecchia.

Weizmann was a politician and he knew he had to give as well as take. His own rather unreliable autobiography tells that Mussolini 'talked freely of a Rome–Paris–London combination, which, he said, was the logical one for Italy. He spoke also of the chemical industry, and of the Italian need of pharmaceuticals, which we could produce in Palestine'.[7]

He wrote those words in 1947; after the war the President of the WZO could scarcely admit that he had offered to build a pharmaceutical industry in Fascist Italy, but the record is clear. Victor Jacobson, the WZO's representative at the League of Nations, had accompanied Weizmann to Italy and sent a detailed report of the interview to the Zionist Executive. Weizmann told Mussolini:

I shall be able to place at your disposal a whole team of chemists of the highest scientific standing; expert, trustworthy and loyal men with only one desire – to help Italy and harm Germany. If necessary, we will also be able to find the necessary capital.[8]

The Italians appointed Nicola Paravano to meet Weizmann the next day. Marquis Theodoli, the Chairman of the League of Nations Mandate Commission, was present and his memoirs record that Weizmann and the Fascists reached complete agreement on the plan. In the end nothing came of the arrangement, and in his autobiography Weizmann blamed the British:

I repeated the substance of this conversation to my British friends in London but it had no consequences . . . I do not know whether detaching Rome from Berlin would have prevented the outbreak of the war, but it certainly might have made a great difference to the war in the Mediterranean, might have saved many lives and shortened the agony by many months.[9]

Certainly the British were not interested in his scheme; furthermore, it is highly unlikely that he could have raised the capital to support his offer of direct economic collaboration with Fascism. He was always a diplomatic speculator; later he would make an equally fantastic offer of a $50 million Jewish loan to the Turks, if they, too, would ally with London. He worked on a principle that, if he could generate interest at one end of an alliance, something might happen at the other. It is doubtful if any of his pre-war diplomatic ploys, which were always tailored to suit the interest of the other side, but carefully designed to make Palestinian Zionism a central pivot of Britain's Mediterranean defence, were accepted by his negotiating partners.

Goldmann's Secret Diplomacy

Zionist diplomacy continued to lean on Mussolini to ward off future catastrophes, and Nahum Goldmann was next to visit the Palazzo Venezia on 13 November 1934. Goldmann cherished secret diplomacy, and he later vividly described the encounter in his *Autobiography*. He had three concerns: Hitler was about to take over the Saar, the Poles were about to rescind the minority-rights clauses in their constitution imposed at Versailles; and the Austrians were blatantly discriminating against Jews in their civil service. Since an Italian happened to be the chairman of the League of Nations Saar Commission, he had no difficulty in persuading Mussolini to agree to force the Germans to permit the Jews to take out all of their wealth with them in francs. He also persuaded him to agree that, if the Poles came to him, which, of course they did not, he would say 'no, no, no'.[10] The Austrian situation was that over which Mussolini had the most control, as the Christian Social government was dependent on the Italian Army at the Brenner Pass to protect it against a German invasion. Goldmann told Mussolini that American Jews were proposing public protests, but that he was discouraging this for the time being. Mussolini replied:

That was very wise of you. Those American Jews and gentiles are always ready to make protests and outcries and meddle in European affairs, which they don't understand at all.

Goldmann continued:

> I said that while I agreed this was not the moment for public protest against the Austrian government, we must nevertheless demand a change in its attitude to the Jews and here we counted strongly on him.

Mussolini responded:

> Herr Schuschnigg will be here next week, sitting in the chair you're sitting in now, and I'll tell him I don't want to see a Jewish problem created in Austria.[11]

Mussolini was in an anti-Nazi phase in late 1934. Perhaps the WZO could act as a bridge between him and the British; he no longer talked of a German–Jewish compromise. He told Goldmann:

> You are much stronger than Herr Hitler. When there is no trace left of Hitler, the Jews will still be a great people. You and we . . . The main thing is that the Jews must not be afraid of him. We shall all live to see his end. But you must create a Jewish state. I am a Zionist and I told Dr Weizmann so. You must have a real country, not that ridiculous National Home that the British have offered you. I will help you create a Jewish state.[12]

The Fascist leader was gulling the Zionist in every respect. As early as June 1933 he had given up any hope of convincing Hitler to compromise with the Jews, and he told the Germans that they should persist, as any retreat would be dangerous: 'certainly there had been much clumsiness and exaggeration at the beginning, but on no account must weakness be shown'.[13] He was also partly responsible for the discrimination in Austria, since he had told the Prime Minister to throw a 'dash of anti-Semitism' into his politics as the way to keep the Christian Socials' following away from the Nazis.[14] Also, he certainly did not tell Goldmann that he had just started subsidising the Mufti. But Goldmann was the perfect foil for an intriguer like Mussolini. In 1969, after he had stepped down from twelve years as President of the WZO, he was to write in his *Autobiography* that:

foreign affairs are so lacking in elegance in a democratic age when governments depend upon the mood of the people. There is something undeniably right in the principle of secret diplomacy, even if it is hardly feasible today.[15]

'Jewry Remembers with Thanks the Loyalty of the Fascist Government'

With the Ethiopian war Mussolini sought to call in his marker with the WZO. In autumn 1935, the League of Nations was about to impose sanctions and the Italian Foreign Ministry hastily commissioned Dante Lattes, the Italian Zionist Federation's representative in its dealings with the regime, and Angelo Orvieto, a prominent Zionist literary figure, to convince the European Jewish bourgeoisie to oppose an embargo. They had two arguments: sanctions would drive Mussolini to Hitler and, in addition, he was outspokenly in favour of an immediate Jewish state and a practical friend of the Zionist movement. They saw Weizmann and the leaders of official Anglo-Jewry, but to no avail. The Jewish leaders had to back Britain, if for no other reason than the fact that Italy was no match for Britain in the Levant.[16]

Rome sent a non-Zionist Fascist Jew, Corrado Tedeschi, a journalist, to Palestine to contact the broad Zionist right-wing. Arguing the same case, he added that the Zionists would improve their own position *vis-à-vis* Britain by taking a pro-Italian stand, as London would then be compelled to buy them off. He found little support outside Revisionist circles. Ittamar Ben-Avi, the famous 'Zionist baby', the first child in centuries whose earliest words were all in Hebrew, ran a pro-war piece in his sensationalist daily paper, *Doar Ha'Yom*, on 21 February 1936.[17] But from Italy's practical point of view, Ben-Avi's eager co-operation meant nothing. His paper had been a Revisionist organ, then he drifted away from them, and now had no personal following. Other rightists listened to Tedeschi's appeal, but the Ethiopian campaign was so clearly another sign of the coming world conflict in which the two Fascist regimes seemed certain to ally that there was no chance of the non-Revisionist right supporting the Italian position.

Hitler always saw Mussolini in more realistic terms than any wing of the Zionist movement. They had all thought that the Austrian question would keep the two dictators apart, but Hitler understood that their common hatred of Marxism would eventually draw them together. The Ethiopian conquest gave Hitler a chance to show that he would stand by his fellow authoritarian, but it was the Spanish Civil War that finally convinced Mussolini that he had to ally with Hitler; the workers' take-over in Madrid and Barcelona in the wake of the military's rising heralded a major left-wing victory, unless there was massive foreign assistance to Franco's forces. Mussolini began to appreciate that he could neither afford to have Hitler lose the next war nor win it without his assistance. Zionism henceforward could no longer be of service to Fascism. If Italy lined up with Germany, the Jews would become Mussolini's enemies regardless of anything he would say or do about a Jewish state. Nevertheless the Zionists sought to restore good relations. In March 1937, Goldmann's Geneva office still chose publicly to:

> emphasise that world Jewry as a whole, or through its various organisations, never opposed the Italian government. On the contrary, Jewry remembers with thanks the loyalty of the fascist Government.[18]

Goldmann came to Rome for one last discussion with Count Ciano, the *Duce*'s son-in-law and Foreign Minister, on 4 May 1937. Ciano assured him that Italy was neither anti-Semitic nor anti-Zionist, and proposed another visit by Weizmann.[19] But the comedy was over and Weizmann never bothered to come again.

'So? Is it Good for the Jews?'

No Zionist element, right or left, understood the Fascist phenomenon. From the first, they were indifferent to the struggle of the Italian people, including progressive Jews, against the blackshirts and Fascism's larger implications for European democracy. Italy's Zionists never resisted Fascism; they ended up praising it and undertook diplomatic negotiations on its behalf. The bulk of the Revisionists and a few other right-wingers became its enthusiastic adherents. The moderate bourgeois Zionist leaders — Weizmann, Sokolow and Goldmann — were uninterested in Fascism itself. As Jewish separatists they only asked one question, the cynical classic: 'So? Is it good for the Jews?' which implies that something can be evil for the general world and yet be good for the Jews. Their only concern was that Rome could be either their friend or enemy at the League of Nations and Mussolini was allowed to become their friend and patron. Given his importance in their cosmos prior to the Nazi triumph, it was hardly surprising that they should have continued to court him blindly after 1933.

Notes

1. Daniel Carpi, 'Weizmann's Political Activity in Italy from 1923 to 1934', *Zionism* (Tel Aviv, 1975), p. 239.
2. Nahum Goldmann, *Autobiography*, p. 111.
3. Chaim Weizmann, *Trial and Error*, p. 372.
4. Carpi, 'Weizmann's Political Activity in Italy', p. 217.
5. Meir Michaelis, *Mussolini and the Jews*, p. 64.
6. Carpi, 'Weizmann's Political Activity in Italy', p. 217.
7. Weizmann, *Trial and Error*, p. 372.
8. Carpi, 'Weizmann's Political Activity in Italy', p. 220.
9. Weizmann, *Trial and Error*, p. 372.
10. Goldmann, *Autobiography*, p. 161.
11. Ibid., p. 159.
12. Ibid., p. 160.
13. Michaelis, *Mussolini and the Jews*, p. 72.
14. Ibid., p. 67.
15. Goldmann, *Autobiography*, p. 105.
16. Michaelis, *Mussolini and the Jews*, p. 84; and Michael Ledeen, 'The Evolution of Italian Fascist Anti-Semitism', *Jewish Social Studies* (Winter 1976), p. 13.
17. Michaelis, *Mussolini and the Jews*, pp. 86-7.
18. Leon Harris, 'Mussolini in Hitler's Footsteps', *Jewish Life* (September 1938), p. 17.
19. Michaelis, *Mussolini and the Jews*, p. 136.

15 AUSTRIA AND THE 'GENTILE FRIENDS OF ZIONISM'

The First World War destroyed four empires and created a string of new states in Central Europe. Of all these the one with the least rationale was Austria. Its population was virtually entirely German and, in 1919, the Austrian Parliament, with only one dissenting vote, voted for union with Germany; the Allies, however, refused to countenance the merger and the Social-Democratic-dominated coalition reluctantly continued to rule. In the summer of 1920, the anti-Semitic Christian Socials took control of the national government, although the leftists were able to maintain a grip on the Viennese city administration.

Three ideological currents competed for power in the truncated republic. The Communist Party was one of the weakest in Europe, and the Social Democrats saw their enemies to the right in the Catholic Christian Socials — the party of the peasantry and the urban lower middle class — and the anti-Semitic German nationalists, with their base in the professions and the white-collar workers. Although both bourgeois groupings were hostile to democracy, the enormous strength of the Socialists in Vienna and Austria's financial dependence on Britain and France, precluded any *coup d'état*. But both the Social Democrats and the Christian Socials were careful to maintain substantial party militias.

'This Great Patriot and Leader of his Country'

The Social Democrats' first major leader, Victor Adler, was a Jew; so was its leading theoretician, Otto Bauer, and Jews comprised almost half of the party leadership. Inevitably, the movement always saw threats to the Jews as a mortal danger to itself and acted accordingly. The worker ranks were extremely loyal to their Jewish comrades and had not the least hesitation in physically combating the anti-Semites, as Hitler records himself in *Mein Kampf*, writing of his experiences in his first job, on a construction site in pre-war Vienna:

These men rejected everything: the nation as an invention of the

160

'capitalistic' (how often was I forced to hear this single word!) classes; the fatherland as an instrument of the bourgeoisie for the exploitation of the working class; the authority of law as a means of oppressing the proletariat . . . There was absolutely nothing which was not drawn through the mud . . . I tried to keep silent. But at length . . . I began to take a position . . . one day they made use of the weapon which most readily conquers reason . . . A few of the spokesmen on the opposing side forced me either to leave the building at once or be thrown off the scaffolding.[1]

From the beginning the Social Democratic workers fought the Nazis when the first signs of the new party appeared in Vienna in 1923. Bands of hoodlums carrying the swastika flag had started to beat up Jews and on one occasion they killed a worker; this brought the Social Democrats out for battle by the thousands. A writer for the American *Menorah Journal*, one of the leading Jewish magazines of its day, described the result:

> No pogrom meetings can now be held undisturbed. The organised workingmen, social democrats and communists, frequently storm the meetings of the anti-Semites, not because of their friendship for the Jews, but because they believe the life of the republic at stake.[2]

The vast majority of Austrian Jews identified with the Social Democrats. Amongst the few who did not were the Zionists of the *Judische-nationale Partei* (JnP). But the Jews were only 2.8 per cent of the entire Austrian population, and no more than 10 per cent of Vienna's voters, and the tiny JnP succeeded only once in electing a candidate to the Austrian Parliament. It was he, Robert Stricker, who cast the sole vote opposing unity with Germany in 1919, a move which guaranteed his defeat in 1920. Three more Zionists were elected to the city council in the early 1920s; in 1920 the Zionists polled 21 per cent of Vienna's Jewish vote and in 1923 their percentage even increased to 26 per cent, but after that the Zionist vote fell away strongly, and by 1930 it polled a mere 0.2 per cent of the total vote.[3] Although the JnP's role in Austrian political life was insignificant, its short career is illustrative of the insularity and the petty-bourgeois character of European Zionism. Most of the JnP's supporters never thought of themselves as emigrating to Palestine. Many of Vienna's Jews had only recently arrived from Galicia. The Zionism of the JnP represented the last vestige of their ghetto mentality. It was not a protest against the anti-Semites; that cause was fought out in the streets in the Social Democratic militia. Austrian Zionism was a petty-bourgeois protest against socialism, and the Christian Socials were always delighted to see the JnP draw some votes away from their radical foes. In turn the Zionists did not see the Christian Socials as their enemies. Sokolow was in Durban, South Africa, in 1934, when he heard of the murder of Austria's Prime Minister, Engelbert Dollfuss, during the Nazis' unsuccessful *putsch* of 25 July; he asked his audience at the Jewish Club to rise in the memory of:

> this great patriot and leader of his country, whom I knew very well and met very often . . . was one of the friends of our cause. He was one of those who established, with my help, the organisation of Gentile Friends of Zionism in the Austrian capital.[4]

The Gentile Friends had been set up in 1927. In 1929 Fritz Lohner-Beda, the former president of the Zionist Hakoah Athletic Club, warned the Jews that they would be punished for their support for the Social Democrats when the reactionaries finished off the socialists. He continued with a promise that Jews would support the Fascist *Heimwehr* militia, if the rightists would only give up their anti-Semitism. He claimed that the socialists, as atheists, anti-nationalists and anti-capitalists were really the Jews' greatest enemies.[5]

'We Condemn Dissemination of Atrocity Stories from Austria Abroad'

While the Christian Socials feared Nazism as a threat to their own power, Hitler's success convinced Dollfuss that dictatorship was the coming thing, at least in Central Europe, and he finally heeded Mussolini's constant advice and provoked the Social Democrats into a rising in February 1934, which he crushed in a three-day battle. Over a thousand workers were murdered when the Heimwehr shelled the famous Karl Marx housing project. The Zionists' response to the massacre was quite clear. Robert Stricker, in a talk on the events before a party gathering, denounced the reports circulating abroad concerning persecution of Jews. He insisted this was false, saying that during those fateful days Austria had manifested a high level of culture rarely found elsewhere.[6] In fact the Dollfuss regime embarked on a policy of severe discrimination against the Jews, particularly in government employment, and many professionals were dismissed. However, the Zionist antagonism against the assimilationist socialist Jews made them the local and international apologists for the Christian Socials. In 1935 the government announced plans for segregating Jewish students in cases of 'overcrowding'. While the assimilationist Jewish leaders naturally opposed the scheme as the first step towards total school segregation, Stricker welcomed the new ghetto schools.[7] That same year, when the Austrian Foreign Minister inveighed against 'atrocity stories' appearing in the world press, *Der Stimme*, the organ of the Austrian Zionist Federation, hastened to explain that:

It is impossible nowadays to seal hermetically any country and hide events including anti-Jewish agitation. We condemn dissemination of atrocity stories from Austria abroad. This however, has never been done by Jews but by Austrian newspapers which are read abroad.[8]

The Christian Socials knew that they were no match for Hitler without foreign guarantors. While they looked to Mussolini to protect them militarily, they also required loans from the London and Paris banks and they had to persuade potential foreign backers that they were not an imitation of the Nazis. In May 1934 Dollfuss appointed Desider Friedmann, a veteran Zionist and head of the Viennese Jewish community organisation, to the State Council. There were other similar gestures by the regime towards Zionism. The Revisionists were permitted to use an estate given to them by a rich member as a training centre. A Revisionist writer later remembered the scene at the spacious country seat as taking on 'the appearance of a disciplined military camp' and, in September 1935, the government allowed the Revisionists to hold the founding congress of the New Zionist Organisation in Vienna.[9]

For reasons of foreign policy the regime always denied that it was discriminating against the Jews while coming up with absurd pretexts, as with the alleged overcrowding, to justify its anti-Semitism. Jews were even legally entitled to join the Fatherland Front which had replaced all the political parties including, technically, the Christian Socials after 1934. However, once Mussolini had decided to ally with Hitler, and it was clear that he was not prepared to protect Austria any longer, the regime had to desperately struggle to ward off a Nazi take-over. In January 1938 the Austrians tried to prove to Hitler that, although they were determined to stay independent, nevertheless they were still a 'German-Christian' state, and they established a segregated section in the Fatherland Front for Jewish youths. The *Encyclopedia Judaica* remarks laconically that 'the Zionists accepted willingly, but it angered those in favor of assimilation'.[10] However, although it was thus becoming more anti-Semitic in its efforts to keep the German Nazis out, the regime had no hesitation in using the Zionists to seek foreign financial support. Desider Friedmann was rushed abroad in early 1938, in the last weeks before the *anschluss*.[11] Dollfuss's successor, Kurt von Schuschnigg, tried a last ploy, announcing on 9 March a plebiscite on independence for 13 March, and the Zionist-dominated Jewish community organisation hastened to draw up a list of every Jew in Vienna to contribute to a fund to pay for Schuschnigg's campaign. Hitler had a much more realistic measure of Herr Schuschnigg and simply commanded him to resign, which he did on 11 March, and the German Army moved into Austria on 12 March.

The Folly of Zionist Reliance on the Christian Socials

Was the Zionists' support for the Austrian right ever justified? One might claim that the Christian Socials were the only barrier between the Jews and a Nazi take-over, but the alliance with them had begun in the 1920s when Hitler was not yet a threat. The establishment of the Gentile Friends cannot be defended in anti-Nazi terms. In fact the Austrian right, Dollfuss and Schuschnigg, were never an obstacle to a German take-over, but were a guarantee of a final Nazi victory. Joseph Buttinger, in the 1930s the leader of the Social Democratic underground, described the reality in his book, *In the Twilight of Socialism*. There was an anti-Nazi majority in Austria, but Schuschnigg was 'unable to use the political opportunity inherent in this circumstance'. He had to prevent any 'mass mobilisation against the brown fascism, because in a true fight for freedom he himself would inevitably be crushed'. This mass mobilisation was what mattered, said Buttinger, writing at that time, 'in so far as Austria matters at all, for in the final analysis the fate of Austria will be decided by international forces'. Hitler would attack Austria at a favourable moment, which he was cheerfully awaiting, with the Schuschnigg regime 'as his guarantee against the organisation of a defense in the meanwhile'.[12]

Austrian Jewry had only one hope: a resolute alliance, locally and internationally, with the Social Democrats. Unlike the discredited German socialists, the Austrian Social Democrats remained largely intact after their heroic, if poorly organised, resistance in 1934. Dollfuss's regime was the weakest of the Fascist states, and even after the massacre of the socialists on 12 February the new government was sustained, not so much by its own police power, as by the overawing presence of the Italian and Hungarian Armies on the borders that would fight for Dollfuss, and the equal certainty that the German Army would intervene rather than see the Social Democrats come to power. Clearly, neither the difficult international setting nor the strength of the Austrian regime can be minimised, but there were giant socialist demonstrations about Austria in Europe and America. However, instead of looking to the socialists, in Austria and abroad, for succour, the local Zionists looked to the regime, which was ultimately to surrender to Hitler without firing a shot. Nahum Goldmann, the representative of the WZO, consciously discouraged foreign Jews from demonstrating over Austrian anti-Semitism, choosing instead to place reliance on backstage whispers from Benito Mussolini.

Notes

1. Adolf Hitler, *Mein Kampf*, p. 40.

2. Eugen Hoeflich, 'Morale in Austria', *Menorah Journal* (August 1923), pp. 235-6.

3. Walter Simon, 'The Jewish Vote in Austria', *Leo Baeck Institute Year Book*, vol. XVI (1961), p. 114.

4. 'Sokolow Honours Memory of Dollfuss', *Palestine Post* (13 August 1934), p. 4.

5. Herbert Solow, 'Unrest in Austria', *Menorah Journal* (February 1930), pp. 141-2.

6. 'Austria – the Key to Jewish Politics', *South African Ivri* (March 1934), p. 1.

7. 'Austria', *American Jewish Year Book* (1935-6), p. 189.

8. 'Vienna Papers take Issue on Press Threats', *Jewish Daily Bulletin* (11 January 1935), p. 1.

9. Otto Seidman, 'Saga of Aliyah Beth', *Tagar* (Shanghai, 1 January 1947), p. 7.

10. 'Austria', *Encyclopedia Judaica*, vol. 3, col. 898.

11. 'Desider Friedmann', *Encyclopedia Judaica*, vol. 7, col. 191.

12. Joseph Buttinger, *In the Twilight of Socialism*, p. 427.

Czechoslovakia – 2.4 Per Cent of an Empire

With the downfall of the three great empires of Eastern Europe in the wake of the First World War a new arrangement of power emerged under the domination of French and British imperialism. Isolation of Germany and the Soviet Union were their two main goals, and their determination to confine the Germans led the Allies to encourage the Lithuanians, Poles and Czechs to carve themselves pieces of ethnic German land. Hungary and Bulgaria, as allies of the Germans, also suffered territorial losses. The result was the creation of a group of states cursed with intense national cleavages. Anti-Semitism was inevitable in this maelstrom of communal hatred.

Zionism succeeded in generating enough strength in the Jewish communities of Eastern Europe to send representatives to the parliaments of Latvia, Lithuania, Poland, Czechoslovakia, Romania and Austria; even in Yugoslavia, where the total Jewish population was less than 70,000, efforts were made to run Jewish slates in the municipal council elections in Zagreb. However, Zionism – as the separatist ideology of the weakest of the ethnic groups in the region – was never able to cope with the crisis of East European nationalism.

Czechoslovakia had a fine reputation in the 1930s as a democratic oasis amid the region's dictatorships, but it was little more than a Czech version of the Habsburg Empire. The Czech bourgeoisie dominated the Slovaks and crudely incorporated pieces of German, Hungarian, Polish and Ukrainian territory into their mini-empire. The Czech leaders were also *sui generis* anti-Semites; the Jews were seen as German and Magyar culture agents, and the early days of the Czech republic saw anti-Semitic riots.[1] The army was dominated by former Czech legionaires who had deserted the Habsburgs for the Russians during the First World War, and then fought alongside the White Guards on their way out of Russia; the generals were outspoken anti-Semites. The Hasidic youths of Carpatho-Ukrainia, where Jews made up 15 per cent of the population, were always the butt of their officers' ill-humour, and a Jew from Slovakia was assumed to be a Magyariser. It was unthinkable that a Jew could become a high officer. No one had any rights in the Czechoslovak Army except Czechs and those Slovaks who accepted Czech domination.[2]

The Czech bourgeoisie did not want the Jews to mix with the Germans or Magyars, but only the Czech Social Democrats encouraged Jews to enter the Czech community.[3] The bourgeois formula was patronage of 'national Jewry', and Jews were allowed to list themselves as Jews by nationality on the census. There were 356,820 Jews in the country in 1930 — 2.4 per cent of the total population; of these 58 per cent listed themselves as Jews, 24.5 per cent as Czechs, 12.8 per cent as Germans and 4.7 per cent as Magyars.

The Czechoslovakian Zionists operated in local politics through the Jewish Party, the *Židovska Strana*. From 1919 they were able to put members on the municipal councils in Prague and other cities and towns, but it always proved impossible to elect anyone to the national Parliament on a straight Jewish vote. In the 1920 elections a United Jewish Parties ballot received only 79,714 votes, and in the 1925 poll the Jewish Party, standing alone, garnered 98,845 votes. By 1928 even the most committed Jewish separatists realised that they had to ally themselves to some non-Jews if they were ever going to get into Parliament, and they found suitable partners in the Polish Middle-Class Party and the Polish Social Democrats of the Cieszyn area. In 1929 their joint effort won 104,539 votes, enough to send two Zionists and two Poles to Parliament. But the alliance was strictly for the election: the Zionists remained loyal to the Czech government, whereas the Poles oriented toward Poland. In Parliament the Zionists ran into another problem, because speaking rights in debates were alloted by voting strength. They were therefore compelled to find refuge in the Czech Social Democratic faction as 'guests'. The Social Democrats already had Jews in their party as good Czechs, and they took in the two Zionists simply to get two more votes for the government which they supported. The Jewish Party's extremely narrow interests, opposition to Sunday closing laws and their efforts to get the government to subsidise Hebrew-language schools in the Carpatho-Ukraine, did not disturb Czech domination of the state. The Zionists always looked toward the Czechs for fulfilment of their ambitions, and they never saw themselves as the allies of the subordinate ethnic groups, not even the Poles with whom they had an electoral pact. For all their Jewish nationalism, they were simply an adjunct of the Czech supremacy. In their own fight against linguistic assimilation they had come to regard the fight for the rights of the other nationalities as a form of radical assimilationism. Their prime goal was central government support for their fledgeling school system, and to get this they remained loyal to the Czechoslovakian state and Thomas Masaryk and Edvard Beneš.

After the surrender of the Sudeten in 1938, and the concomitant fall of Beneš's government, the patronage of the rump Czech state for 'national' Jewry evaporated. The new Czech leaders, actually the right wing of the previous government, were determined to adapt to the new reality of Nazi domination of Central Europe, and they knew that Hitler would never consider coming to terms with them if the Jews had the free run of their new 'Czecho-Slovakia'. The new Prime Minister, Rudolph Beran, leader of the Agrarian Party, which had been the dominant party in the Cabinet under the Beneš Republic, informed Parliament after the Munich Conference that anti-Semitism would now be the official policy of his government. It was necessary to 'limit the tasks of the Jews in the life of the nations which are the bearers of the state idea'. His declaration was accepted with one dissenting vote. A Czech rightist rose in defence of the Jews, but the deputy of the Jewish Party, who had never spoken up on behalf of the oppressed under Beneš, now did not raise his voice in defence of his own people.[4]

Romania — 'Yids to Palestine!'

Romania before 1914 was determinedly anti-Semitic. Most of its Jews had come as refugees from Russia, and the Romanian government simply denied them and their descendants the right to become citizens. The fact that Romania sided with the Allies during the First World War provided new territories at Versailles, which brought many thousands of additional Jews into the expanded state. Now the Jews received citizenship rights, as the Versailles powers insisted that Bucharest grant minimal rights to its millions of new non-Romanian subjects. Discrimination against the Jews continued of course, and began for the other non-Romanians, but ethnic hostility was only one of the country's problems. Apart from the fundamental economic problems, the government was notably corrupt: 'Rumania is not a country, it is a profession', became a celebrated Yiddish proverb of the day.

Throughout the 1920s and early 1930s there was some improvement in the status of the Jews. They were 5.46 per cent of the population and the politicians began to court their vote; the King, Carol II, even took a Jewish mistress, the famous Magda Lupescu. All progressive elements saw anti-Semitism as an integral part of the general backwardness that the country had to overcome. Although the Social Democrats were extremely timid, the National Peasant Party (NPP) and the Radical Peasant Party were more vigorous in opposing anti-Semitism.

They wanted land reform and more democracy, and realised that those who would deny the Jews their rights were also opposed to democracy in general.

Jews supported all parties except the extreme anti-Semites. Many of the prosperous Romanian-speakers even voted for the more moderate anti-Semitic parties, as long as they used the police against hoodlums. Other Jews, in Transylvania, were passionate Hungarian nationalists. A minority voted for the Social Democrats or backed the outlawed Communists. The Zionists, based on the non-Romanian-speakers, slowly put together a Jewish Party which, after some experience in the local elections, ran for the national Parliament in 1931. They did well, in their own terms, and gained 64,175 votes — over 50 per cent of the Jewish vote, and four seats in the Parliament, although this only amounted to 2.19 per cent of the total vote. In the July 1932 elections they did slightly better, getting 67,582 votes or 2.48 per cent of the poll, and they held their four seats.

The leaders of the Jewish Party were from the small-town middle class. They appreciated that the NPP opposed anti-Semitism and they allied themselves loosely with the peasants in the Parliament, but they were, at best, only lukewarm supporters of the peasant cause. Their middle-class base saw itself threatened economically by the co-operative movement, which always followed on the heels of a peasant awakening. Instead of facing up to the real political challenge confronting Romania during the inter-war period, the Zionist leaders busied themselves in Jewish communal activities, not realising that they were weakening the Jewish position by remaining isolated from the struggle for democratic changes.

The extreme anti-Semites were already violent in the 1920s. Corneliu Codreanu, the founder of the Legion of the Archangel Michael and its terrorist Iron Guard, had been acquitted of murdering the chief of police in Jassy in 1924. A Jewish student had been murdered in 1926 and the killer acquitted, and there were riots in 1929 and 1932, but there was no chance of the extreme right coming to power until after the impact of Hitler's victory in 1933. With the Nazi triumph, the slow trend away from anti-Semitism was sharply reversed. The Fascist forces now had a number of psychological advantages. If Germany, a highly civilised state, could turn anti-Semitic, the local extremists could no longer be written off as backward fanatics; nor were the Iron Guard part of the universal corruption.

Although the erosion of parliamentary democracy was fairly rapid, there was substantial resistance. The National Peasant Party spoke out against anti-Semitism until the 1937 election, when it suddenly changed direction and formed an alliance with the anti-Semites. The Radical Peasants continued to speak out and even, in some cases, physically defended the Jews, but they were no match for the far right.

'Put up their own . . . Candidates and Vote among Themselves'

Disaster had already hit the Jewish Party in the December 1933 elections. Hitler's triumph in Berlin made the election of Codreanu in Bucharest much more of a possibility, and many of the party's supporters realised that if they were going to live in safety in Romania they would have to have the protection of Romanian allies. The Jewish Party vote dropped to 38,565 (1.3 per cent) and all four seats were lost. In 1935 the Social Democrats raised the call for a Popular Front of all liberal forces, but excluding the Communists. They, in their turn, supported an alliance with the socialists and the NPP. Both parties wanted to combine with the NPP, not the other, but the NPP refused to unite with either, and signed a 'non-aggression pact' with the Fascists for the December 1937 elections. The Socialists, Radical Peasants and the Jewish Party all stood individually and the Communists, consistent with their view that the NPP were absolutely necessary for an anti-Fascist government, told their supporters to vote for the NPP.[5] The election was a rout for the fractured anti-Fascists; the Social Democrat vote dropped from an already anaemic 3.25 per cent to 1.3 per cent and they were wiped out as a parliamentary group. The Jewish Party hoped to go back into Parliament with the votes of Jews who could not now vote for the NPP. But their gain was too tiny, and they only achieved 1.4 per cent of the poll.

Had the Jewish Party and the Social Democrats joined forces, they at least would have gained the statutory 2 per cent required to obtain one seat but, of course, a united-front effort would have drawn other forces to them as well. For a separate Jewish party to stand for election alone was political suicide. It was exactly what the anti-Semites wanted; Octavian Goga, who became Prime Minister after the election, had told the Jews during the campaign to 'remain in their homes or put up their own lists of candidates and vote among themselves'.[6]

'Emigration Deals are in Order'

No wing of the Zionist movement had shown any interest in the struggle against the anti-Semitic wave in Romania. In November 1936 the American *Labor Zionist Newsletter*, which expressed the ideological guidance of Enzo Sereni and Golda Myerson (Meir), who were then the

Poale Zion emissaries in the United States, stated the strategic position of the dominant tendency in the WZO: 'Unless the Peasant Party seizes power immediately the country will be taken over by the Nazis, and will become a satellite of Germany. Emigration deals are in order.'[7] A pact was envisioned with the incumbent regime or its successor – be it the NPP or the Fascists – to encourage some of the Jews to emigrate to Palestine as a method of relieving some of the 'pressure' of the presence of 'too many Jews'. But such a 'deal' would have been taken by the anti-Semites to mean that if they tried harder they would be able to get rid of even more Jews, and it would have triggered further demands by the anti-Semites in other countries for the Jews to start 'voluntarily' leaving Europe. Rather than help organise the struggle against the oncoming Fascists, the WZO was projecting a disastrous extension of its Ha'avara strategy to Eastern Europe.

'Jidanii in Palestina!' (Yids to Palestine!) had long been the warcry of the Iron Guards and other anti-Semites. The only sensible way for the Jews to respond to the menace was to seek unity with all others who were willing to make a common stand for liberty; but the Zionists, who had the electoral support of the majority of the Jews at the start of the right-wing upsurge, never made a move in that direction. Fascism did come to power, and the country was to witness the horrors of the Holocaust.

In January 1941 the Iron Guard broke with its allies in the government, and a short but furious civil war was waged in the capital. The Guard used the occasion to slaughter at least 2,000 Jews in the most barbaric fashion. Some 200 Jews were led to the slaughterhouse and had their throats cut in imitation of the Jewish rites of animal slaughter. Yet there was another side to the story. The dairy farmers of Dudesti Cioplea, a little village near Bucharest, sent messengers to the Jewish quarter: any Jews who could escape to their town would be protected. Over a thousand Jews fled there and were protected by peasants using their hunting rifles. The Iron Guard tried to break in, but was resolutely turned back.[8] That there were not more Dudesti Ciopleas was due to the failure of the anti-Fascist forces, including the Jewish Party, to unite against Codreanu's killers in the 1930s.

Notes

1. Aharon Rabinowicz, 'The Jewish Minority' in *The Jews of Czechoslovakia*, vol. I, p. 247; and Gustav Fleischmann, 'The Religious Congregation, 1918–1938'

in *The Jews of Czechoslovakia*, p. 273.

2. Yeshayahu Jelinek, 'The Swoboda Army Legend: Concealed Realities', *Soviet Jewish Affairs* (May 1980), pp. 76–7.

3. J.W. Brugel, 'Jews in Political Life', *The Jews in Czechoslavakia*, vol. II, p. 244.

4. Solomon Goldelman, 'The Jews in the new Czecho-Slovakia', *Contemporary Jewish Record* (January 1939), p. 13.

5. Bela Vago, 'Popular Front in the Balkans: Failure in Hungary and Rumania', *Journal of Contemporary History*, vol. V, no. 3 (1970), p. 115.

6. Bela Vago, 'The Jewish Vote in Rumania between the two World Wars', *Jewish Journal of Sociology* (December 1972), p. 241.

7. 'Diaspora', *Labor Zionist Newsletter* (15 November 1935), p. 12.

8. William Perl, *The Four Front War*, p. 349.

Both Hitler and Mussolini recognised the full implications of the Spanish Civil War; a victory for the left there would have galvanised their enemies, and not the least of these the workers of Germany and Italy. They moved with alacrity, and later Hitler was to boast that the intervention of the 14,000 men of his Condor Legion was decisive in the struggle. Another 25,000 Germans were to serve with Franco's tank corps and artillery, and the Italians sent in another 100,000 'volunteers'. The Loyalist left also received substantial foreign support; individual radicals crossed the Pyrenees on their own to join the workers' militias; the Communist International organised 40,000 volunteers of the International Brigades (although by no means all were Communists); and ultimately the Soviets were to send in both men and material, although never in the quantities supplied by the Fascist states.

There is no certainty as to the number of Jews who fought in Spain. They identified themselves as radicals rather than as Jews, and few thought then to count them as Jews. The considered estimate of Professor Albert Prago, himself a veteran of the conflict, is that they provided 16 per cent of the International Brigades, proportionately the highest figure for any ethnic group.[1] It is believed that of the 2,000 Britons, at least 214 or 10.7 per cent were Jewish, and the numbers given for American Jews are between 900 and 1,250, about 30 per cent of the Abraham Lincoln Brigade. The largest single Jewish national grouping consisted of Poles living in exile from the savagely anti-Communist regime in Warsaw. Of the approximately 5,000 Poles, 2,250 or 45 per cent were Jews. In 1937 the Brigades, for propagandist reasons, set up the Naftali Botwin Company, almost 200 Yiddish-speakers in the Polish Dombrowski Brigade. Strangely, no one has ever estimated a figure for the Jews among the German Ernst Thaelmanns, the second largest national contingent, but they were well represented.

A few of the Italians were also Jews; the most notable of these was Carlo Rosselli, whom Mussolini considered his most dangerous opponent among the exile community. A maverick liberal who went to Spain some time before the Communists, he organised the first Italian column of 130 men – mostly Anarchists, with a few clusters of liberals and Trotskyists – to fight in the ranks of the militia of the Catalonian

Anarcho-Syndicalists. Mussolini finally had Carlo and his brother Nello assassinated by thugs of the *Cagoulards*, a French Fascist group, on 9 July 1937.[2]

'The Question is not Why They Went, But Rather Why Didn't We Go?'

There were 22 Zionists from Palestine in Spain when the Civil War broke out. These were members of *HaPoel*, the Labour Zionist athletic association, who had come for a Workers' Olympiad scheduled to be held in Barcelona on 19 July 1936 as a protest against the forthcoming Olympic Games in Berlin.[3] Almost all of them took part in the battles in Barcelona when the workers crushed the rising of the local garrison.[4] Albert Prago mentions two other Zionists by name as having come to fight and doubtless there were others, but they came strictly as individuals. The Zionist movement not only opposed their members in Palestine going to Spain, but on 24 December 1937 *Ha'aretz*, the Zionist daily newspaper in Palestine, denounced the American Jews in the Lincoln Brigades for fighting in Spain rather than coming to Palestine to work. [5] There were, however, Jews in Palestine who ignored the strictures of the Zionist movement and went to Spain, but no one is certain of their number; estimates run from 267 to 500, proportionately the highest number for any country.[6] The *Encyclopedia of Zionism and Israel* describes them as 'about 400 Communists'.[7] It is known that some Zionists, acting as individuals, were amongst their number, but almost all were members of the Palestine Communist Party.

In 1973 the Israeli veterans of the conflict held a reunion and invited veterans from other countries to attend. One of these, Saul Wellman, an American Jew, later described the most dramatic incident of the event, which occurred when they toured Jerusalem and met the mayor, Teddy Kolleck. They had been debating whether they had been right to go to Spain in the midst of the Arab revolt and Kolleck had his own answer to their discussion: 'The question is not why they went, but rather why didn't we go as well?'[8]

There were several reasons, all deeply rooted in Zionism – and particularly Labour Zionism – which explain why they did not go, when it was clear that the Nazis were crucially involved on Franco's side. All Zionists saw the solving of the Jewish question as their most important task, and they sharply counterposed Jewish nationalism to any concept of international solidarity; none despised 'red assimilation' more vigorously than the Labour Zionists. During the Spanish Civil

War, in 1937, Berl Katznelson, the editor of the Histadrut's daily paper, *Davar*, and a senior figure in the movement, wrote a pamphlet, entitled *Revolutionary Constructivism*, which was primarily an attack on their own youth for their growing criticism of the party's supine line on Revisionist Fascism and its increasing racism towards the Arabs. Katznelson's polemic was also an assault on the very heart of Marxism: its internationalism. He denounced the youths in no uncertain terms:

> They do not have the capacity to live their own lives. They can live only someone else'e life and think someone else's thought. What queer altruism! Our Zionist ideologists have always denounced this type of Jew — this revolutionary middleman, who pretending to be an internationalist, a rebel, a warrior, a hero, is actually so abject, so cowardly, and spineless when the existence of his own nation hangs in the balance . . . The revolutionary speculator is continually begging, 'See my modesty, see my piety, see how I observe all significant and trivial revolutionary precepts.' How prevalent is this attitude among us and how dangerous at this hour when it is imperative that we be honest with ourselves and straight-forward with our neighbors.[9]

Nominally the Labour Zionists were part of the Socialist International, but for them international workers' solidarity only meant workers' support for them in Palestine. They raised small sums of money for Spain, but none of their number officially went to fight in 'someone else's battles'. At the 1973 veterans' conference they had taken up the question of whether they had been justified in going off to Spain 'in the face of some criticism from Zionist and Histadrut leaders in 1936 . . . at a time of anti-Jewish riots'.[10] But given the statements by Enzo Sereni and Moshe Beilenson in *Jews and Arabs in Palestine*, which was published in July 1936, the very month that the Fascists revolted in Spain, it is apparent that the Labour Zionists' thinking at that time was not defensive; their ambition was to conquer Palestine and economically dominate the Middle East. The 'riots' were the natural defence response to their ambitions and not the other way around. Although the Histadrut's ranks did sympathise with the left in Spain, with their ambitions the Zionist leaders were as far removed as ever from the fight against international Fascism. It was during the Spanish conflict that their approaches to the Nazis reached their height with the request in December 1936 that the Nazis testify on their behalf before the Peel Commission and then the further offers, by the

Labour-dominated Haganah, to spy for the SS in 1937.

Only one Zionist tendency, the Hashomer Hatzair, ever tried to grapple with the deeper implications of the Spanish revolution. Its members had devoted considerable efforts to try to win over the British Independent Labour Party (ILP) to a pro-Zionist position, and they closely followed the fate of the ILP's sister party in Spain, the *Partido Obrero de Unificación Marxista* (POUM). The political failure of the Popular Front strategy in Spain prompted a broad critique of the Stalinists and Social Democrats. However, there is no evidence that any of their members went to Spain, certainly not in an official capacity, or that they did anything for the struggle there beyond the raising of an insignificant donation, in Palestine, for the POUM. Throughout the 1930s Hashomer's members took no part in political life, not even Jewish communal affairs, outside Palestine and were, in this regard, the most narrowly focused of all the Zionist groupings. Far from providing any theoretical leadership, on the Spanish question or on the larger problems of Fascism and Nazism, they lost followers to both the Stalinists and the Trotskyists as they offered nothing beyond isolationist and utopian rhetoric in the midst of a world catastrophe.[11]

In later years the bravery of the Jewish left-wingers who fought and died in Spain has been used to prove that 'the Jews' did not go as sheep to the slaughter during the Holocaust. Most zealous in pursuing this line have been those Jewish ex-Stalinists who have since sought to make their peace with Zionism. They cannot bring themselves to repudiate their venture or to claim that the Zionists were correct in denouncing them for fighting in Spain, but in retrospect they have sought to emphasise the 'national' Jewish aspect of their involvement and they have carefully counted every Jew in the long lists of those who fought. The majority of those who went to Spain went because they were committed Communists and they had become radicalised on the basis of many issues, of which Nazism was only one. Their bravery proves nothing about how 'the Jews' reacted to the Holocaust, any more than their involvement with the Communist movement implicates 'the Jews' in the systematic murder of the leaders of the POUM by the Soviet secret police.

Stalin's crimes in Spain are part of the Civil War and they cannot be minimised. Nevertheless, those leftists were fighting and dying in the front lines of the world struggle against international Fascism, while the Labour Zionists were receiving Adolf Eichmann as their guest in Palestine and offering to spy for the SS.

Notes

1. Albert Prago, *Jews in the International Brigades in Spain*, p. 6.

2. Charles Delzell, *Mussolini's Enemies*, pp. 147–61.

3. 'Anti-Nazi World Olympic Games in Spain on July 19', *Palestine Post* (13 July 1936), p. 1.

4. Prago, *Jews in the International Brigades in Spain*, pp. 6–7.

5. Morris Schappes, 'An Appeal to Zionists: Keep War Out of Palestine', *Jewish Life* (April 1938), p. 11.

6. Prago, *Jews in the International Brigades in Spain*, p. 5.

7. 'Communists is Israel', *Encyclopedia of Zionism and Israel*, vol. 2, p. 204.

8. Saul Wellman, 'Jewish Vets of the Spanish Civil War', *Jewish Currents* (June 1973), p. 10.

9. Berl Katznelson, *Revolutionary Constructivism* (1937), p. 22.

10. Wellman, 'Jewish Vets of the Spanish Civil War'.

11. Zvi Loker, 'Balkan Jewish Volunteers in the Spanish Civil War', *Soviet Jewish Affairs*, vol. VI, no. 2 (1976), p. 75.

18 ZIONISM'S FAILURE TO FIGHT NAZISM IN THE LIBERAL DEMOCRACIES

Zionism and the British Union of Fascists

There was no Western state that did not see the rise of pro-Nazi movements after 1933, but the extent of their influence varied from country to country. Although Western capital preferred Nazi Germany to a Communist take-over, there was never as much support in business circles for Hitler as for Mussolini. Hitler was too revanchist in his attitude toward Versailles, and Germany too potentially powerful, for there not to be strong ambivalence toward this latest anti-Communist saviour. Furthermore, Hitler's anti-Semitism was never popular with the capitalists. As long as the Jews were only a small element within their societies it was assumed that they would eventually be assimilated. The mass migration from Eastern Europe had revived anti-Semitism in the West, but if there was more prejudice against Jews in British and American ruling circles in 1933 than, say, 1883, none would go as far as Hitler. Nevertheless, during the Depression both Britain and America saw the rise of substantial anti-Semitic movements which physically threatened the Jewish communities.

In Britain the menace came from Sir Oswald Mosley and the British Union of Fascists (BUF). The Board of Deputies of British Jews tried to deal with the danger by ignoring it. From the beginning it told the Jews not to heckle at Mosley's meetings. The leaders insisted that Jews as such had no reason to quarrel with Fascism, and Neville Laski, President of the Board and chairman of the administrative committee of the Jewish Agency, emphasised that 'there is Fascism in Italy under which 50,000 Jews live in amity and safety . . . the Jewish community, not being a political body as such, should not be dragged into the fight against Fascism as such'.[1] The British Zionist Federation supported his position in the *Young Zionist* with an article on the question in its September 1934 issue. The Communists and the Independent Labour Party had been actively engaging the Mosleyites in the streets with at least 12,000 hostile demonstrators outside the BUF's Olympia rally on 7 June, and no less than 6,937 police had to protect 3,000 Fascists from 20,000 opponents in Hyde Park on 9 September. The East End Jewish community saw the Communist Party as its protector against the BUF supporters, and there was a growing mood amongst the Zionist youth to join the anti-Mosley campaign. However, the Zionist leadership was determined that this should not come about. What would happen if the Jews fought Mosley and the BUF won?

> Suppose that under a Fascist regime reprisals are used against anti-Fascists, all Jews must suffer . . . So the question looms up once more — *should* we? . . . Meanwhile there are three ideals which cry out aloud for the support of all Jews . . . 1. The unity of the Jewish People. 2. The need for a stronger Jewish pride. 3. The building of Eretz Yisrael. And we are wasting our time wondering whether we should join anti-Fascist societies![2]

The next issue restated their case more 'thoroughly and unmistakenly':

> Once we have realised that we cannot root out the evil, that our efforts so far have been in vain, we must do everything to defend ourselves against the outbursts of that infamous disease. The problem of anti-Semitism becomes a problem of our own education. Our defence is in the strengthening of our Jewish personality.[3]

In fact the Jewish masses largely ignored the Zionists' passive advice and backed the Communists. Eventually the Zionist position was reversed and some Zionists joined a community defence group called the Jewish People's Council (JPC), but anti-Fascism never became the priority for the Zionist movement.

The famous battle of Cable Street on 4 October 1936, when over 5,000 police failed to push a BUF march through 100,000 Jews and leftists, was the turning-point in the fight against Mosley. William Zukerman, one of the most distinguished Jewish journalists of the age and then still a Zionist, was present and wrote an account of it for New York's *Jewish Frontier*:

> no English-speaking city has ever seen anything like the scenes which marked this attempted demonstration . . . Those who like myself had the privilege of taking part in the event will never forget it. For this was one of those great communal acts of a mass of people aroused by a profound emotion or by a sense of outraged justice, which makes history . . . It was indeed the great epic of the Jewish East End.[4]

He reported that the demonstration had been called by the JPC which included 'synagogues, friendly societies, and *Landsmanschaften*' (immigrant societies). He wrote about the presence of Jewish ex-servicemen. He continued: 'The Communists and the Independent Labour Party must be given the credit for being the most active fighters of Mosley's Fascist anti-Semitism.'[5] Others among the local Zionists thought as he did and must have been there, but it is significant that a Zionist journalist, writing for a Zionist magazine, does not even mention the Zionists as being there. Gisela Lebzelter's book, *Political Anti-Semitism in England, 1918-1939*, mentions only that 'Zionist organisations' were present at the founding conference of the JPC on 26 July 1936.[6] She is silent about any further role they might have played in the campaign which lasted for several years. She confirms Zukerman's evaluation and fully acknowledges the leading role of the Communists.

The British Zionist movement of that day was not small. It sent 643 settlers to Palestine between 1933 and 1936. It had the strength to play a prominent role in the street-fighting, but in fact it did very little to defend the Jewish community, even after the abandonment of its 1934 stance. It was Cable Street – that is, the illegal resistance of the Jews, led primarily by the Communists and the ILP – that forced the government to stop protecting the 'rights' of the BUF and finally ban uniformed private militias.

Zionism and the German-American *Bund*

Fascist currents in the United States had been growing throughout the 1930s. The traditional Ku-Klux-Klan was still strong in the South, and many of the Irish in North America had become infected with Father Coughlan's clerical Fascism as Franco's armies smashed into Barcelona. Italian neighbourhoods saw organised Fascist parades, and many German immigrant organisations were under the influence of the Nazis' German-American '*Bund*'. Anti-Semitism was growing powerful, and the Bund determined on a show of their new strength with the announcement of a rally in New York's Madison Square Garden for 20 February 1939. Other rallies were to follow in San Francisco and Philadelphia. Would the Jews respond?

The Jews in New York numbered at least 1,765,000 (29.56 per cent of the population) and there were additional hundreds of thousands in the near suburbs; yet not one Jewish organisation thought to organise a counter-demonstration. One, the right-wing American Jewish Committee, even sent a letter to the Garden's management supporting the

Nazis' right to hold their meeting.[7] Only one group, the Trotskyists of the Socialist Workers Party (SWP), issued a call for a counter-demonstration. The SWP was a tiny group, with no more than a few hundred members, but as Max Shachtman the organiser of the action explained, it knew enough to 'mesh the small gear which it represents into the huge gear which the militant workers of New York represent, thus setting the latter into motion'.[8] The public found out about the SWP's demonstration when the city announced that the police would defend the Nazis against attack, and the press played up the possibility of violence.

There were two Yiddish daily newspapers then which were identified with Zionism: *Der Tog*, one of whose editors, Abraham Coralnik, had been a prime organiser of the anti-Nazi boycott; and *Der Zhournal*, whose manager, Jacob Fishman, had been one of the founders of the Zionist Organisation of America. Both papers opposed a protest against the presence of the Nazis. *Der Tog* begged its readers: 'Jews of New York, do not let your sorrows guide you! Avoid Madison Square Garden this evening. Don't come near the hall! Don't give the Nazis the chance to get the publicity they desire so much.'[9] The *Socialist Appeal*, the SWP's weekly paper, described the *Zhournal*'s plea as combining the same language with 'an additional nauseating touch of rabbinical piety'.[10] Nor was the response of the Zionist organisations any more militant. During the preparations for the encounter a group of young Trotskyists went to the Lower East Side headquarters of the Hashomer Hatzair, but they were told: 'Sorry we can't join you, our Zionist policy is to take no part in politics outside Palestine.'[11]

Then as now, the Hashomer claimed to be the left wing of Zionism, but only ten months before, Hashomer's magazine had defended their rigid policy of abstentionism:

> We can't divide our position as Jews from our position as socialists; in fact we place the stabilisation and normalisation of the first condition as a necessary preference to our work for the second condition . . . thus we don't take part in the socialist activities in which we could only participate as bourgeois, as an unstable, non-basic element, not imbedded in the true proletariat and speaking 'from above' . . . This does not call for the phrase-slinging, demonstration staging, castle building program of the usual 'radical' organisation . . . We are, and must be, essentially non-political.[12]

Over 50,000 people turned up at Madison Square Garden. Most were

Jews, but by no means all of them. A contingent from the Universal Negro Improvement Association, the nationalist followers of Marcus Garvey, came from Harlem. Although the CPUSA refused to support the demonstration through hatred for Trotskyism and their support for the Democratic mayor, Fiorello La Guardia, whose police were protecting the Bund, many of its multinational rank and file did attend. The area was the scene of a furious five-hour battle as the mounted police, part of a contingent of 1,780 armed police, repeatedly rode into the anti-Nazis. Although the anti-Nazis were unable to break the police lines, the victory was theirs. The 20,000 Nazis and Coughlanites in the Garden would have been mauled, had not the police been present.

The SWP immediately followed up its New York success by calling for another demonstration in Los Angeles on 23 February outside a Bund meeting at the *Deutsche Haus*. Over 5,000 people trapped the Fascists in their hall until the police came to their rescue. The Bund's offensive soon came to a halt and, thoroughly humiliated, they had to cancel their scheduled San Francisco and Philadelphia rallies.

The fact that, as late as February 1939, the SWP was alone in calling for a demonstration against a storm-trooper meeting in New York City testifies to a reality during the Nazi epoch: individual Zionists certainly took part in the battle of the Garden, but the entire range of Jewish organisations – political or religious – were never prepared to fight their enemies.

Notes

1. Gisela Lebzelter, *Political Anti-Semitism in England, 1918–1939*, p. 142.

2. Raphael Powell, 'Should Jews join Anti-Fascist Societies?', *Young Zionist* (London, August 1934), p. 6.

3. C.C.A., 'Should Jews join Anti-Fascist Societies?', *Young Zionist* (London, September 1934), pp. 12, 19.

4. William Zukerman, 'Blackshirts in London', *Jewish Frontier* (November 1936), p. 41.

5. Ibid., pp. 42–3.

6. Lebzelter, *Political Anti-Semitism in England*, p. 140.

7. 'Review of the Year 5699 – United States', *American Jewish Year Book, 1939–40*, p. 215.

8. Max Shachtman, 'In This Corner', *Socialist Appeal* (28 February 1939), p. 4.

9. 'The Craven Jewish Press', *Socialist Appeal* (24 February 1939), p. 4.

10. Ibid.

11. 'An End to Zionist Illusions!', *Socialist Appeal* (7 March 1939), p. 4.

12. Naomi Bernstein, 'We and the American Student Union', *Hashomer Hatzair* (April 1938), p. 16.

ZIONISM AND THE JAPANESE EAST ASIA
CO-PROSPERITY SPHERE

There were 19,850 Jews in China in 1935: one community in Shanghai
and another in Manchuria. The Shanghai community was dominated
by Sephardim of Iraqi origin, descendants of Elias Sassoon and his
clerks, who had set themselves up in business after the Opium War and
had grown fabulously wealthy in the development of Shanghai. The
Manchurian community at Harbin was of Russian origin and dated from
the construction of the tsarist Chinese Eastern Railway. It had later
been swollen by refugees from the Russian civil war.

Zionism was weak among the 'Arabs', who were one of the wealthi-
est ethnic communities in the world, as they had no interest in leaving
their good life. The Zionists in China were Russians. They, too, were
part of the imperialist presence and had no desire to assimilate into the
Chinese nation. Capitalist and middle class, they had no interest in
returning to the Soviet Union, and their Jewish identity was reinforced
by the presence of thousands of White Guard anti-Semitic refugees
throughout northern China. Zionism's separatism had a natural attraction, and within the movement Revisionism had the most appeal. The
Russian Jews were traders in an imperialist and militarised environment,
and the Betar combined an enthusiastic capitalist and imperialist
orientation with a militarism that was extremely practical in a context
of White Guards who had become lumpenbandits. Revisionism seemed
ideally suited to the harsh world they saw around them.

'An Active Part in the Construction of the New Order of East Asia'

The Harbin community thrived until the Japanese conquest of Manchuria in 1931. Many of the senior Japanese officers had taken part in
the 1918–22 expedition, which had fought the Bolsheviks by the side
of Admiral Alexander Kolchak's army in Siberia, and they had picked
up the White Guards' Jewish obsession. Soon the local White Russians
became a central prop for Japan's puppet 'Manchukuo' kingdom, and
many were directly recruited into the Japanese Army. White Russian
gangs, protected by the Japanese police, started extorting money from
the Jews, and by the mid-1930s most of Harbin's Jews had fled south

into Nationalist-held China, rather than endure the severe anti-Semitism.

The flight of the Jews seriously affected the Manchurian economy, and by 1935 the Japanese had to reverse their course. The military had their own distinctive version of anti-Semitism: there was a world Jewish conspiracy, and it was very powerful, but it could be made to work in the Japanese interest. The Japanese would dangle Manchukuo before world Jewry as a potential haven for German Jewish refugees and they would also take a pro-Zionist line. Then, it was believed, American Jews would invest in Manchukuo and mollify American opinion over the invasion of China and even the growing Japanese friendship with the Nazis. This was a forlorn hope, as the Jews had little influence on American policy; furthermore, Stephen Wise and the other American Jewish leaders were deeply opposed to collaborating with the Japanese, whom they saw as the inevitable allies of the Nazis.

The Japanese had much more success convincing Manchukuo's remaining Jews that it was in their interest to collaborate, not least by curbing the White Russians and closing down *Nash Put*, the organ of the Russian Fascist Association. The leader of Harbin's Jews was a pious doctor, Abraham Kaufman, who was deeply involved in the local community. He was greatly encouraged by the change in Japanese policy and, according to a Japanese Foreign Office report, in 1936-7 he and friends asked permission to set up a Far Eastern Jewish Council. Its aims were to organise all the Jews in the Orient and to disseminate propaganda on Japan's behalf, particularly in taking a stand with Japan against Communism.[1]

The first of three conferences of the Jewish communities in the Far East was held in Harbin in December 1937. The decor of these conferences is seen in photographs in the January 1940 issue of *Ha Dagel* (The Banner) which, in spite of its Hebrew title, was the Russian-language magazine of Manchukuo Revisionism. The platforms were always festooned with Japanese, Manchukuo and Zionist flags. Betarim acted as guards of honour.[2] The meetings were addressed by such people as General Higuchi of the Japanese Military Intelligence, General Vrashevsky for the White Guards, and Manchukuo puppet officials.[3]

The 1937 conference issued a resolution, which it sent to every major Jewish organisation in the world, pledging to 'cooperate with Japan and Manchukuo in building a new order in Asia'.[4] In return, the Japanese acknowledged Zionism as the Jewish national movement.[5] Zionism became a part of the Manchukuo establishment, and the Betar was given official colours and uniforms. There were moments of embarrassment in the new relationship, as, for example, when the Betar had to be excused from the parade celebrating Germany's recognition of Manchukuo.[6] But, in general, the local Zionists were quite happy with their cordial relationship with the Japanese regime. As late as 23 December 1939, an observer at the third conference reported 'joy all over town'.[7] The gathering passed several resolutions:

> This Convention hereby congratulates the Japanese Empire for her great enterprise of establishing peace in East Asia, and is convinced that when the fighting has ceased the people of East Asia will set on their national construction under the leadership of Japan.[8]

They went on to say that:

> The Third Conference of Jewish Communities calls upon the Jewish people to take an active part in the construction of the New Order of Eastern Asia, guided by the fundamental ideals laid down of a struggle against the Comintern in close collaboration with all nations.[9]

Verdict: the Zionists Collaborated with the Enemy of the Chinese People

Did the Manchukuo Zionists gain anything for the Jews by their collaboration with the Japanese? Herman Dicker, one of the leading specialists on Far Eastern Jewry, concluded that: 'It cannot be said, in retrospect, that the Far Eastern Conference made it easier for large numbers of refugees to settle in Manchuria. At best, only a few hundred refugees were permitted entry.'[10] In the last days of the Second World War the Soviets marched into Manchuria and Kaufman was arrested; ultimately he served eleven years in Siberia for collaboration. Certainly Manchukuo Zionism was deeply enmeshed in the Japanese structure in Manchukuo. The Zionists had not supported the Japanese conquest, but once the White Russians were curbed they no longer had any grievance against the Japanese presence. They had nothing to gain from a return of the Kuomintang, and they dreaded a Communist revolution. They were never pleased with Tokyo's connection with Berlin, but they hoped to temper that by using their influence with American Jewry to promote a compromise with Washington in the Pacific. There is no doubt that, despite their dissent from Japan's German policy, the Japanese saw the Manchurian Zionists as their willing collaborators.

Notes

1. Herman Dicker, *Wanderers and Settlers in the Far East*, pp. 45–7.
2. 'Otkrytiye Tryetyevo Syezda Yevryeiskikh Obshchin Dalnovo Vostoka', *Ha Dagel* (Harbin, 1 January 1940), pp. 21–8.
3. Dicker, *Wanderers and Settlers in the Far East*.
4. Marvin Tokayer and Mary Swartz, *The Fugu Plan*, p. 56.
5. David Kranzler, 'Japanese Policy towards the Jews, 1938–1941', *Forum on the Jewish People, Zionism and Israel* (Winter 1979), p. 71.
6. Dicker, *Wanderers and Settlers in the Far East*, p. 56.
7. David Kranzler, *Japanese, Nazis and Jews*, p. 220.
8. Kranzler, 'Japanese Policy towards the Jews', p. 77.
9. *Ha Dagel*, p. 26.
10. Dicker, *Wanderers and Settlers in the Far East*, p. 51.

20 POLAND, 1918-1939

The collapse of the three empires ruling Poland gave the Polish capitalists an independent state that they had long ceased to want. After the failure of the 1863 insurrection against tsarism, they had begun to see the Russian empire as a huge market and saw no reason to cut themselves off from it. The enemy, they argued, was not Russia but the Jews and the German Protestants who dominated 'their' home market. Nationalism became the preserve of the working class and its *Polska Partja Socjalistyczna* (PPS). The First World War saw the capitalist National Democrats, the so-called *Endeks*, backing the Tsar, and the right wing of the PPS, lead by Józef Pilsudski, setting up a Polish Legion for the Germans as the lesser of the two evils, since they intended to turn later on Germany. However, the imperialist collapse compelled the two factions to unite in order to set up a reborn Polish state. Pilsudski had left the PPS during the war and moved to the far right; thus the two camps could now agree on a programme of anti-Bolshevism and the recreation of a Polish empire. 'Marshall' Pilsudski had welcomed Jewish soldiers into his legion and still despised anti-Semitism, which he identified with tsarist backwardness; however, he had no control over those generals who came into the army via the Endeks' tsarist military, and he backed Petliura's pogromists. Murder and persecution of Jews reached such proportions that the Allies had to intervene and impose a minority-rights clause into the Polish constitution as a condition of recognition. Only when the Endeks realised that Jewish pressure could affect Warsaw's credit with foreign bankers did the pogroms tail off. But the end of the pogroms only meant that anti-Semitism was changing its form. The regime determined to 'Polonise' the economy, and thousands of Jews lost their jobs as the government took over the railways, cigarette and match factories and the distilleries.

In the early 1920s the Polish Jewish community amounted to 2,846,000 − 10.5 per cent of the population. It was far from politically homogeneous. On the far left were the Communists (KPP). Although the proportion of Jews in the KPP was always greater than 10.5 per cent, the Communists were never a significant proportion of the Jewish population. Although the PPS had always welcomed Jews into its ranks, it was imbued with Polish nationalism and was hostile to Yiddish; as a result the post-war PPS had little Jewish following. Instead the largest left-wing force among the Jews were the Yiddishists of the Bund, whose Polish section had survived its defeat in the Soviet Union, but they were still a distinct minority in the larger community. In the 1922 elections for the Polish Parliament (*Sejm*) they received only a fraction over 87,000 votes and were unable to win a single seat. On the right stood Agudas Yisrael, the party of traditional orthodoxy, with approximately one-third of the community loosely behind it. Its members took the position that the Talmud required loyalty to any Gentile regime that did not interfere with the Jewish religion. With their passive conservatism they could have no influence on any of the more educated elements who sought an activist solution to anti-Semitism. A small following, primarily intellectuals, followed the Folkists, a group of Diaspora Yiddish nationalists. All of these elements, though each for different reasons, were anti-Zionist.

The dominant political force within the Jewish community were the Zionists. They had taken six of the thirteen Jewish seats in the 1919 Sejm, and the 1922 elections gave them an opportunity to demonstrate that they could counter the still virulent anti-Semitism. The largest faction within the movement, led by Yitzhak Gruenbaum of the Radical Zionists, organised a 'Minorities Bloc'. The non-Polish nationalities constituted almost one-third of the population and Gruenbaum argued that if they united they could be the balance of power within the Sejm. The Bloc, comprising Gruenbaum's Zionist faction, together with elements from the German, Byelorussian and Ukrainian nationalities, had 66 of its candidates elected, including 17 Zionists. Superficially the pact seemed to have succeeded, but in fact it quickly demonstrated the divisions both within the Zionist movement and the minorities in general. The Ukrainian majority in Galicia refused to recognise the Polish state and boycotted the elections. None of the other nationalist politicians would support the Ukrainians' fight and the Galician Zionists, anxious not to antagonise the Poles, stood in the election as rivals to the Minorities Bloc. The Galician Zionists won 15 seats, but as their success was due to the Ukrainian abstention they could not pretend to represent the region. Even within the Minorities Bloc there was no commitment to long-term unity, and after the election it fell apart. There were now 47 Jews in both houses of the Sejm, 32 of them Zionists, but their electoral opportunism had discredited them.

The failure of the Minority Bloc opened the way for another adventure to be organised by the Galician General Zionist leaders, Leon Reich and Osias Thon. In 1925 they negotiated a pact, the *'Ugoda'* (compromise) with Wladyslaw Grabski, the anti-Semitic Prime Minister. Grabski was seeking an American loan, and needed to prove that he was not an unmovable fanatic. The deal with these two Zionists made it look, at least to unwary foreigners, as if his regime was capable of change. In fact the government only agreed to minor concessions: Jewish conscripts could have kosher kitchens and Jewish students would not have to write on Saturdays as all other students had to do. Even within the Zionist movement Thon and Reich were seen as having betrayed the Jewish community.[1]

Anti-Semitism was only a part of the reactionary line of the post-1922 governments, and the majority of the people, including the Jews, backed Pilsudski's May 1926 *coup d'état* in the hope of a change for the better. The entire Jewish Sejm delegation voted for him for President on 31 May.[2] The position of the Jews did not improve, but at least Pilsudski made no efforts to increase discrimination and his police suppressed anti-Semitic riots until his death in 1935. The 1928 Sejm election was the last more or less free national election in Poland. The General Zionists were again split: Gruenbaum's faction entered another Minority Bloc, and the Galicians supported their own candidate. Pilsudski was popular with conservative Jews for putting down attacks and many voted for his supporters out of gratitude. This, together with the entry of the Galician Ukrainians into the electoral arena, served to reduce the Jewish representation to 22, of whom 16 were Zionists.[3] By 1930 the Pilsudski regime had tightened into an intense police state with severe brutality towards political prisoners. Pilsudski kept the Sejm alive, but he rigged the election and ruled above it and the results of the 1930 elections were largely meaningless. The Jewish representation declined again, to eleven, six of whom were Zionists.

With the intensification of the dictatorship the Zionist parliamentarians showed more interest in the anti-Pilsudski opposition, but these tendencies were brought short by Hitler's victory in neighbouring Germany. Polish Zionism had originally underestimated the Nazis. Before he came to power the Zionist daily newspapers *Haint, Der Moment* and *Nowy Dziennik* had assured their readers that once he took office Hitler would be restrained in his anti-Semitism by the presence of the conservatives like von Papen and Hugenburg in his coalition Cabinet. They thought the needs of the German economy would soon make him adopt a more moderate approach.[4] A few weeks of the New Order destroyed such fantasies and the Polish Zionists' next worry was that the Nazis' success would trigger a wave of extremism in Poland. All interest in an opposition bloc ceased, and

Pilsudski became the man of the hour again as he made sounds against the regime in Berlin.[5] The Zionists' sharp reversal of opinion toward the dictator brought cries of protest from the opposition parties resisting Pilsudski. The Jewish Telegraphic Agency reported on a debate on the Jewish question in the Sejm on 4 November 1933:

> Deputy Rog, the leader of the Peasant Party . . . denounced the anti-Jewish attitude of Hitler Germany. The crime which is being committed against the German Jews is a world crime, he said. Poland will never, he declared, take an example from Hitler Germany. He could not understand, however, he went on, how Jewish politicians who are fighting against German dictatorship can reconcile with their conscience the support they are giving in Poland to the Polish dictatorship. It is not a good thing, he said, for the Polish masses to bear in mind how the Jews are supporting their oppressors.[6]

On 26 January 1934 Pilsudski signed a ten-year peace pact with Hitler. That same year the Warsaw authorities, observing the impotence of the League of Nations in dealing with the German problem, decided to repudiate the Minorities Treaty signed under duress at Versailles. Nahum Goldmann met Józef Beck, the Polish Foreign Minister, in Geneva on 13 September 1934, to try to persuade him to change his mind, but without success. As usual the WZO refused to organise mass protest demonstrations abroad, and relied instead on diplomatic intervention from London and Rome.[7] The Polish Zionists remained loyal to Pilsudski until his death on 12 May 1935, and then Osias Thon and Apolinary Hartglas, the President of the Polish Zionist Organisation, proposed a 'Pilsudski Forest' in Palestine in his memory.[8] The Palestinian Revisionists announced that they were going to build an immigrants' hostel to be named in his honour.[9]

'The Workers have not been Contaminated'

Hitler's victory excited the extremists among the Polish anti-Semites, but as long as the marshall lived his police were under strict orders to repress any kind of street agitation. However, his sucessors, the 'Colonels', could no longer afford politically to maintain his policy. They lacked his prestige and knew that they had to adopt a policy with popular appeal or they would be overthrown. Anti-Semitism was an obvious choice as it pandered to the traditional prejudices of much of the Polish middle class. However, they still tried to maintain order; restrictions on the Jews would have to proceed strictly according to law. The hard-core anti-Semites of the Endeks and their offshoot, the pro-Nazi National Radicals or *Naras*, understood that the Colonels' capitulation to the anti-Semitic mood stemmed from their weakness, and they frequently defied the police. The country soon was swept by a wave of pogroms. The outrages frequently started in the universities, where the Endeks and Naras tried to establish 'ghetto benches' and a *numerus clausus* for the Jews. Soon a boycott of Jewish stores was set into effect and roving bands of Jew-haters began terrorising Poles who patronised Jewish shops. Street assaults on Jews became an everyday occurrence.

The Jewish resistance to the pogromists was largely the work of the Bundists. Although they were numerically much smaller than the Zionists until the mid-1930s, nevertheless they had always been the dominant force in the Jewish labour movement. Now they organised 24-hour flying squads at their Warsaw headquarters. On hearing of an attack their *Ordener-grupe* would sally out, sticks and pipes in hand to enter into combat. At times there were hundreds of Bundists, Jewish unionists and their friends from the PPS militia, the *Akcja Socjalistyczna*, engaged in pitched battles with the Endek and Nara supporters.[10] The most important of these street fights was the battle in the Saxonian Garden, Warsaw's famous park, in 1938, when the Bund found out that the Naras planned a pogrom in the park and the streets surrounding it. Bernard Goldstein, the leader of the Ordener-grupe, later described the battle in his memoirs.

We organised a large group of resistance fighters which we concentrated around the large square near the Iron Gate. Our plan was to entice the hooligans to that square, which was closed off on three sides, and to block the fourth exit, and thus have them in a trap where we could give battle and teach them an appropriate lesson ... When we had a fair number of Nara hooligans in the square ... we suddenly emerged from our hiding places, surrounding them from all sides ... ambulances had to be called.[11]

Earlier, on 26 September 1937, the Naras bombed the Bund's headquarters. The Bund promptly put together a group of thirty: ten Bundists, ten members of a Zionist splinter group, the Left Poale Zion, and ten Poles from the PPS. They went to the Nara's headquarters. The Poles, pretending to be repairmen, went in first and cut the phone wires. Then the rest of the attackers raided the place. Hyman Freeman, one of the Bundists, later told of the raid:

> There was a fight, but they really did not have a chance to put up much of a resistance. We attacked them in blitzkreig fashion. We really ruined the place and beat them up quite badly . . . It was really an extraordinary piece of work.[12]

Although there is a common misconception that anti-Semitism was endemic to all classes in Polish society, the evidence shows that anti-Semitism was primarily a middle-class and, to a much lesser extent, a peasant phenomenon. The bulk of the Polish working class followed the PPS, and they understood from the beginning that the Bund's fight was their fight and their aid to the beleaguered Jews was, as in the retaliation against the Naras, vital. In 1936 the *Palestine Post* told its readers that whenever the Fascist student gangs would swarm out of their sanctuaries in the universities to start a pogrom:

> the non-Jewish Polish workers and students speedily come to the aid of the Jews. Recently the Polish Socialist Party [PPS] has arranged a number of huge propaganda meetings . . . very stirring addresses were heard from non-Jewish Poles who seemed pathetically eager to disassociate themselves from the 'Endek' rowdyism.[13]

Jacob Lestchinsky, one of the leading Zionist scholars of the day, described the Polish labour movement's mentality to the readers of *Jewish Frontier* in a July 1936 article:

> the Polish labor party may justly boast that it has successfully immunised the workers against the anti-Jewish virus, even in the poisoned atmosphere of Poland. Their stand on the subject has become almost traditional. Even in cities and districts that seem to have been thoroughly infected by the most revolting type of anti-Semitism the workers have not been contaminated.[14]

There were others who were pro-Jewish. Among the Ukrainian masses, anti-Semitism had grown alarmingly as many nationalists had become pro-Nazi. They deluded themselves that Germany, out of hostility to both the Polish Colonels and Stalin, would help them win their independence at some unspecified time in the future. However, the tiny stratum of Ukrainian students, who had to confront the chauvinism of the Polish middle class in its university strongholds, never became infected with the folk anti-Semitism. They understood what would happen to their career chances, if the Endeks and Naras triumphed. In December 1937 the *Palestine Post* reported that:

> In Wilno and in Lemberg [Lvov] Universities the White Russian and Ukrainian students have joined almost in a body the anti-Ghetto front and are helping the Jews in their fight against the medieval measures.[15]

The peasants were divided on the Jewish question. The richer ones tended toward anti-Semitism, particularly in western Poland. In the south, and to a lesser degree in the central region, the rural masses followed the Peasant Party. In 1935 the Peasants had taken an inconsistent position, simultaneously insisting on the principle of democratic rights for all Jews in the country and calling for Polonisation of the economy and Jewish emigration to Palestine and other places.[16] However, by 1937 the party was insisting that the anti-Semitic campaign was nothing but a ruse to divert attention from the real political issues, particularly the need for land reform. In August 1937 a large proportion of the peasantry came out in a ten-day general strike. Although the police killed fifty demonstrators, in many areas the strike was complete. Alexander Erlich of Columbia University, then a Bund youth leader, reports that: 'During the strike you could see bearded Chassidim on the picket lines together with peasants.'[17] The government was only able to survive because the old-guard Peasant leaders were unwilling to work with the socialists.

The Bund and the PPS involved the masses in the struggle against the anti-Semites. The murder of two Jews and serious injury to dozens more in Przytyk on 9 March 1936 compelled a definitive response, and the Bund called a half-day general strike for 17 March with the PPS supporting the action. All Jewish businesses — a significant proportion of the economic life of the country — stopped. The PPS unions in Warsaw and most of the major cities supported the strike, and much of Poland closed down. It was truly the 'Sabbath of Sabbaths!' as it was described in the Jewish press.

In March 1938 the Bund declared a two-day protest strike against the ghetto benches and the continual terror in the universities. Despite Fascist attacks, which were driven off, many of Poland's most distinguished academics joined the Jewish community and the PPS unions in the streets, a magnificent accomplishment in a country where mothers quietened their children by threatening to have a Jew take them away in a sack.

Electoral Victories that Lead Nowhere

The masses began moving towards the Bund in the Jewish community elections in 1936, and the Bund and the PPS both registered a strong increase in support in the municipal elections that same year. However, here the severe limitations of the PPS were sharply revealed. In Lodz, Poland's most industrialised city, the PPS refused to unite electorally with the Bund, because its leadership was concerned that they would lose votes if they identified with the Jews. Nevertheless, in practice, the two parties did ally themselves in daily working life and they continued to gain support. The Social Democratic reformists of the PPS could never abandon their electorally opportunist mentality and again they refused to run a joint slate in the city council elections of December 1938 and January 1939. The Bund had to run separately, but they then cross-endorsed in areas where either was a minority. *De facto* allied, they won majorities in Lodz, Cracow, Lvov, Vilna and other cities, and prevented a government majority in Warsaw. The PPS won 26.8 per cent of the vote, the Bund another 9.5 per cent and, although they were only loosely combined, their 36.3 per cent was seen as socially much more influential than the 29.0 per cent for the Colonels' slate or the Endeks' 18.8 per cent. The *New York Times* wrote of the 'striking victory' of the left, and the loss of ground suffered by the deeply divided anti-Semites.[18] In the Jewish districts the Bund devastated the Zionists and received 70 per cent of the vote, which gave them 17 of the 20 Jewish seats in Warsaw with the Zionists holding only one seat.[19]

'I Wish that a million Polish Jews might be Slaughtered'

The Jewish masses began abandoning the Zionists in the late 1930s. When the British cut the immigration quotas after the Arab revolt, Palestine no longer seemed a solution to their problems. Polish emigration to Palestine fell from 29,407 in 1935 to 12,929 in 1936, and to 3,578 in 1937, and finally to 3,346 in 1938. However, there was another basic reason for the move away from Zionism. The movement was discredited by the fact that all the anti-Semites, from the government to the Naras, favoured emigration to Palestine. 'Palestine' took on a morbid quality in Polish political life. When Jewish deputies spoke in the Sejm the government and Endek representatives would interrupt with shouts of 'go to Palestine!'[20] Everywhere the anti-Jewish boycott pickets carried the same sign: *'Moszku idz do Palestyny!'* (Kikes to Palestine!)[21] In 1936 the Endek delegates to the Piotrkow city council typically made a symbolic gesture proposing an allocation of one *zloty* 'to further the mass-emigration of the Jews of Piotrkow to Palestine'.[22] On 31 August 1937, *ABC*, the organ of the Naras, declared:

> Palestine alone will not solve the question but it may be the beginning of mass emigration of Jews from Poland. Consequently it must not be neglected by Polish foreign policy. The voluntary emigration of Jews to Palestine can reduce the tension of Polish Jewish relations.[23]

The Colonels were hardly in need of any prompting from the Naras; they had always been enthusiastic philo-Zionists and warmly supported the Peel Commission's proposed partition of Palestine. Weizmann met Józef Beck in September 1937 and was assured that, when the frontiers of the new state were defined, Warsaw would do its utmost to guarantee the Zionists the largest territory possible.[24]

The Zionist movement had never believed it was possible for Poland's Jews to solve their problems on Polish soil. Even in the 1920s, while he was manoeuvring with the other national minorities, Gruenbaum had become notorious for his proclamations that the Jews were just so much 'excess baggage' in the country and that 'Poland has a million more Jews than it can possibly accommodate'.[25] When the British discovered Abba Achimeir's diary after the Arlosoroff murder, they found that view expressed more forcefully: 'I wish that a million Polish Jews might be slaughtered. Then they might realize that they are living in a ghetto.'[26]

The Zionists consistently played down the efforts of the PPS to help the Jews. The *Palestine Post*, in the same article in January 1936 which recorded the workers' street battles against the anti-Semites, wrote that 'it is decidedly worth while putting on record this hopeful manifestation slight as it admittedly is'.[27] In June 1937 the American *Labor Zionist Newsletter* reiterated this scepticism:

> It is true that the PPS is now showing its soldarity with the Jewish

masses in Poland with unprecedented courage and vigor. But it is very doubtful whether the Socialists and genuinely liberal elements in Poland are in a position to muster enough effective resistance to block the forward march of the Polish brand of Fascism.[28]

In fact, although the Labour Zionists were supposed to be a part of the same Socialist International as the PPS, they hoped to be able to ignore the latter and negotiate a deal directly with the enemies of the Polish socialists. In an editorial in its 20 September 1936 issue the *Newsletter* wrote:

> Attention was attracted in the world of international politics by a statement that the Polish government is preparing to press its demand for colonies . . . Realistic observers are of the opinion that the question of the redistribution of colonies is on the way to becoming a vital one. For this reason such plans and proposals on the part of countries with large Jewish populations should be given due attention by Jewish world leadership.[29]

In reality, Poland had no possibility of 'a place in the sun', but in giving credence to the lunatic fringe of the Polish right the Zionists hoped to persuade world opinion that the answer to Polish anti-Semitism lay outside the country.

Although the WZO was eager to accommodate the Warsaw regime, after the British had abandoned the Peel partition plan and cut the immigration quotas, its followers no longer had anything to offer the Polish Colonels and it was the Revisionists who became the most intimate collaborators with the regime. Jacob de Haas summed up the Revisionists' attitude to the Polish Jews in October 1936:

> Of course it is unpleasant to be told that the Jews are anywhere 'superfluous'. On the other hand to be thinskinned about the phrases that are being used, and will be used, in matters of this kind is to expose oneself to unnecessary pain. We ought to be capable of swallowing a whole lot more if a healthy result is produced.[30]

Jabotinsky had proposed to 'evacuate' 1½ million Jews from Eastern Europe over a ten-year period, and most of these would come from Poland. He tried to put a good gloss on this surrender to anti-Semitism, but in 1937 he admitted that he had difficulty in finding an appropriate term for his proposition:

I had first thought of 'Exodus', of a second 'departure from Egypt'. But this will not do. We are engaged in politics, we must be able to approach other nations and demand the support of other states. And that being so, we cannot submit to them a term that is offensive, that recalls Pharaoh and his ten plagues. Besides, the word 'Exodus' evokes a terrible picture of horrors, the picture of a whole nation-mass-like disorganised mob that flees panic stricken.[31]

In 1939 the Revisionists sent Robert Briscoe, then a *Fianna Fail* member of the Irish Parliament (later famous as the Jewish Lord Mayor of Dublin) to make a proposition to Colonel Beck:

On behalf of the New Zionist Movement . . . I suggest that you ask Britain to turn over the Mandate for Palestine to you and make it in effect a Polish colony. You could then move all your unwanted Polish Jews into Palestine. This would bring great relief to your country, and you would have a rich and growing colony to aid your economy.[32]

The Poles did not waste their time asking for the Mandate. It will be recalled that Jabotinsky planned to invade Palestine in 1939. That operation was first planned in 1937, when the Poles agreed to train the Irgun and arm it for an invasion of Palestine in 1940.[33] In spring 1939 the Poles set up a guerrilla training camp for their Revisionist clients at Zakopane in the Tatra Mountains.[34] Twenty-five members of the Irgun from Palestine were taught the arts of sabotage, conspiracy and insurrection by Polish officers.[35] Weapons for 10,000 men were provided, and the Revisionists were preparing to smuggle the guns into Palestine when the Second World War broke out. Avraham Stern, the prime mover behind the Zakopane camp, told the trainees that a passage to Palestine through Turkey and Italy was a 'matter of diplomatic negotiations that have possibilities', but there is no evidence that the Italians, and certainly not the Turks, were involved.[36] Stern was one of the hard-core Fascists within Revisionism, and he thought that if Mussolini could see that they really meant to challenge the British he could be induced to revive his pro-Zionist policy. The invasion had originally been planned as a serious bid for power, and when Jabotinsky proposed to turn it into a symbolic gesture aimed at creating a government-in-exile there was a bitter debate within the Irgun command. The discussion was cut short by their arrest by the British on the eve of the war.

It will be difficult to believe that any Jewish group could have seriously concocted such a utopian plan and persuaded the Poles to back them. However, it did have the advantage to the regime of keeping thousands of Betarim out of action against the anti-Semites. They boxed and wrestled and did a little shooting but, unless they were attacked, they never fought the Fascists. According to Shmuel Merlin, who was then in Warsaw as the NZO's Secretary-General:

> It is absolutely correct to say that only the Bund waged an organised fight against the anti-Semites. We did not consider that we had to fight in Poland. We believed the way to ease the situation was to take the Jews out of Poland. We had no spirit of animosity.[37]

The Failure of the Socialists and the Betrayal of the Zionists

It must not be thought that the Polish workers were all strong sup-porters of the Jews. The PPS was hostile to Yiddish and looked upon the fanatic Hasids with good-natured contempt. However, the party always had assimilated Jewish leaders, as with Herman Liebermann, its most prominent parliamentarian, and many of its leaders were married to Jews. In 1931 the PPS made a momentous offer to the Bund: the PPS militia, the Akcja Socjalistczyna, would protect the Bund's section of their joint May Day demonstration and the Bund's Ordener-grupe would protect the PPS's contingent. The Bund turned down the magnificent proposal. It appreciated the spirit of the gesture, but declined on the grounds that it was the duty of Jews to learn to protect themselves.[38] The unwillingness of the leaders of the PPS to build a united front with the Bund for the last crucial municipal elections was not based on their own anti-Semitism but on a Polish application of the uniformly baneful Social Democratic preoccupation with winning votes. Instead of trying to win the votes of the most back-ward workers, they should have been calling for the unity of the most advanced workers and peasants for an assault on the regime. But by its incapacity to recognise the immense potentials that flowed from the 1931 defence proposal, and its general inability to understand that the Jews could never irrevocably defeat their foes — nor attain socialism — with their own party, isolated from the Polish working class, the Bund also contributed to the nationalist rift in the working class. Both parties were reformist in essence; the Colonels had suffered a severe defeat in the municipal elections, but they had no forward thrust, and they waited passively for the regime to fall of its own weight. In the interests of 'national unity' they called off their 1939 May Day rallies when Poland's only possible salvation lay in their militantly putting the masses before the regime with the demand for the arming of the entire people.

But if the Bund and the PPS failed the ultimate test, at least they did fight the Polish anti-Semites. The Zionists did not. On the contrary, they competed for the support of the enemies of the Jews.

Notes

1. Ezra Mendelsohn, 'The Dilemma of Jewish Politics in Poland: Four Responses' in B. Vago and G. Mosse (eds.), *Jews and non-Jews in Eastern Europe*, p. 208.

2. Joseph Rothschild, *Pilsudski's Coup D'Etat*, p. 207.

3. 'Zionism in Poland', *Encyclopedia of Zionism and Israel*, vol. II, p. 899.

4. Nana Sagi and Malcolm Lowe, 'Research Report: Pre-War Reactions to Nazi anti-Jewish Policies in the Jewish Press', *Yad Vashem Studies*, vol. XII, p. 401.

5. Pawel Korzec, 'Anti-Semitism in Poland as an Intellectual, Social and Political Movement', *Studies on Polish Jewry, 1919-1939*, p. 79.

6. 'Jewish Debate in Polish Parliament', *Jewish Weekly News* (Melbourne, 29 December 1933), p. 5.

7. Zosa Szajkowski, 'Western Jewish Aid and Intercession for Polish Jewry, 1919-1939', *Studies on Polish Jewry*, p. 231.

8. Ezra Mendelsohn, 'The Dilemma of Jewish Politics in Poland: Four Responses', p. 26.

9. 'Pilsudski Wood', *Palestine Post* (16 May 1935), p. 1.

10. Leonard Rowe, 'Jewish Self-Defense: A Response to Violence', *Studies on Polish Jewry*, p. 121.

11. Ibid., p. 123.

12. Ibid., p. 124.

13. 'The Anti-Jewish Excesses in Poland', *Palestine Post* (29 January 1936), p. 3.

14. Jacob Lestchinsky, 'Night over Poland', *Jewish Frontier* (July 1936), pp. 11-12.

15. William Zukerman, 'Jews in Poland', *Palestine Post* (1 December 1937), p. 4.

16. Joel Cang, 'The Opposition Parties in Poland and their Attitudes toward the Jews and the Jewish Problem', *Jewish Social Studies* (April 1939), p. 248.

17. Alexander Erlich *et al.*, *Solidarnosc, Polish Society and the Jews*, p. 13.

18. 'Democrats win in Polish Elections', *New York Times* (20 December 1938); and *The Times* (London, 20 December 1938).

19. Bernard Johnpoll, *The Politics of Futility*, p. 224; and Edward Wynot, *Polish Politics in Transition*, pp. 234-5.

20. *American Jewish Year Book 1937-1938*, p. 392.

21. S. Andreski, 'Poland' in S. Woolf (ed.), *European Fascism*, p. 179.

22. 'Endeks propose mass emigration of Jews', *World Jewry* (London, 13 March 1936), p. 5.

23. 'The Jewish Situation in Poland during August and September 1937',

Information Bulletin (American Jewish Committee), nos. 8–9 (1937), p. 3.

24. 'Agreement Outside Mandate Sought', *Palestine Post* (15 September 1937), p. 8.

25. Szajkowski, ' "Reconstruction" vs. "Palliative Relief" in American Jewish Overseas Work (1919–1939)', *Jewish Social Studies* (January 1970), p. 24.

26. *Jewish Daily Bulletin* (8 September 1933), p. 1.

27. *Palestine Post* (29 January 1936), p. 3.

28. 'Poland', *Labor Zionist Newsletter* (4 June 1937), pp. 1–2.

29. 'The Diaspora', *Labor Zionist Newsletter* (20 September 1936), p. 10.

30. Jacob de Haas, 'They are willing to go', *Chicago Jewish Chronicle* (2 October 1936), p. 1.

31. Vladimir Jabotinsky, 'Evacuation – Humanitarian Zionism' (1937), published in *Selected Writings of Vladimir Jabotinsky* (South Africa, 1962), p. 75.

32. Robert Briscoe, *For the Life of Me*, p. 28.

33. J. Bower Bell, *Terror Out of Zion*, p. 28.

34. Daniel Levine, *David Raziel, The Man and His Times*, pp. 259–60.

35. Nathan Yalin-Mor, 'Memories of Yair and Etzel', *Jewish Spectator* (Summer 1980), p. 33.

36. Levine, *David Raziel*, p. 260.

37. Author's interview with Shmuel Merlin, 16 September 1980.

38. Rowe, 'Jewish Self-Defense', pp. 113–14.

As soon as the Nazis invaded Poland, the Jews were doomed. Hitler intended that the conquest of Poland would provide 'lebensraum' for German colonists. Some Poles, the racially better stock, would be forcibly assimilated to the German nation, the rest would be ruthlessly exploited as slave labourers. Given these radical goals for the Slav population, it was obvious that there could be no place for the Jews in the expanded Reich. The Nazis permitted, and even forcibly encouraged, Jewish emigration from Germany and Austria until late in 1941, but from the beginning emigration from Poland was reduced to a trickle in order that the flow from Greater Germany would not be obstructed. At first the occupiers allowed American Jews to send in food packages, but that was only because Hitler needed time to organise the new territory and conduct the war.

The Working Class does not Capitulate

Within days of the German invasion the Polish government declared Warsaw an open city, and ordered all able-bodied men to retreat to a new line on the River Bug. The Bund's central committee considered whether it would be better for the Jews to fight to the end in Warsaw rather than see their families fall to Hitler, but they doubted that the Jews would follow them in resisting, nor would the Poles tolerate their bringing ruin to the city; thus they decided to fall back with the army. They appointed a skeleton committee to remain, and ordered all other party members to follow the military eastward. Alexander Erlich has explained their position:

> It must sound naive, because we now know that Stalin was about to invade from the East, but we thought the lines would stabilize. We felt certain we would be more effective even with a beleaguered army than we could ever be in territory held by the Germans.[1]

When the Bund Committee drew near the Bug, they heard that the evacuation order had been countermanded. Mieczyslaw Niedzialkowski and Zygmunt Zaremba of the PPS had convinced General Tshuma, the military commandant, that it was psychologically crucial for the future resistance movement that Poland's capital should not fall without a fight. The Bund instructed two of its senior leaders, Victor Alter and Bernard Goldstein, to return to Warsaw. The road back was hopelessly clogged, and they decided to head south and then try to approach Warsaw again from that position. They got as far as Lublin, where they split up. Alter never succeeded, but Goldstein did reach Warsaw on 3 October. By then the city had fallen, but only after a determined defence by troops from the surrounding area and worker battalions organised by the PPS and the Bund.

The Zionist Leadership Disperses

Most of the prominent Zionist leaders left Warsaw when the army evacuated the city but, unlike the Bundists, none returned when they heard that the capital was to be held. After the Soviets crossed the border, they either escaped into Romania or fled northward to Vilna, which they heard had been handed over to Lithuania by the Soviets. Among the refugees were Moshe Sneh, the President of the Polish Zionist Organisation, Menachem Begin, then the leader of Polish Betar, and his friends Nathan Yalin-Mor and Israel Scheib (Eldad).[2] Sneh went to Palestine and was to command the Haganah from 1941 to 1946. Begin was eventually arrested in Lithuania by the Russians and, after an ordeal in Stalin's camps in Siberia, he was released when Germany invaded the Soviet Union. He left the USSR as a soldier in a Polish army-in-exile and arrived in Palestine in 1942; later he headed the Irgun in the 1944 revolt against Britain. Nathan Yalin-Mor and Israel Scheib (Eldad) later rose to become two of the three commanders of the 'Stern Gang', a group which had split from the Irgun. Of the Zionists only the youth of Hashomer and HeChalutz sent organisers back into the Polish maelstrom. The others sought, and some obtained, Palestine certificates and left the carnage of Europe.

Did they abandon their people to push on to Palestine? With Begin the record is clear. He told an interviewer, in 1977:

> With a group of friends, we reached Lvov [Lemberg] in a desperate and vain effort to try to cross the border and try to reach Eretz Yisroel − but we failed. At this point, we heard that Vilna would be made the capital of an independent Republic of Lithuania by the Russians.[3]

When Begin was arrested, in 1940, he was intending to continue on his journey to Palestine and he had no plans to return to Poland. In his book, *White Nights*, he wrote that he told his Russian jailors in Vilna's Lukishki Prison that:

I had received a *laissez-passer* from Kovno for my wife and myself. and also visas for Palestine. We were on the point of leaving, and it is only my arrest that prevented me from doing so.

A few pages later he added: 'We were about to leave . . . but we had to surrender our places to a friend.'[4]

Two of his most recent biographers, fellow Revisionists Lester Eckman and Gertrude Hirschler, have recorded that he was condemned by his movement for his flight, but they claim he thought of returning:

he received a letter from Palestine criticizing him for having fled from the Polish capital when other Jews were stranded there. As captain of Betar, the letter stated, he should have been the last to abandon the sinking ship. Begin was torn by feelings of guilt; it took strenuous efforts on the part of his comrades to keep him from this impulsive act, which probably would have cost him his life.[5]

Begin does not refer to this in *White Nights*, but explains that 'there is no doubt that I would have been one of the first to be executed had the Germans caught me in Warsaw'.[6] In fact there was no special persecution against Zionists in general or Revisionists in particular in Warsaw or anywhere else. On the contrary, even as late as 1941, after the invasion of the Soviet Union, the Germans appointed Josef Glazman, the head of the Lithuanian Betar, as the inspector of the Jewish police in the Vilna ghetto. Begin wanted to go to Palestine because he had been the one at the 1938 Betar Congress who had shouted the loudest for its immediate conquest. An interesting postscript to this emerged on 2 March 1982, during a debate in the Israeli Parliament. Begin solemnly asked: 'How many people in Parliament are there who had to wear the Star of David? I am one.'[7] Begin fled from the Nazis and there were no yellow stars in Lithuania when he was there as a refugee.

The Judenrats

Upon their arrival in Warsaw the Germans found Adam Czerniakow, a Zionist and President of the Association of Jewish Artisans, as the head of the rump of the Jewish community organisation and they ordered him to set up a *Judenrat* (Jewish Council).[8] In Lodz, Poland's second city, Chaim Rumkowski, also a minor Zionist politician, was similarly designated. They were not, in any way, authorised representatives of the Zionist movement, and both were insignificant figures prior to the war. Not all the councils were headed by Zionists; some were headed by assimilationalist intellectuals or rabbis and even, in one city (Piotrkow), by a Bundist. However, more Zionists were chosen for membership or leadership of the puppet councils than all the Agudists, Bundists and Communists combined. The Nazis most despised the pious Hasids of the Aguda, and they knew the Bundists and the Communists would never act as their tools. By 1939 the Nazis had a number of dealings with the Zionists in Germany and also in Austria and Czechoslovakia, and they knew that they would find little resistance in their ranks.

The vacuum of experienced Zionist leadership was augmented by the fact that for some months the Nazis permitted certificate-holders to leave Poland for Palestine. The WZO used the opportunity to pull out more of the local leadership, including Apolinary Hartglas, who had preceded Sneh as head of the Zionist Organisation. In his *Diary* Czerniakow told how he had been offered one of the certificates and how he had contemptuously refused to abandon his post.[9] In February 1940 he recorded how he raged at one man who left when he came to pay his final farewells:

> You louse, I will not forget you, you louse, how you pretended to act as a leader and are now running away with the others like you, leaving the masses in this horrid situation.[10]

Yisrael Gutman, one of the scholars at Israel's Yad Vashem Holocaust Institute, has written on this subject.

> It is true that some of the leaders had good reason to fear for their personal safety in a country which had fallen to the Nazis. At the same time there was in the departure of these leaders an element of panic, which was not counterbalanced by an attempt to concern themselves with their replacement and the continuation of their former activities by others ... Those left behind were mostly second or third rank leaders, who were not always capable of tackling the acute problems of the times, and they also lacked vital liaison

contacts with the Polish public and its leadership. The leaders who remained included some who held aloof from underground activity and tried to obliterate traces of their past.[11]

Some scholars have shown that not all leaders or members of the Jewish Councils collaborated, but the moral atmosphere within them was extremely corrupting. Bernard Goldstein, in his memoir *The Stars Bear Witness*, described the Warsaw Council in the early months before the establishment of the ghetto; the council, in order to mitigate the terror of the press gangs, provided the Germans with labour battalions. They set up a subpoena system. Everyone was supposed to serve in rotation, but:

> the operation very quickly became corrupt . . . rich Jews paid fees running into thousands of zlotys to be freed from forced labor. The Judenrat collected such fees in great quantity, and sent poor men to the working battalions in place of the wealthy.[12]

By no means every branch of the council apparatus was corrupt. They applied themselves briskly to education and social welfare, but few councils did anything to engender a spirit of resistance. Isaiah Trunk, one of the most careful students of the Judenrats, succinctly summed them up.

> I explicitly said that most of the Judenrats had a negative approach to the matter of resistance . . . In the eastern regions the geographical proximity to partisan bases offered possibilities of rescue, and this to a certain extent influenced the attitude of the Judenrats . . . where there was no possibility of rescue through the partisans, the attitude of the great majority of the Judenrats toward the resistance was absolutely negative.[13]

There were some outright collaborators, like Avraham Gancwajch in Warsaw. At one time a 'right' Labour Zionist, he headed the '13', so-called after their headquarters at 13 Leszno Street. Their job was to catch smugglers, spy on the Judenrat and generally ferret out intelligence for the Gestapo.[14] In Vilna, Jacob Gens, a Revisionist, chief of the ghetto police and *de facto* head of the ghetto, certainly collaborated. When the Nazis heard about a resistance movement in the ghetto, Gens tricked its leader, the Communist Itzik Wittenberg, into coming to his office. Gens then had him arrested by Lithuanian policemen.[15] The

General Zionist Chaim Rumkowski of Lodz ran his ghetto in singular style and 'King Chaim', as his subjects referred to him, put his portrait on the ghetto postage. Not all were as debased as these. Czerniakow co-operated with the Nazis and opposed resistance, but during the great '*aktion*' in July 1942, when the Germans took 300,000 Jews, he committed suicide rather than co-operate further. Even Rumkowski insisted on going to his death with his ghetto, when the Nazis made it clear that not even collaboration would lead to the survival of a 'core' of his charges. In their minds they were justified in what they were doing, because they thought that only by abject co-operation could a few Jews survive. However, they were deluded; the fate of individual ghettos, and even of individual councils, was determined in almost every case either by Nazi whim or regional policy and not by whether a ghetto had been docile.

'The Parties haven't any Right to Give Us Orders'

All Jewish resistance has to be seen in the context of Nazi policy towards the Poles. Hitler never sought a Polish Quisling; the country was to be ruled by terror. From the beginning thousands were executed in collective punishments for any act of resistance. PPS members, ex-officers, many priests and academics, many of these likely to be believers in solidarity with the Jews, were murdered or sent to concentration camps. At the same time the Nazis sought to involve the Polish masses in the persecution of the Jews through material rewards, but there were always those who were prepared to help the Jews. The most important group was the PPS, which had stolen every type of official stamp and forged Aryan papers for some of its Bundist comrades. The Revisionists maintained contact with elements in the Polish military. Thousands of Poles hid Jews at the risk of certain death, if they were caught.

The most important advantage the Germans had was the absence of guns in the hands of the people, as the Colonels had always ensured that weapons were kept out of civilian reach. The PPS and the Bund had never developed their militias beyond occasional target shooting, and were now to pay the penalty. Effectively the only guns available were those hidden by the retreating army and these were now in the custody of the *Armia Krajowa* (AK), the Home Army, which took its orders from the government-in-exile in London. Under British pressure the exiles had to include token representation from both the PPS and the Bund, but control of the AK remained with the anti-Semites and their allies. They were loath to arm the people for fear that, after the Germans were driven out, the workers and peasants would turn the weapons against the rich; they developed the strategic doctrine that the time to strike was when the Germans were suffering defeat on the battlefield. They insisted that premature action would serve no purpose and just bring down Nazi wrath on the people. Naturally this meant that aid to the Jews was always ill-timed. The PPS, having no weapons of its own, felt obliged to join the AK, but they were never able to obtain sufficient weapons to assist the Jews independently in any serious way.

Those Jews who had resisted pre-war Polish anti-Semitism were the first to resist the Nazis. Those who had done nothing continued to do nothing. Czerniakow insisted that the Bund provide one member of the Warsaw Judenrat. The Bundists knew from the start that the council could only be a tool of the Germans, but felt obliged to agree and nominated Shmuel Zygelboym. Zygelboym had been the party leader in Lodz and had fled to Warsaw in the hope of continuing to fight after the Polish Army had withdrawn from his city. He then helped to mobilise the remnants of the Warsaw Bund alongside the PPS.

Zygelboym had reluctantly agreed to the setting up of a forced-labour roster as preferable to arbitrary seizures by press gangs, but in October 1939, when the Judenrat was ordered to organise a ghetto, he would no go further. He told the council:

I feel I would not have the right to live if . . . the ghetto should be established and my head remained unscathed . . . I recognise that the chairman has an obligation to report this to the Gestapo, and I know the consequences this can have for me personally.[16]

The council feared that Zygelboym's stance would discredit them among the Jews if they meekly accepted the Nazi order, and they rescinded their initial decision to comply. Thousands of Jews arrived outside their headquarters to get further information, and Zygelboym used the occasion to speak. He told them to remain in their homes and make the Germans take them by force. The Nazis ordered him to report to the police the next day. The Bund understood this to be a death sentence and smuggled him out of the country; however, his action did succeed in having the order to establish a ghetto temporarily cancelled.

The last gallant battle of the Bund took place just before Easter

1940. A Polish hoodlum attacked an old Jew and began to tear his beard out of his face. A Bundist saw the incident and beat the Pole. The Nazis caught the Bundist and shot him the next day. Polish pogromists started raiding Jewish neighbourhoods as the Germans stood by. They wanted the raids to continue to prove that the Polish people supported them in their anti-Jewish policy. The assaults on the Jews far exceeded anything the Naras had ever mounted in independent Poland; the Bund felt it had no choice but to risk the wrath of the Nazis and went out to fight. To make sure no Polish deaths would be used as a pretext for further forays, no knives or guns were used; only brass knuckles and iron pipes. Hundreds of Jews, and PPS members in the Wola district, fought the pogromists over the next two days, until finally the Polish police broke up the street war. The Nazis did not interfere. They had taken their propaganda pictures and for the moment they chose not to punish the Jews for their action.[17] This episode marked the end of the leadership of the Bund within Polish Jewry.

Within a few months of the German occupation the leaders of the Hashomer and HeChalutz Zionist youth groups, who had also fled to Lithuania, sent representatives back into Poland, but not with any idea of organising a rising. They saw their duty as suffering with the people in their duress and in trying to maintain morale through maintaining high moral standards. The first military actions by a Zionist group came from *Swit* (Dawn), a Revisionist veterans' grouping. They had ties to the *Korpus Bezpieczenstwa* (KB or Security Corps), a small Polish unit then loosely connected with the AK, and as early as 1940 the KB sent several Jews, among them a number of physicians, into the area between the Rivers Bug and the San, where they worked with elements of the AK.[18] However, neither Swit nor the KB had any plans for large-scale resistance or escape from the ghettos.[19]

Serious consideration of armed Jewish resistance only began after the German invasion of the Soviet Union. From the onset the Nazis abandoned all restraints in their activities in the Soviet Union. *Einsatz-gruppen* (Special Duty Units) started systematically slaughtering Jews and by October 1941, four months after the invasion, over 250,000 Jews had been killed in mass executions in White Russia and the Baltic states. By December 1941 the first reports of gassings on Polish soil, at Chelmno, convinced the youth movements, the Bund, the Revisionists and the Communists that they had to assemble some military groups, but the bulk of the surviving leaders of the mainline WZO parties either did not believe that what had happened elsewhere would happen in

Warsaw or else they were convinced that nothing could be done. Yitzhak Zuckerman, a founder of the Jewish Fighting Organisation (JFO) which united the WZO's forces with the Bund and the Communists, and later a major historian of the Warsaw rising, has put it baldly: 'The Jewish Fighting Organisation arose without the parties and against the wish of the parties.'[20] After the war some of the writings of Hersz Berlinksi, of the 'left' Poale Zion, were posthumously published. He told of an October 1942 conference between his organisation and the youth groups. The question before them was whether the JFO should have just a military command or a military-political committee, and the youth groups wanted to avoid the domination of the parties:

> The comrades from Hashomer and HeChalutz spoke out sharply about the political parties: 'the parties haven't any right to give us orders. Except for the youth they will do nothing. They will only interfere.'[21]

At the Conference on Manifestations of Jewish Resistance at the Yad Vashem Remembrance Authority in April 1968, bitter words were exchanged between those historians who had partaken in the struggle and those who still sought to defend the passive approach. Yisrael Gutman challenged one of the latter, Dr Nathan Eck:

> Do you believe that if we had waited until the end and acted according to the advice of the party leaders, the revolt would still have taken place, or that there would then have been no point in it whatsoever? I believe there would have been no revolt at all and I challenge Dr Eck to offer convincing proof that the party leaders intended at all that there should be an uprising.[22]

Emmanuel Ringelblum, the great historian of the destruction of Jewish Warsaw, described the thinking of his friend Mordechai Anielewicz of Hashomer, the commander of the JFO:

> The Mordechai who had matured so rapidly and risen so quickly to the most responsible post as commander of the Fighters Organisation now greatly regretted that his fellows and he had wasted three war years on cultural and educational work. We had not understood that new side of Hitler that is emerging, Mordechai lamented. We should have trained the youth in the use of live and cold

ammunition. We should have raised them in the spirit of revenge against the greatest enemy of the Jews, of all mankind, and of all times.[23]

The debate within the resistance focused on the key question of where to fight. Generally speaking, it was the Communists who favoured getting as many of the youth as possible into the forests as partisans, whereas the young Zionists called for last stands in the ghettos. The Communists had always been the most ethnically integrated party in the country and, now that the Soviet Union had itself been attacked, they were wholly committed to the struggle against Hitler. The Soviets had parachuted Pincus Kartin, a Spanish Civil War veteran, into Poland to organise the Jewish underground. The Communists argued that the ghettos could not be defended and the fighters would be killed for nothing. In the woods they might not only survive, but be able to start attacking the Germans. The Zionist youth raised real questions about retreating to the forests. The Red Army was still a long way off and the Polish Communist *Gwardia Ludowa* (Peoples' Guard) was viewed with great suspicion by the Polish masses, because of their previous support for the Hitler–Stalin pact which had led directly to the destruction of the Polish state. As a result the Gwardia had very few weapons and the countryside was full of anti-Semitic partisans, often Naras, who had no hesitation about killing Jews. However, there was an additional sectarian element in much of the young Zionists' thinking. Mordechai Tanenbaum-Tamaroff of Bialystok was the most vehement opponent of the partisan conception, yet the town was in an immense primeval forest.[24] He wrote:

> In the vengeance that we want to exact the constant and decisive element is the Jewish, the national factor . . . Our approach is – fulfillment of our national role within the ghetto (not to leave the old people to their bloody fate!) . . . and if we remain alive – we will go out, weapon in hand, to the forests.[25]

This line was maintained in Warsaw where Mordechai Anielewicz, feeling that thoughts of a last-minute escape would destroy the iron will required to stand and face certain death, deliberately made no plans to retreat.[26]

The results were disillusioning; the Hashomer and HeChalutz had hoped their example would rally the ghettos, but they did not understand that the spirit of the people had been broken by the four years of humilation and pain. The ghettos could not be armed, and therefore they saw revolt as only increasing the certainty of their death. Yisrael Gutman was quite correct when he insisted:

> The truth is that the Jewish public in most of the ghettoes neither understood nor accepted the path and assessment of the fighters . . . Everywhere the fighting organisations were engaged in bitter argument with the Jewish public . . . The youth movements achieved in Warsaw what they did not in other places of revolt.[27]

The Warsaw ghetto had two potential sources of arms: the People's Guard, which wanted to help but had few guns, and the Home Army that had guns but did not want to help. They ended up with few weapons, mostly pistols, and they battled bravely for a few days as long as their sparse arsenal held out. The Revisionists had to form their own separate 'National Military Organisation', because the other political tendencies refused to unite with a group they considered Fascist. However, the Revisionists were able to provide one of their detachments with German uniforms, three machine guns, eight rifles and hundreds of grenades. Some of their fighters escaped through tunnels and sewers and were driven to the forest by some Polish friends, were trapped by the Germans, escaped again, took refuge back in the Gentile sector of Warsaw and were finally surrounded and murdered. The end came for Anielewicz, in the ghetto, on the twentieth day of the rising. Marek Edelman, then a Bundist and deputy commander of the JFO, says he and 80 other fighters shot themselves in a bunker.[28] Zuckerman, another deputy commander, says Anielewicz was killed by gas and grenades tossed into the hide-out.[29]

'Jews Dream of Getting into the Homes of Workers'

Emmanuel Ringelblum, a Labour Zionist, had also returned to Poland from abroad. He was in Switzerland for the Zionist Congress in August 1939 when the war broke out, and he chose to return to Poland via the Balkans. He then set about the task of recording the momentous events. The value of his work was obvious to the entire political community and he was eventually chosen for a hiding-place on the Aryan side of Warsaw. He died in 1944, when his hiding-place was discovered, but not before he had written his masterpiece, *Polish–Jewish Relations during the Second World War*. The writing was blunt: 'Polish Fascism and its ally, anti-Semitism, have conquered the majority of the Polish people', but he took great pains to analyse Poland class by class and even region by region.[30]

> The middle-class population *in toto* has continued to adhere to the ideology of anti-Semitism and rejoices at the Nazi solution to the Jewish problem in Poland.[31]

He confirmed the pre-war evaluation of Lestchinsky and the other observers concerning the steadfastness of the workers in the struggle against anti-Semitism:

> Polish workers had long before the war grasped the class aspect of anti-Semitism, the power-tool of the native bourgeoisie, and during the war they redoubled their efforts to fight anti-Semitism . . . There were only limited possibilities for workers to hide Jews in their homes. Overcrowding in the flats was the greatest obstacle to taking in Jews. In spite of this, many Jews did find shelter in the flats of workers . . . It must be stressed that in general Jews dream of getting into the homes of workers, because this guarantees them against blackmail or exploitation by their hosts.[32]

Ringelblum's testimony, that of an eyewitness and of a trained historian, shows the path the Jews should have taken both before and during the war. Whatever the failings of the PPS and KPP as parties, there is no doubt that many Polish workers stood with the Jews to the death, and that many workers did more in defence of the Jews than many Jews. It is not suggested that more than a few hundred or a couple of additional thousand Jews might have been added to those who were in fact saved, but revolts in the ghettos, when they lacked arms, never had a chance of success even as symbolic gestures. The Nazi commandant's internal report on the Warsaw rising acknowledged only sixteen deaths among the Germans and their auxiliaries and, although this figure may be too low, the rising was never a serious military matter.

Mordechai Anielewicz's apotheosis to historic immortality is entirely justified, and no criticism of his strategy should be construed as attempting to detract from the lustre of his name. He voluntarily returned from Vilna. He dedicated himself to his stricken people. However, the martyrdom of the 24-year-old Anielewicz can never absolve the Zionist movement of its pre-war failure to fight anti-Semitism

— in Germany or in Poland — when there was still time. Nor can his return make us forget the flight of the other Zionist leaders, even in the first months of the occupation, nor the unwillingness of the remaining party leaders to initiate an underground struggle.

Notes

1. Author's interview with Alexander Erlich, 3 October 1979.

2. Yitzhak Arad, 'The Concentration of Refugees in Vilna on the Eve of the Holocaust', *Yad Vashem Studies,* vol. IX, p. 210.

3. Hyman Frank, 'The World of Menachem Begin' (*Jewish Press,* 2 December 1977).

4. Menachem Begin, *White Nights,* pp. 84–5, 87.

5. Lester Eckman and Gertrude Hirschler, *Menachem Begin,* p. 50.

6. Begin, *White Nights,* p. 79.

7. David Shipler, 'Israel Hardening Its Stand on Visits', *New York Times* (3 March 1982), p. 7.

8. Bernard Goldstein, *The Stars Bear Witness,* p. 35; and N. Blumenthal, N. Eck and J. Kermish (eds.), *The Warsaw Diary of Adam Czerniakow,* p. 2.

9. Blumenthal, Eck and Kermish, *The Warsaw Diary of Adam Czerniakow,* p. 117.

10. Ibid., p. 119.

11. Yisrael Gutman, 'The Genesis of the Resistance in the Warsaw Ghetto', *Yad Vashem Studies,* vol. IX, p. 43.

12. Goldstein, *The Stars Bear Witness,* pp. 35–6.

13. Isaiah Trunk (in debate), *Jewish Resistance During the Holocaust,* p. 257.

14. Emmanuel Ringelblum, *Notes from the Warsaw Ghetto,* p. 250.

15. Lester Eckman and Chaim Lazar, *The Jewish Resistance,* p. 31.

16. Bernard Johnpoll, *The Politics of Futility,* p. 231.

17. Goldstein, *The Stars Bear Witness,* pp. 51–3.

18. Wladyslaw Bartoszewski, *The Blood Shed Unites Us,* p. 32.

19. Reuben Ainsztein, *Jewish Resistance in Nazi Occupied Europe,* pp. 565–70.

20. Yitzhak Zuckerman (in debate), *Jewish Resistance During the Holocaust,* p. 150.

21. Hersz Berlinski, 'Zikhroynes', *Drai* (Tel Aviv), p. 169.

22. Yisrael Gutman (in debate), *Jewish Resistance During the Holocaust,* p. 148.

23. Emmanuel Ringelblum, 'Comrade Mordechai' in Yuri Suhl (ed.), *They Fought Back,* p. 102.

24. Joseph Kermish, 'The Place of the Ghetto Revolts in the Struggle against the Occupier', *Jewish Resistance During the Holocaust,* p. 315.

25. Ibid.

26. Yisrael Gutman, 'Youth Movements in the Underground and the Ghetto Revolts', *Jewish Resistance During the Holocaust,* p. 280.

27. Ibid., pp. 275, 279.

28. Marek Edelman, 'The Way to Die', *Jewish Affairs* (September 1975), p. 23.

29. Yitzhak Zuckerman, 'The Jewish Fighting Organisation — ZOB — Its Establishment and Activities', *The Catastrophe of European Jewry,* p. 547.

30. Emmanuel Ringelblum, *Polish-Jewish Relations During the Second*

World War, p. 247.
    31. Ibid., p. 197.
    32. Ibid., pp. 199, 203.

22 ZIONIST COLLUSION WITH THE POLISH GOVERNMENT-IN-EXILE

News of the German invasion of the Soviet Union reached Menachem Begin while he was travelling on a prison train towards Siberia. He had been arrested by the Russians with all the other Polish non-Communist political acivists who had fled into the territories allotted to Stalin by the German–Soviet Pact in 1939. The Polish government-in-exile and the Soviets were bitter enemies until the German invasion of the Soviet Union, but even then there were still irreconcilable conflicts between them, most notably over the eastern territories. Nevertheless Stalin announced a general amnesty for all Polish prisoners, and the Polish Prime Minister, Wladyslaw Sikorski, ordered all males to join a Polish army-in-exile.

'Those of Moses' Faith Step Forward'

In the last months prior to the war the Revisionists, prominent among whom was Begin (then heading Polish Betar), had negotiated with Captain Runge, head of the Security Police in Warsaw, to set up separate Jewish army units under Polish commanding officers.[1] They hoped that, after the Poles and Jews had beaten the German Army, the Jews, without their Polish commanders, would go on to conquer Palestine.[2] The scheme failed because of the hostility of the Bund, who opposed such plans to segregate the Jews.[3] In September–October 1941, in the Volga region of the Soviet Union, while the Nazis were stalking towards Moscow, the proposal was raised again by Miron Sheskin, Commander-in-Chief of the *Brith HaChayal* (Union of Soldiers), the Revisionists' veterans organisation, and Mark Kahan, editor of the Warsaw Yiddish daily newspaper *Der Moment*. The Polish exile army was dominated by anti-Semites, who were concerned to keep Jews out of their army, and this proposal of Jewish self-segregation was attractive to them. However, at the highest levels around the army's commander, General Wladyslaw Anders, it was understood that the proposal would not be acceptable to either the Soviets or the British. Nevertheless some of the officers at the army's staging area in Samara Oblast were old associates of the

Revisionists and believed they would be doing the Jews a favour by separating them into their own units; and Colonel Jan Galadyk, the former commandant of the pre-war infantry officers' school, volunteered to lead such a battalion. After the war Kahan described the unit as a model for the hoped-for Jewish Legion and he gave a positive picture of it as a successful example of Jewish–Polish relations. But Yisrael Gutman has researched the history of 'Anders' Army' and warns us that Kahan is unreliable.[4] The truth was better served by rabbi Leon Rozen-Szeczakacz, an Agudist but a supporter of the Legion idea, in his *Cry in the Wilderness*.

On 7 October 1941, at Totzkoye, all Jews were summoned to a field and an officer called out 'those of Moses' faith step forward'. Most of those who did so suddenly found themselves dismissed from the army. Those few, including Rozen-Szeczakacz who were not summarily discharged were totally segregated from the rest of the army. Barbarities commenced immediately. The majority of Jews were issued boots that were too small for them which meant that they had to try to protect themselves with rags in the −40° Soviet winter. They were transferred to another location and left out in the fields for days on end, and the army would 'forget' to feed them.[5] When Rozen-Szeczakacz, whom the army's top command had made into a chaplain, arrived at the battalion's new location at Koltubanka, his first task was to start burying the large number of dead.[6] Eventually, after much suffering and death, things improved as word of their plight reached the Polish ambassador and the exiled Bundist leaders, and the battalion turned into a smart military unit. However, the larger plan for a Jewish Legion disappeared.

Anders' Army finally left the Soviet Union for Iran, where they linked up with the British military; the anti-Semites tried to leave behind as many Jews as possible and healthy youths were rejected for service. Approximately 114,000 people were evacuated in March–April and August–September 1942. About 6,000 were Jews, 5 per cent of the soldiers and 7 per cent of the civilians. To put this into perspective, in the summer of 1941, before the anti-Semitic recruiting line was imposed, Jews had comprised about 40 per cent of the army's enlistees. Despite the discrimination against the Jewish troops, the Revisionists Kahan, Sheskin and Begin managed to get out through their military connections.[7]

Zionist Acceptance of Anti-Semitism in the Polish Army

One of the ironies of the Second World War is that a Polish Army-in-exile, with its large contingent of anti-Semites, was finally glad to arrive in Palestine. It was still there on 28 June 1943, when Eliazer Lieben-stein (Livneh), then editing the Haganah's paper *Eshnab*, ran a secret Order of the Day that General Anders had issued in November 1941. He had told his officers that he 'fully understood' their hostility toward the Jews; however, they had to realise that the Allies were under Jewish pressure but, he reassured them, when they got back home 'we shall deal with the Jewish problem in accordance with the size and indepen-dence of our homeland'.[8] This was understood to mean that he was hinting at the post-war expulsion of any Jews who might have escaped Hitler's claws. The presence of the Polish Army in Palestine made it impossible for the WZO to ignore the scandal and finally, on 19 September, the 'Representation of Polish Jewry' confronted Anders with the Order at the home of the Polish Consul in Tel Aviv. The General declared that the whole thing was a forgery. He then spoke of the desertions of Jews from his army while in Palestine. He told them that he did not care that 3,000 of the 4,000 Jews in his ranks had walked away, he was not going to search for them, and the Zionists took the hint.[9] Shortly after the encounter the Consul sent the Polish Foreign Ministry in London a memorandum about another meeting between his deputy and Yitzhak Gruenbaum, then on the Jewish Agency Executive. The Deputy Consul had repeated the lie about the Order and asked the Zionist to help hush up the whole affair. After discussing the situation with the other members of his Executive, Gruenbaum agreed to concur with the Polish deception.[10] Later, on 13 January 1944 in London, Dr Ignacy Schwarzbart, the Zionist representative on the Polish National Council, and Aryeh Tartakower of the World Jewish Congress, met Stanislaw Mikolajczyk, a Peasant Party politician who had succeeded Sikorski as Prime Minister and, again, the Zionists agreed to lie about the Order. Schwarzbart told the Pole that:

> there are witnesses, among them ministers, who fought against the order when it was issued. We know that one of the cables referred to the order as a forgery. I have no objection against making such a claim for external consumption, but on the inside, no one should expect me to believe that it was a forgery.[11]

Even in Britain Jewish soldiers were told by their commanders that they would be shot in the back when they went into battle, and Polish officers repeatedly made statements about deporting Jews after the war. Some bluntly announced that those Jews who might survive Hitler would be massacred; in January 1944, some of the Jews finally had enough. Sixty-eight deserted and threatened to go on hunger strikes, and even commit suicide, rather than stay with the Polish forces, although they had no objection to fighting in the British Army. In February, 134 more Jews deserted and in March more soldiers walked out. The Poles' first reaction was just to let them go, but finally they announced that 31 men would be court-martialled and that no further transfers would be allowed. Some Labour Party members took up their cause and Tom Driberg put down a question on the subject in the House of Commons. No sooner had he done so than Schwarzbart phoned, begging him to withdraw the question so as not to attract further attention to the matter.[12] Driberg ignored this suggestion; both he and Michael Foot denounced the forthcoming trials at a mass meeting on 14 May, and there were demonstrations in Downing Street. The government-in-exile was compelled to back down and drop the charges. Years later Driberg touched upon the incidents in his book, *Ruling Passions*. He was still amazed at the behaviour of the Anglo-Jewish misleadership:

> The odd thing was that we had pursued this matter in the House against the advice — the almost lachrymose pleading — of the official spokesmen of the Jewish community in Britain. They felt that any publicity about this might lead to more anti-Semitism, perhaps directed against their own flock.[13]

Driberg's interpretation of the Anglo-Jewish leaders' motivation is undoubtedly correct. They eventually spoke out, but only after the Labour members had roused the public and they could be absolutely sure that it was safe to do so.

Schwarzbart had earlier participated in another rather shameful episode in Polish Jewish affairs. In 1942 Mme Zofia Zaleska, an Endek, had proposed to the exile Sejm that a Jewish homeland be established outside Poland and that the Jews be asked to emigrate. Rather than oppose this, Schwarzbart tried to amend Zaleska's resolution to name Palestine specifically as the homeland. His suggestion was defeated and Zaleska's original motion was accepted by the Sejm. Only Shmuel Zygelboym of the Bund and a representative of the PPS voted against it. Schwarzbart abstained.[14]

The Polish exiles were dependent on Britain and, after the arrival of the Polish Army in Palestine, the Zionists could have put extra pressure on the British. Anders was right when he told his officers that the Jews always had the ability to pressurise the British on the question of anti-Semitism in the Polish armed forces, and the success of the Driberg-Foot intervention in 1944 shows what could be done. Instead the WZO, in both Palestine and London, colluded with the Poles to conceal the Anders' Order of the Day and intervened to persuade the Labour members to call off their protest. Similarly the Revisionists connived with the Polish Army while still in the Soviet Union, in the interests of a Jewish Legion to help conquer Palestine; in 1943 their good friend, Colonel Galadyk, helped train the Irgun in Palestine.[15] Those who had sought the patronage of the anti-Semites in pre-war Poland never fought Polish anti-Semitism, even in Britain and Palestine where the advantages were all on their side.

Notes

1. 'Menachem Begin Writes', *Jewish Press* (13 May 1977), p. 4.
2. Yisrael Gutman, 'Jews in General Anders' Army in the Soviet Union', *Yad Vashem Studies*, vol. XII, pp. 255-6.
3. Bernard Johnpoll, *The Politics of Futility*, p. 248.
4. Gutman, 'Jews in General Anders' Army', pp. 262, 265 and 269.
5. Leon Rozen-Szeczakacz, *Cry in the Wilderness*, pp. 92-3.
6. Gutman, 'Jews in General Anders' Army', p. 266.
7. Rozen-Szeczakacz, *Cry in the Wilderness*, pp. 157-8.
8. Reuben Ainsztein, 'The Sikorski Affair', *Jewish Quarterly* (London, Spring 1969), p. 31.
9. Gutman, 'Jews in General Anders' Army', p. 295.
10. Ibid., p. 279.
11. Ibid., p. 280.
12. Bernard Wasserstein, *Britain and the Jews of Europe 1939-1945*, p. 128.
13. Ibid.
14. Johnpoll, pp. 247-8.
15. Mark Kahan, 'An Utmost Historical Documentation', in *Cry in the Wilderness*, app. p. 237.

23 ILLEGAL IMMIGRATION

It is not known exactly how many illegal immigrants were smuggled into Palestine before and during the Second World War. Yehuda Bauer estimates that approximately 15,000 illegal immigrants entered in the years 1936-9.[1] He breaks down this number to 5,300 brought in by Revisionist ships, 5,000 by the Labour Zionists and 5,200 by private vessels.[2] The British listed 20,180 as having arrived prior to the end of the war. William Perl, the prime organiser of the Revisionist effort, doubles that figure to more than 40,000.[3] Yehuda Slutzky gives 52,000 as having reached Palestine during the war, but his number includes both legals and illegals.[4]

The first illegal boat, the *Velos*, organised by the Palestinian kibbutzim, arrived in July 1934. It tried again in September, but was intercepted and both the WZO and Labour Zionist leaderships opposed any further attempts; by 1935 the British were letting in 55,000 legal immigrants and they saw no reason to antagonise London for the sake of a few more. The first Revisionist effort was the *Union*, which was intercepted while landing in August 1934. These two failures discouraged any additional exertions, until the Revisionists tried again in 1937.

After the Holocaust, the post-1937 illegal immigration acquired a reputation as part of Zionism's contribution to the rescue of European Jewry from Hitler. However, at the time neither the Revisionists nor the WZO saw themselves as *rescuing* Jews *per se*; they were bringing in specially selected settlers to Palestine.

'Priority Went to Members of our own Betar'

The Revisionists returned to illegal immigration during the Arab revolt. The immigrants were mostly Betarim brought in as reinforcements for the Irgun, which was engaged in a terrorist campaign against the Arabs.[5] The first three groups, comprising 204 passengers, left Vienna in 1937 before the Nazi occupation. Except for four Austrians, they were all Eastern Europeans. All had been given weapon-training earlier at their camp at the Revisionist estate at Kottingbrunn, in preparation for what they knew would some day be 'the final battle against the

British occupiers'.[6] Their focus had always been the military needs of Palestinian Revisionism. *Die Aktion*, the Viennese group organising the 'free immigration', passed a resolution proclaiming that they would only take young people: 'For the upcoming battle for the liberation of our Jewish homeland from the British colonial yoke, the first ones to be saved must be Jews able and willing to carry arms.'[7]

In the years to come there were occasions when the Revisionists did take others besides Betarim, but these were only accepted because of the contingencies of the situation. The money for the first expedition after the *anschluss* came from the Vienna Jewish community organisation, which was dominated by a right-wing Zionist coalition; Die Aktion was therefore sometimes compelled by political and financial considerations to include members of other groups among the passengers, but preference was always given to Betarim. William Perl, Die Aktion's main organiser, later discussed their first post-*anschluss* boat in his book, *Four Front War*, and he candidly admitted that:

Priority went to members of our own Betarim . . . next, to those whom we expected to stand the strain of the trip, to adjust to life in Palestine. One day these youngsters would have to be ready and be able to rise up in arms with the Betar.[8]

In dealing with events during the summer of 1939 Perl wrote further of: 'Jabotinsky himself . . . who now took a most active role in trying to arrange the escape of more Jews from Poland, particularly of as many as possible of our Betarim there'.[9] Yitshaq Ben-Ami, who had come from Palestine to assist the operations in Vienna, and then went to the USA to raise money for their vessels, has recently spoken of 'big arguments and tension' between himself and Jabotinsky over how to appeal to the American public. Ben-Ami knew there would be a war in Europe and wanted to organise a rescue operation, whereas Jabotinsky saw fund-raising as a party project.[10] Even in November 1939, two months after the outbreak of the war, Perl, far from rescuing Jews as such, was still thinking: 'If paying fully, the Betarim always had preference.'[11] He mentions one case where they took 'a few' Zionist-Socialists, and he and other Revisionist writers list some members of the right-wing Macabbi sports club and General Zionist groups as part of their convoys, but there were only two ways non-Zionists managed to board a Revisionist boat. Either the Nazis − or some other government along the Danube − insisted that they be taken along or else, as in the case of some Agudists from Budapest, a shortage of cash obliged Perl to go outside the Zionist orbit for paying customers so that one of his stranded Betar contingents might continue its trip. Even here his central concern for Palestine came through. Although the Aguda hated Zionism, he felt that 'for the sake of the future state they were valuable. To them Palestine was not just a temporary haven.'[12] The 1947 statement of Otto Seidmann, the former leader of the Viennese Betar, who wrote that: 'We had to save the lives of Jews — be they Communists or capitalists, members of Hashomer Hatzair or General Zionists', was simply untrue.[13] Betarim were always preferred over any other Zionists, right Zionists over left Zionists, and any kind of Zionist over a non-Zionist.

'Whom a Jewish Homeland in the Process of Construction Needs Most'

The German Zionist Federation opposed illegal immigration until Kristallnacht. They were legalists who had done nothing to oppose Nazism and they were not about to turn against the British. When the WZO re-entered the field of illegal immigration again, it was with great trepidation, and even after Kristallnacht Ben-Gurion warned the Director of the ZVfD Central Committee: 'We shall never be able to fight both the Arabs and the British.'[14] Weizmann, after years of collaboration with the British, was instinctively against anything illegal. At first the WZO could not bring themselves to accept that a Britain seriously preparing for war could not afford to antagonise the Arab and Muslim world by any further patronage of Zionist immigration. What finally compelled the Labour Zionists to move was the prestige which the Revisionists were gaining inside the Zionist camp by their putting European Jews on Palestine's coast. But even then their strictly selective approach remained unchanged. In 1940 the Emergency Committee for Zionist Affairs, the WZO's official voice in America during the Second World War, published a pamphlet, *Revisionism: A Destructive Force*, which gave their full case for selectivity:

> It is quite true that Palestine should be a refuge for every homeless Jew. Is there a Jew or Zionist who would wish otherwise? But we are faced by the tragic compulsion of facts. Only a number of those who seek entrance can for the present be taken. Selection is inevitable. Shall the choice be haphazard, dependent merely on the accident of who clambered abroad first, or shall profounder motives determine the nature of the immigration? We know that in emigration from

Germany preference is given to the Youth Aliyah. Is the reason for this preference a brutal disregard for the aged, or does it spring from the difficult but honest effort to save those whose need is greatest and whom a Jewish Homeland in the process of construction needs most?

When the force of events places on human beings the terrible burden of allocating salvation, the question is not solved by a helter-skelter opening of doors to whoever manages to crowd in. That too is a choice − a choice against the present and the future.[15]

The selection process for WZO-chartered boats was later spelt out by Aaron Zwergbaum in his description of an expedition from Nazi-occupied Czechoslovakia:

> The Zionist authorities treated this *Aliya Bet* like regular migration; it was highly selective, demanding [at least of younger people] *Hakshara* [agricultural training], a certain knowledge of Hebrew, affiliation to a Zionist body, good health, and so on. There was a rather low age limit, and the passage money was fixed on the principle that the well-to-do should pay not only for themselves but also for those without means.[16]

Again, as with the Revisionists, there had to be exemptions to the rules. Some veteran Zionists were rewarded for their services by a place in the boats, sometimes other forms of influence performed the necessary miracle, as with relatives of Zionists who were taken along, or a rich Jew, carried for financial reasons. And, of course, those imposed upon them by the Nazis and other governments. Not being nearly as military-minded as their rivals, children were less frowned upon; some day they would have their own children in Palestine, thus increasing the Jewish percentage of the population. But, for an example, a 45-year-old non-Zionist piano-tuner, without the ability to pay for someone else, and unrelated to a Zionist, would never be considered for such a voyage.

'They will Co-operate with Us in Matters in which We are vitally Interested'

The Revisionists were more daring in organising the illegal immigration, because they did not care what London thought. They had come to understand that they would have to fight Britain, if they were ever to realise their Zionist state; the WZO, however, still expected to get a Jewish state with the approval of the British at another Versailles Conference after the Second World War. They argued that Britain would only reward them if they accommodated to her plans during the war, and London most definitely did not want more refugees in Palestine. Therefore, in November 1940, when the British Navy tried to deport 3,000 illegals to Mauritius in the Indian Ocean, Weizmann tried to convince the Zionist Executive that 'they must not have anything to do with this business just for the sake of getting an additional 3,000 people into Palestine — who might later turn out to be a millstone around their neck'.[17] He claimed to be concerned about the Gestapo's involvement in the voyages.[18] Obviously the ships could not have left German-held territory without their permission, but it is doubtful that he seriously believed the British imputation that the Nazis were putting spies aboard these squalid boats. However, Weizmann's argument was consistent with his lifetime strategy of getting British patronage for Zionism. He knew that a serious illegal operation would jeopardise his relations with the British and, in particular, make it impossible to attain London's assent for a Jewish Legion within the British Army.

The British, who had learnt from the experience of having worked with the Zionists for decades, decided to use the Zionist ambition for a Jewish state to eliminate illegal immigration. They knew the WZO hoped to attend the post-war peace conference with an impressive war record, so British Intelligence concocted an ingenious plan. The *Mossad*, the organisation behind the WZO immigration, owned one boat, the *Darien II*. In 1940, it had been arranged that the vessel would be sent up the Danube to pick up some refugees stranded in Yugoslavia. The British proposed instead that the ship should be loaded with scrap iron and explosives. Jewish refugee boats had become part of the river's life, and no one would suspect the *Darien*. When it reached a narrow point upstream, it would blow up, thereby blocking Romanian oil and grain from getting to the Reich. The corollary to this would be that refugee boats would no longer be able to come down the Danube, and the Nazis, who had been co-operating with the Mossad by clearing out Zionist training camps, would blame them for the explosion. Despite the grisly revenge which the Nazis were likely to exact, the WZO leadership decided to agree to the ploy being executed. However, there was a hitch. Some of the Mossad workers involved refused to co-operate. The ship was registered in the name of one of their number, an

American, and he refused to sign the boat over to the British. David HaCohen, a member of the Jewish Agency Executive, was rushed to Istanbul to try to persuade them to agree. Ruth Kluger, who was present with the Mossad, later gave HaCohen's arguments in her memoir, *The Last Escape*:

'I've come with an order. From Shertok [Political Secretary of the Jewish Agency] himself . . . Shertok would not have given the *Darien* so much time and consideration if he did not feel that the matter was one which came into his realm of operations. He feels, we all feel, that the plan proposed for the *Darien* will, without doubt, end the war sooner. And the sooner it ends, the more lives will be saved. Including Jewish lives. Furthermore – and this point I cannot stress enough – if we co-operate with British Intelligence in this matter, one in which they happen to be vitally interested, we have every reason to believe' – he repeated the words slowly, '*every reason to believe* that they will co-operate with us in matters in which we are vitally interested. [Yehuda] Arazi has mentioned a Jewish Brigade in the British Army . . . There are many others which I'm not permitted to go into at this point. But I *can* say this, Zameret, the matter of the *Darien* is one which might even have bearing on our postwar future. Whether or not we Jews ever have our own nation may be in the lap of the gods. But it's definitely in the hands of the British. If we go back on our promises to them and use the ship in direct contradiction to British law – if they see that the man who would be, in all likelihood our first Foreign Minister has no control over his countrymen in so vital a matter' – HaCohen let the sentence hang, like a noose around our necks.[19]

The local Mossad agents would not comply, and the WZO had to use the *Darien* for one more voyage to save some more of its own members. However, that last voyage was the last successful illegal expedition during the war. William Perl is of the strong conviction that the *Darien* proposal was designed to ensnare the WZO into a situation whereby the trickle of refugees would be stopped by the Nazis.[20] Certainly HaCohen could not have put the point more forcefully: 'the matter of the *Darien* is one which might even have a bearing on *our* post-war future'. British Intelligence had appreciated the simple truth that the WZO would compromise their rescue operation, if it meant a significant step towards their supreme ambition.

The saga of the illegal immigrant ships ended on 24 February 1942, when the derelict *Struma*, carrying 767 Jews, was towed back into the Black Sea by the Turks, under British pressure, and sank with only one survivor. Dalia Ofer, an Israeli scholar, remarks: 'there was still no real perception of the nature of events in Nazi-occupied Europe, and hence there were no attempts to reorganise'.[21] Rescue attempts did not start again until 1943, during the full fury of the Holocaust.

Dogs Fight Dogs, but They Unite against the Wolf

As long as America was neutral, it would have been possible to raise large sums from American Jews for the rescue and relief of their fellows in occupied Europe, but such fund-raising could only have been done on a strictly non-partisan and humanitarian basis. Instead, the WZO, through its Emergency Committee for Zionist Affairs and other outlets, attacked the Revisionist involvement in illegal immigration. They denounced their rivals' Fascist tendencies and accused them of not being selective about whom they let aboard their ships. Apparently the Revisionist propagandists concealed the political and even military basis of their selection process, and the WZO's publicists were fooled. The Emergency Committee's pamphlet of 1940 accused the Revisionists of 'an incorrigible love of dramatic gestures':

> Among other things, the Revisionists made a virtue of the fact that their immigrants are not 'selected'. They take all – the old, the sick, the psychologically unfit for pioneering – whereas the responsible Aliyah presumes to choose.[22]

By what authority could the WZO denounce anyone for trying to rescue the old and the sick, or even the psychologically unfit for pioneering? Had the WZO apparatus in America proposed unity with the Revisionists for a genuine non-exclusionary effort, the Revisionists would have had to live up to their propaganda or risk being exposed. However, the WZO was not interested in humanitarian rescue. Its leaders were openly picking and choosing strictly on the basis of what they saw as the interests of Zionism.

Notes

1. Yehuda Bauer, *From Diplomacy to Resistance*, p. 391.

2. Yehuda Bauer, 'Illegal Immigration', *Encyclopedia of Zionism and Israel*, vol. I, p. 532.

3. William Perl, *The Four Front War*, p. 1.

4. Yehuda Slutzky, 'The Palestine Jewish Community and its Assistance to European Jewry in the Holocaust Years', *Jewish Resistance During the Holocaust*, p. 421.

5. Daniel Levine, *David Raziel, The Man and His Times*, pp. 226, 229.

6. Perl, *The Four Front War*, p. 16.

7. Ibid., p. 23.

8. Ibid., pp. 60–1.

9. Ibid., p. 226.

10. Author's interview with Yitshaq Ben-Ami, 16 December 1980.

11. Perl, *The Four Front War*, p. 306.

12. Ibid., p. 302.

13. O. Seidmann, 'Saga of Aliyah Beth', *Tagar* (Shanghai, 1 January 1947), p. 7.

14. David Yisraeli, 'The Third Reich and Palestine', *Middle Eastern Studies* (May 1971), p. 348.

15. Emergency Committee for Zionist Affairs, *Revisionism: A Destructive Force* (1940), p. 24.

16. Aaron Zwergbaum, 'From Internment in Bratislava and Detention in Mauritius to Freedom', *The Jews of Czechoslovakia*, vol. II, p. 601.

17. Bernard Wasserstein, *Britain and the Jews of Europe 1939-1945*, p. 65.

18. Ibid.

19. Ruth Kluger and Peggy Mann, *The Last Escape*, pp. 456–7.

20. Perl, *The Four Front War*, p. 193.

21. Dalia Ofer, 'The Activities of the Jewish Agency Delegation in Istanbul in 1943', *Rescue Attempts During the Holocaust*, p. 437.

22. Emergency Committee for Zionist Affairs, *Revisionism: A Destructive Force*, p. 24.

24 THE WARTIME FAILURE TO RESCUE

Aid to European Jewry during the Second World War can only be dealt with in the context of the general war aims of the Allies. At all times, the main concern of Britain and France, and then the United States, was the preservation of their empires and the capitalist system. The Soviet Union had no quarrel with this vision, except where its own troops actually penetrated Central Europe. London and Paris entered the war on the defensive, fearing both victory and defeat: the First World War had led to the collapse of four empires and the rise of Communism.

The attitude of the British government towards helping Jews escape the Nazi fury was carefully set down by Roosevelt's intimate, Harry Hopkins. He told of a meeting on 27 March 1943 between the President, Anthony Eden and others, at which the question of at least saving the Jews of Bulgaria had arisen. Eden said:

> we should move very cautiously about offering to take all Jews out of a country like Bulgaria. If we do that, then the Jews of the world will be wanting us to make similar offers in Poland and Germany. Hitler might take us up on any such offer and there simply are not enough ships and means of transportation in the world to handle them.[1]

Britain's prime concern was that rescuing Jews would create problems with the Arabs, who feared that Jewish immigration to Palestine would lead to a post-war Jewish state. Naturally, London's solicitous regard for Arab sensitivities in this respect was solely based on imperial calculation; according to Churchill, the Arabs were no better than 'a backward people who eat nothing but camel dung'.[2] The British understood that the Zionists also saw the war and rescue through the Palestinian prism. The Zionists knew that the Arabs would be opposed to their British overlords, and they hoped to curry favour with Britain by their own loyalty. Their main wartime goal was the creation of a Jewish Legion, and with it they hoped to establish a military record which would compel Britain to grant them statehood as a post-war reward. Their first thought was how to turn the war to their advantage in Palestine. Yoav Gelber of the Yad Vashem Institute gives a good account of this view among the Labour Zionists in September 1939:

> the majority of the leaders tended to view Palestine and its problems
> as the touchstone of their attitude towards the war. They were
> inclined to leave the front-line fighting as such, if unconnected to
> Palestine, to the Jews of the Diaspora.[3]

Hashomer Hatzair took the same position, and opposed any volunteer-
ing that involved service outside Palestine. As one of their writers,
Richard Weintraub, put it on 28 September 1939: 'it would be politically unwise to attempt to revive an updated version of Jewish
"missions" in the world at large and to make sacrifices for their sake'.[4]

During 1940 and 1941 the Jewish Agency Executive rarely discussed
the Jews of occupied Europe and, aside from their half-hearted efforts
at illegal immigration, the Agency did nothing for them.[5] Nor were
their colleagues in neutral America much more helpful, despite the fact
that Goldmann had arrived there for the duration in 1940 and both
Ben-Gurion and Weizmann went there for several extended visits in
1940 and 1941. Furthermore, the American Zionist leadership cam-
paigned against those Jews who were trying to aid the stricken. Aryeh
Tartakower, who was in charge of aid work for the World Jewish Congress in America in 1940, has told some of the story in an interview with
the distinguished Israeli historian, Shabatei Beit-Zvi:

> we received a call from the American Government, from the State
> Department, and they brought to our attention that sending parcels
> to the Jews in Poland was not in the interests of the Allies ... The
> first one to tell us to stop immediately was Dr Stephen Wise ...
> He said: 'We must stop for the good of England.'[6]

The British decided that it was the 'duty' of the Germans as belli-
gerents to feed the population in the territories they occupied. Food
packages from the outside only aided the German war efforts. The
WJC–AJC apparatus not only stopped sending food, but it pressurised
the non-Zionist Jewish relief agencies to stop as well, and almost all
did except the Aguda. They told the Zionists that Britain was no
authority on what was good for the Jews and sent more packages. This
aroused Joseph Tanenbaum, a Zionist and leader of the barely existent
Jewish anti-Nazi boycott. He had not previously seen food packages as
his responsibility until the State Department had suggested it. He then
attacked the Agudists in the Zionist daily newspaper, *Der Tog* in July

and August 1941:

> Why then do the English send, or the Yugoslavian representatives
> collect money to send food to the *prisoners-of-war*. This is a com-
> pletely different issue. The prisoners-of-war are under the auspices
> of the Red Cross international convention which has already a long
> gray beard.[7]

Aguda's own grey beards continued to defy Tanenbaum, and his
Joint Boycott Council of the AJC and the Jewish Labor Committee and
– eventually – the British realised that they could never stop the
Agudists and let them send 10,000 monthly packages. The anti-
Semitism of British policy was later exposed when they supplied
Canadian wheat to occupied Greece from 1942 to its liberation. The
Greeks were conquered allies; the Jews were not.

Wise Suppresses News about Extermination of Jews

When did the Western Jewish establishment and the Allies discover
that Hitler was systematically killing Jews? Reports of slaughter in
the Ukraine started reaching the Western press in October 1941, and in
January 1942 the Soviets issued a detailed report, the 'Molotov
Announcement', which analysed the workings of the *Einsatzgruppen*.
The memorandum was dismissed by the WZO in Palestine as 'Bolshevik
propaganda'.[8] In February 1942 Bertrand Jacobson, the former representative of the Joint Distribution Committee in Hungary, held a press
conference on his return to the USA and relayed information from
Hungarian officers about the massacre of 250,000 Jews in the Ukraine.
In May 1942 the Bund sent a radio message to London that 700,000
Jews had already been exterminated in Poland, and on 2 July the BBC
broadcast the essence of the report in Europe. The Polish government-
in-exile used the Bund alarm in its own English-language press propaganda. Yet on 7 July 1942, Yitzhak Gruenbaum, then leading the
Jewish Agency's *Vaad Hazalah* (Rescue Committee), refused to believe
similar accounts of massacres in Lithuania, because the numbers of the
estimated dead were larger than the pre-war Jewish population in the
country.[9] On 15 August Richard Lichtheim in Switzerland sent a
report to Jerusalem, which was based on German sources, about the
scope and methods of extermination. He received a reply, dated 28
September:

Frankly I am not inclined to accept everything in it literally . . . Just as one has to learn by experience to accept incredible tales as indisputable facts, so one has to learn by experience to distinguish between reality — however harsh it may be — and imagination which has become distorted by justifiable fear.[10]

Gruenbaum and his Rescue Committee acknowledged that terrible things were going on, but he kept minimising them as 'only' pogroms.

On 8 August Gerhart Riegner of the Geneva office of the WJC obtained detailed accounts of the gassing programme from reliable German sources, and he forwarded these to the WJC's London and New York offices via British and American diplomats. The WJC in London received the material, but Washington withheld the message from rabbi Wise. On 28 August the British section of the WJC sent Wise another copy, and he called the State Department and discovered that they had kept back the information. They then asked him not to release the news to the public pending verification; he agreed and said nothing until 24 November — 88 days later — when the State Department finally confirmed the report. Only then did Wise make a public announcement of a Nazi plan to exterminate all the Jews in their grasp. On 2 December he wrote a letter to 'Dear Boss', Franklin Roosevelt, asking for an emergency meeting and informing him that:

I have had cables and underground advices for some months, telling of these things. I succeed, together with the heads of other Jewish organisations, in keeping them out of the press.[11]

Wise and Goldmann, who was in the United States throughout the war, never doubted that Riegner's report was true. According to Walter Laqueur, they feared that publicity would add to the despair of the victims.[12] Yehuda Bauer is certain that the American Jewish leaders were already aware of the Bund report.[13]

'There is no Need to Reveal Them in Public'

In November 1942 some 78 Jews holding Palestinian citizenship arrived from Poland in exchange for some Palestinian Templars. The Jewish Agency could no longer doubt the reports that had been coming into the country for months and, like Wise, they finally declared that the Nazis were systematically exterminating the Jews. But, as with Wise, some WZO leaders in Palestine had been convinced of the truth of the reports well before they chose to make the facts public. On 17 April 1942, even before the Bund broadcast, Moshe Shertok wrote to General Claude Auchinleck, the commander of the British Eighth Army in North Africa. He was concerned with what might happen to Palestine's Jews, if the *Afrika Korps* broke through Egypt.

> The destruction of the Jewish race is a fundamental tenet of the Nazi doctrine. The *authoritative reports* recently published show that that policy is being carried out with a ruthlessness which defies description . . . An even swifter destruction, it must be feared, would overtake the Jews of Palestine [my emphasis].[14]

In other words, while Gruenbaum, the official in charge of the rescue efforts of the WZO, was sceptical about the reliability of the reports about the massacre of the people he was supposed to be helping, the head of the Political Department of the Jewish Agency was utilising these same reports to convince the British to arm the Zionist movement in Palestine.

With the announcements by Wise and the Jewish Agency, attention was turned to what could be done about it. The Jewish Agency's statement triggered off a spontaneous feeling of guilt throughout the Yishuv, as the reality of the horror facing their own kin sank in. However, there was no change in political focus amongst the Zionists. A Jewish state after the war remained their priority, and the Holocaust was not going to jeopardise this. Accordingly, when the local Journalists' Union cabled similar organisations abroad asking them to focus on the slaughter, Dov Joseph, the acting director of the Jewish Agency's Political Department, cautioned them against:

> publishing data exaggerating the number of Jewish victims, for if we announce that millions of Jews have been slaughtered by the Nazis, we will justifiably be asked where the millions of Jews are, for whom we claim that we shall need to provide a home in Eretz Israel after the war ends.[15]

Yoav Gelber tells us of the immediate effect of Dov Joseph's intervention: 'Vociferous protests were therefore toned down and instead, ways of responding more "constructively" were sought.'[16] Ben-Gurion talked of 'requests' that the Allies should threaten retribution and try and rescue Jews, particularly children, or exchange Germans for Jews, etc. In the same breath, he continued to call for concentration on building support for the Jewish Army proposal.[17] The Jewish Agency just soldiered on; no special effort was made for the rescue operation. Gruenbaum continued with several other duties in addition to heading the Rescue Committee.[18] Professor Bauer has given a stark scholarly assessment of Gruenbaum's captaincy of their efforts:

> On the basis of research done at the Institute of Contemporary Jewry at the Hebrew University, I would say ... the mood of some of the leaders – especially of Yitzhak Gruenbaum . . . turned to utter despondency. He and some of his close associates thought that nothing could be done to save Europe's Jews, and that money sent to Europe for escape, resistance, or rescue would be wasted. But they felt that the effort was worthwhile in order to be able to say after the war that everything possible had been done. It should be stressed they did not say the effort should not be made; but they felt it would inevitably fail.[19]

But did Gruenbaum really do anything? There were many in Palestine who were appalled at the WZO's defeatism and its continuing preoccupation with the goals of Zionism while their relatives were being slaughtered, and these people cried out for action. They were no immediate threat to the hegemony of the WZO leaders, but the leadership felt the pressure. Most of it was directed at Gruenbaum, who finally gave way at a meeting of the Zionist Executive on 18 February 1943. He accused his critics and his friends of letting him take the blame, while they did nothing either. Later he set down his incredible speech in his post-war book, *Bi-mei Hurban ve Sho'ah* (In the Days of Holocaust and Destruction).

> However, among us – permit me to speak of this side of the picture – there is one solution that is universal to every bad event, to every Holocaust. First of all, we attack the leaders; they are to blame ... had we cried, had we demanded, everything possible would have been done to save, to help. And if nothing was done, that was because we did not cry or make demand ...
> I want to destroy this assumption ... in order to save, to take out people from the occupied countries ... it would be necessary for the neutral countries to provide refuge, that the warring nations open their gates to the refugees. And when we suggested demanding this through the help of our friends . . . there were those who said:

'Don't touch this matter; you know they won't admit Jews onto North Africa, to the United States, don't put our comrades into such a situation. The public is unable to accept these considerations, they don't understand them, nor do they wish to understand them' . . .

Meanwhile a mood swept over Eretz Yisrael, that I think is very dangerous to Zionism, to our efforts for redemption, our war of independence. I do not want to hurt any one, but I cannot understand how such a thing could occur in Eretz Yisrael, something that never happened abroad. How is it possible that in a meeting in Yerushalayim people will call: 'If you don't have enough money you should take it from the *Keren Hayesod*, you should take the money from the bank, there is money there.' I thought it obligatory to stand before this wave . . .

And this time in Eretz Yisrael, there are comments: 'Don't put Eretz Yisrael in priority in this difficult time, in the time of destruction of European Jewry.' I do not accept such a saying. And when some asked me: 'Can't you give money from the Keren Hayesod to save Jews in the Diaspora?', I said: no! And again I say no! I know that people wonder, why I had to say it. Friends tell me, that even if these things are right, there is no need to reveal them in public, in time of sorrow and concern. I disagree. I think we have to stand before this wave that is putting Zionist activity into the second row. Have I said this to glorify my own tenets? And because of this, people called me an anti-Semite, and concluded that I am guilty, because we do not give priority to rescue actions.

I am not going to defend myself. The same as I'm not going to justify or defend myself if they would blame me for killing my mother, so I'm not going to defend myself in this case. But my friends did not have to abandon me in this battle and then comfort my soul later: 'If you were connected with any political party we would have put the reins on you.' I think it necessary to say here: Zionism is over everything . . .

I wish to end with suggestions. Naturally, it is incumbent upon us to continue all action for the sake of rescue and not neglect one chance to end the slaughter . . . . At the same time we must guard Zionism. There are those who feel that this should not be said at the time a Holocaust is occurring, but believe me, lately we see worrisome manifestations in this respect: Zionism is above all — it is necessary to sound this whenever a Holocaust diverts us from our war of liberation in Zionism. Our war of liberation does not arise from the fact of a Holocaust in a straightforward manner and does not interlock with actions for the benefit of the Diaspora in its time, and this is to our detriment. This situation does not exist for any other nationality. We have two areas of action, and they connect and interlock, but are actually two separate areas of work though they sometimes touch. And we must guard — especially in these times — the supremacy of the war of redemption.[20]

In 1944 a Hungarian Zionist, Joel Brand, arrived in Jerusalem on an extraordinary mission. (The mission will be described in greater detail in the following chapter; here it is sufficient to state that until 1944 the Germans had not occupied Hungary and that it had become a refuge for those fleeing Nazi territory.) Brand had been a prominent figure in Budapest's own Zionist Rescue Committee and as such had been taken to see Gruenbaum. He later told of one of his pathetic encounters with the director of the WZO's rescue operations:

He said to me at once, 'Why haven't you rescued my son, Herr Brand? You should have been able to get him out of Poland into Hungary.' I replied: 'We have not usually undertaken the rescue of individuals.' 'But you ought to have thought of my son, Herr Brand. It was your duty to do so.' I respected his gray hairs, and I said no more.[21]

'For only with Blood Shall We Get the Land'

The Nazis began taking the Jews of Slovakia captive in March 1942. Rabbi Michael Dov-Ber Weissmandel, an Agudist, thought to employ the traditional weapon against anti-Semitism: bribes. He contacted Dieter Wisliceny, Eichmann's representative, and told him that he was in touch with the leaders of world Jewry. Would Wisliceny take their money for the lives of Slovakian Jewry? Wisliceny agreed for 50,000 in dollars, so long as it came from outside the country. The money was paid, but it was actually raised locally, and the surviving 30,000 Jews were spared until 1944 when they were captured in the aftermath of the furious but unsuccessful Slovak partisan revolt.

Weissmandel, who was a philosophy student at Oxford University, had volunteered on 1 September 1939 to return to Slovakia as the agent of the world Aguda. He became one of the outstanding Jewish figures during the Holocaust, for it was he who was the first to demand that the Allies bomb Auschwitz. Eventually he was captured, but he managed to saw his way out of a moving train with an emery wire; he jumped, broke his leg, survived and continued his work of rescuing Jews. Weissmandel's powerful post-war book, *Min HaMaitzer* (From the Depths), written in Talmudic Hebrew, has unfortunately not been translated into English as yet. It is one of the most powerful indictments of Zionism and the Jewish establishment. It helps put Gruenbaum's unwillingness to send money into occupied Europe into its proper perspective. Weissmandel realised: 'the money is needed here — by us and not by them. For with money here, new ideas can be formulated.'[22] Weissmandel was thinking beyond just bribery. He realised immediately that with money it was possible to mobilise the Slovak partisans. However, the key question for him was whether any of the senior ranks in the SS or the Nazi regime could be bribed. Only if they were willing to deal with either Western Jewry or the Allies, could bribery have any serious impact. He saw the balance of the war shifting, with some Nazis still thinking they could win and hoping to use the Jews to put pressure on the Allies, but others beginning to fear future Allied retribution. His concern was simply that the Nazis should start to appreciate that live Jews were more useful than dead ones. His thinking is not to be confused with that of the Judenrat collaborators. He was not trying to save some Jews. He thought strictly in terms of negotiations on a Europe-wide basis for all the Jews. He warned Hungarian Jewry in its turn: do not let them ghettoise you! Rebel, hide, make them drag the survivors there in chains! You go peacefully into a ghetto and you will go to Auschwitz! Weissmandel was careful never to allow himself to be manoeuvred by the Germans into demanding concessions from the Allies. Money from world Jewry was the only bait he dangled before them.

In November 1942, Wisliceny was approached again. How much money would be needed for all the European Jews to be saved? He went to Berlin, and in early 1943 word came down to Bratislava. For $2 million they could have all the Jews in Western Europe and the Balkans. Weissmandel sent a courier to Switzerland to try to get the money from the Jewish charities. Saly Mayer, a Zionist industrialist and the Joint Distribution Committee representative in Zurich, refused to give the Bratislavan 'working group' any money, even as an initial payment to test the proposition, because the 'Joint' would not break the American laws which prohibited sending money into enemy countries. Instead Mayer sent Weissmandel a calculated insult: 'the letters that you have gathered from the Slovakian refugees in Poland are exaggerated tales for this is the way of the *"Ost-Juden"* who are always demanding money'.[23]

The courier who brought Mayer's reply had another letter with him from Nathan Schwalb, the HeChalutz representative in Switzerland Weissmandel described the document:

> There was another letter in the envelope, written in a strange foreign language and at first I could not decipher at all which language it was until I realized that this was Hebrew written in Roman letters, and written to Schwalb's friends in Pressburg [Bratislava] . . . It is still before my eyes, as if I had reviewed it a hundred and one times. This was the content of the letter:
>
> 'Since we have the opportunity of this courier, we are writing to the group that they must constantly have before them that in the end the Allies will win. After their victory they will divide the world again between the nations, as they did at the end of the first world war. Then they unveiled the plan for the first step and now, at the war's end, we must do everything so that Eretz Yisroel will become the state of Israel, and important steps have already been taken in this direction. About the cries coming from your country, we should know that all the Allied nations are spilling much of their blood, and if we do not sacrifice any blood, by what right shall we merit coming before the bargaining table when they divide nations and lands at the war's end? Therefore it is silly, even impudent, on our part to ask these nations who are spilling their blood to permit their money into enemy countries in order to protect our blood — for only with blood shall we get the land. But in respect to you, my friends, *atem taylu*, and for this purpose I am sending you money illegally with this messenger.'[24]

Rabbi Weissmandel pondered over the startling letter:

> After I had accustomed myself to this strange writing, I trembled, understanding the meaning of the first words which were 'only with blood shall we attain land'. But days and weeks went by, and I did not know the meaning of the last two words. Until I saw from something that happened that the words *'atem taylu'* were from *'tiyul'* [to walk] which was their special term for 'rescue'. In other words: you, my fellow members, my 19 or 20 close friends, get out of Slovakia and save your lives and with the blood of the remainder — the blood of all the men, women, old and young and the sucklings

— the land will belong to us. Therefore, in order to save their lives it is a crime to allow money into enemy territory — but to save you beloved friends, here is money obtained illegally.

It is understood that I do not have these letters — for they remained there and were destroyed with everything else that was lost.[25]

Weissmandel assures us that Gisi Fleischman and the other dedicated Zionist rescue workers inside the working group were appalled by Schwalb's letter, but it expressed the morbid thoughts of the worst elements of the WZO leadership. Zionism had come full turn: instead of Zionism being the hope of the Jews, their blood was to be the political salvation of Zionism.

Minimal Response to the Extermination

Even after Wise's belated announcement of the extermination campaign, the response of the American Jewish establishment was minimal. They heeded a call from one of the Zionist chief rabbis in Palestine for a day of mourning, which they called for 2 December 1942, and the anti-Zionist Jewish Labor Committee added a ten-minute Jewish work stoppage. But much more had to be done before the Roosevelt administration would ever take concrete action. He would have to be pushed hard, if he was going to do anything to help the Jews of Europe.

Roosevelt had ambivalent attitudes toward Jews. He had one in his Cabinet and had appointed another to the Supreme Court, and he had several among his confidential advisers. But he never made the slightest move in the 1930s to amend the anti-Semitic immigration laws. Although Jews were prominent in the northern and western Democratic machines, there were several outspoken anti-Semites among the Dixiecratic contingent in Congress and Roosevelt would never think of separating from them. He never expressed any public anti-Semitic sentiments, but there is no doubt that he held them. Years later, the United States government published the notes of the Casablanca Conference, held in January 1943, and it was revealed that he had told the French:

The number of Jews engaged in the practice of the professions (law, medicine, etc) should be definitely limited to the percentage that the Jewish population in North Africa bears to the whole North African population . . . The President stated that his plan would further eliminate the specific and understandable complaints which the Germans bore towards the Jews in Germany, namely that while they represented a small part of the population, over fifty per cent of the lawyers, doctors, schoolteachers, college professors, etc. in Germany were Jews.[26]

The inadequacy of the Jewish establishment's response was so glaring that it brought forth a furious denunciation by the veteran Labour Zionist, Chaim Greenberg, in the February 1943 issue of the *Yiddishe Kemfer*:

> the few Jewish communities remaining in the world which are still free to make their voices heard and to pray in public should proclaim a day of fasting and prayer for American Jews . . . this American Jewish community has fallen lower than perhaps any other in recent times . . . We did not even display sufficient ability to set up (temporarily, for the duration of the emergency only) some kind of general staff that should meet every day and think and consult and consider ways to engage the help of people who *may, perhaps,* be in a position to help us . . . One clique tries to outmaneuver the other — Zionists and anti-Zionists . . . What has such rescue work to do with political differences and with the entire ideological clap-trap which we have produced during the past couple of generations?[27]

Greenberg's powerful attack on American Jewry's leaders spared no one, least of all his fellow Zionists, who were becoming the strongest force in the community. Without naming names, he denounced the defeatism and obsession with Palestine to be seen in many of the leading Zionist circles.

> There have even appeared some Zionists in our midst who have become reconciled to the thought that it is impossible to stay the hand of the murderer and therefore, they say, it is necessary 'to utilize this opportunity' to emphasise to the world the tragedy of Jewish homelessness and to strengthen the demand for a Jewish National Home in Palestine. (A Home for whom? For the millions of dead in their temporary cemeteries in Europe?)

He attacked Wise's American Jewish Congress:

> at a time when the Angel of Death uses airplanes, the AJCongress

employs an oxcart-express . . . [it] delegated rescue work in Europe to a special committee . . . this committee permits itself the luxury of not meeting *for weeks on end* . . . It displayed a lack of the courage of despair, of that 'aggressiveness of spirit' which characterizes the hour of doom, of the ability to act on its own on a suitable scope or to attract people from other circles and activate them for such a generally self-evident cause as the attempt to rescue those who can still be rescued.

Greenberg lashed out at the Revisionists' Committee for a Jewish Army for expensive advertisements publicising a Jewish Army for 200,000 stateless Jews: 'knowing very well that this is a mythical figure . . . all the Jews in Europe, to the last one, would be murdered long before such a force could be recruited, organised and trained'.[28]

The Emergency Committee

Only one of the Zionist groups understood that rescue had to become their top priority. A small number of Irgunists had gone to the USA to raise funds for their illegal immigration, and when the war broke out they added a demand for a Jewish Legion which they, like the WZO, saw as Zionism's immediate goal. In April 1941 they noticed some articles by Ben Hecht, one of America's most famous journalists, in *PM*, a liberal New York daily paper, deploring the silence of Jewish social, political and literary figures on the situation of European Jewry. The Irgunists convinced Hecht to help them set up a 'Committee for a Jewish Army of Stateless and Palestinian Jews'. Hecht approved of the idea, because he could see they were fighters and that was what he wanted: a Jewish army that would kill Germans in revenge for the Jews Hitler humiliated and murdered. Hitherto the Irgunists had played a very minor role in the Jewish political scene; however, with Hecht on their committee the Revisionists became a semi-serious force. He knew everybody in Hollywood and the publishing world. When their advertisements appeared in the major newspapers they looked as if they were an actual part of wartime politics.

Although the Irgunists had missed the full significance of the earliest massacre reports, Wise's statement convinced their leader, Peter Bergson, that they had to push for American government action specifically on behalf of the Jews. They planned to bring a pageant, *They Shall Never Die*, to Madison Square Garden on 9 March 1943. Some of the most famous theatrical people of the age — Kurt Weill, Billy Rose and Edward G. Robinson amongst many others — started to put it together. This was too much for Wise, who was not willing to be upstaged by any Fascist interlopers. The Jewish establishment suddenly announced its own rally in the Garden for 1 March. The Committee for a Jewish Army tried to bring about unity by offering to withdraw as exclusive sponsor for the 9 March event, if the establishment would agree to co-sponsor it, but it refused.[29] The result was that two separate rallies on the same Jewish tragedy took place in the Garden only nine days apart. Both were well attended; the Hecht-Weill pageant filled the arena twice on the same night. The real difference was that the circle of followers around Wise were primarily moved by their hostility to the Irgunists and had no genuine plans for a sustained mobilisation, whereas the Committee for a Jewish Army toured America's major cities with their pageant. Wise's American Jewish Congress, infuriated by their success, ordered its local branches around the country to try to keep the pageant out of auditoriums wherever it could, and the pageant was denied a performance at Pittsburgh, Baltimore and Buffalo at least.[30]

But what have we really achieved, Kurt Weill asked? 'The pageant has accomplished nothing. I know Bergson calls it a turning point in Jewish history, but he is stage struck. Actually all we have done is make a lot of Jews cry, which is not a unique accomplishment.'[31] In fact the pageant did establish the Committee for a Jewish Army as a force to be reckoned with. Nevertheless, latter-day apologists for the Holocaust Jewish establishment, like Bernard Wasserstein of Brandeis, still would argue that:

> Congress, and the majority of the general public were at one in their adamant refusal to contemplate any tinkering with the strict letter of the national origins quota restrictions . . . It requires a vivid imagination to be convinced that a campaign of Jewish 'activism' would have changed these harsh realities. The more probable consequences would have been to arouse increased antipathy toward Jews . . . Jewish leaders were only too aware of this: hence their general scepticism as to the efficacy of activism.[32]

In fact there is no evidence to suggest that anti-Semitism increased as a result of the committee's activities. Rather the opposite: momentum built in Congress for action. The Irgunists, including the deeply committed Weill, felt that if they put all their strength and energy into rescue they could force the government to start doing something. From spring 1943 to the end of the year, the committee — now renamed the Emergency Committee to Save the Jewish People of Europe — virtually had the rescue field to itself, as the Jewish establishment either did nothing or else tried to sabotage their work.

Their practical experience in mobilising soon taught the committee that they had to move away from the Palestine issue. By 1943 Zionist sympathies were rapidly growing among Jews, but the anti-Zionist elements were still powerful and non-Jews had not the least interest in causing trouble for their British allies in the Middle East, although many ordinary Americans were convinced that their government should try to save the Jews. Now Wise and Goldmann brought a new charge against the Emergency Committee: they had betrayed the sacred cause of Palestine. Bergson tried to reason with Wise: 'If you were inside a burning house, would you want the people outside to scream "save them", or to scream "save them by taking them to the Waldorf Astoria?" ' It was all to no avail; Wise would never concede.[33]

The committee mobilised 450 orthodox rabbis for an October march to the White House, but Roosevelt would not see them; he rushed off to dedicate four bombers to the Yugoslav exile air force, but the campaign continued. Peter Bergson emphasises: 'The rich Jews, the establishment, always fought us. It was always the little Jews — and Gentiles — who sent in the money for our ads.'[34] Sensing that there was now clearly enough public support for the cause, their leading congressional friends, Senator Guy Gillette and Representatives Will Rogers Jr and Joseph Baldwin, put in a Bill for a rescue commission. They pointedly emphasised that their proposal had nothing to do with Zionism. Hearings in the Senate in September were friendly, but in the House Foreign Relations Committee the Chairman, Sol Bloom, a Jewish Tammany Democrat from Brooklyn, bitterly attacked Bergson and the hearings went against the proposition. For good measure, American Zionism's most prestigious figure, rabbi Stephen Wise, came to Washington to testify against the rescue Bill because it did not mention Palestine.

Wise's *Congress Weekly* boasted how the hearings were 'utilised by Dr Wise for lifting the discussion from the plane of abstract plans to the most immediate practical measures of rescue, and in the first place to the opening of Palestine'. But there was more to it; the article denounced the Emergency Committee for 'utter disregard of all existing Jewish organisations and their years of effort thru and with the government agencies created to deal with the rescue problem'.[35] For years the press and the politicians had deferred to Wise as *the* leader of American

Jewry. Now an outsider, Ben Hecht, and a group of the hated Revision-ists were trying to tell Roosevelt how to save the Jews.

Bloom's action against the Bill could not stop the pressure for a rescue commission. Before the Emergency Committee could launch a new plan, the Secretary of the Treasury, Henry Morganthau Jr, handed Roosevelt a report on a plot by a group of State Department officials to suppress information on the massacres. Breckenridge Long, the former ambassador to Italy, a pre-war admirer of Mussolini, whom the department had assigned to handling refugee problems during the Holocaust, had been found to have altered a vital document to obstruct exposure. At the congressional hearings Long had been the administra-tion's main witness against the proposal for a rescue commission, and now Morganthau had to warn the President that the situation could easily 'explode into a nasty scandal'.[36] Roosevelt knew he was beaten, and on 22 January 1944 he announced the establishment of a War Refugee Board.

Credit for the establishment of the Refugee Board has been debated by Holocaust historians. Those who identify with the Zionist establish-ment derogate the work of the Emergency Committee and argue that the Board was wholly the work of Morganthau. Thus Bernard Wasser-stein insists that 'activism' did not and could not get results for the Jews. The Board was the result of Morganthau's intervention and nothing else: 'Morganthau's protests yielded some results . . . It is an example of what was feasible as a result of energetic behind-the-scenes activity by Jewish leaders.'[37] However, Nahum Goldmann conceded that John Pehle, who drafted Morganthau's report and became the Director of the WRB, 'had taken the position that Bergson's Emergency Committee to Save the Jewish People of Europe had inspired the intro-duction of the Gillette–Rogers resolution, which in turn had led to the creation of the War Refugee Board'.[38] Yet Goldmann and Wise con-tinued their own campaign against Bergson. Goldmann went to the State Department on 19 May 1944 and, according to a department memorandum, he 'alluded to the fact that Bergson and his associates were in this country on temporary visitors' visas . . . He added that he could not see why this government did not either deport Bergson or draft him.' In the same memorandum the reporter noted that Wise 'had gone so far as to inform Mr Pehle that he regarded Bergson as equally great an enemy of the Jews as Hitler, for the reason that his activities could only lead to increased anti-Semitism'.[39]

The Board turned out to be only of minimal help to the Jews. Arthur Morse wrote in his book, *While 6 Million Died*, of 50,000

Romanians directly saved, and indirectly, through pressure on the Red Cross, neutrals, clergy and underground forces, the Board saved an additional few hundred thousand.[40] More recent calculations lower the figure to approximately 100,000.[41] The Board was never a powerful agency. It never had more than thirty staff, and it could not circumvent the State Department in dealing with the neutrals or the collapsing Nazi satellites. It had no power to guarantee that escaped Jews would eventually be given refuge in America, where so many had kin. Shmuel Merlin, who directed the public relations aspects of the Emergency Committee's work, has explained why the Board was so relatively weak:

> We knew we were defeated when the Jewish organisations offered to put up the money for the Board. Naturally we had envisioned a serious program on the part of the Administration. That meant the government had to lay out money in exactly the same way it does for anything else it really wanted. Instead Roosevelt and Congress were taken off the hook by the Jewish establishment. They offered to pay the Board's basic expenses. They put up about $4,000,000,000 seed money and a total of $15,000,000 during the WRB's entire existence. The sum was so paltry they could always laugh and say 'first wait until the Jews put up some real money'.[42]

The Joint Distribution Committee put up $15 million of the $20 million spent by the Board. Other Jewish groups added $1.3 million. If the board had more money, it could have done far more. If the Jewish establishment had united with the Irgunists in a further campaign for government funding, it is highly likely that the money would have been forthcoming. Before the Board was set up, the government warded off demands for such a commission on the grounds that other agencies were doing all that could be done. Once the Board had been established, there was a formal government commitment to rescue; however, the Jewish establishment remained implacably opposed to the Irgun activists and they continued to demand the deportation of Bergson, instead of uniting with the Emergency Committee.

In 1946 the Revisionists re-entered the WZO and eventually some of the enmity evaporated, but Bergson, Merlin, Ben-Ami and other committee veterans could never listen to the establishment figures who dominated Israel until 1977 without recalling their previous obstructionism. In recent years, they have been able to prove the perfidious backstage role of Wise, Goldmann and others by means of previously secret documents obtained under the Freedom of Information Act; as a result the controversy over the conflicting rescue efforts has never really died down. Thus Wasserstein insists that the silence of the leaders is a 'myth':

> It is no accident that this legend has grown up. On the contrary, this is an accusation first voiced during and immediately after the war by a specific group: the Revisionist Zionists and their various offshoots . . . This was their rallying cry which they used in their attempts to mobilize Jewish youth in a misguided and morally tainted campaign of invective and terror.[43]

In fact the first explanation of why the establishment was doing nothing came from the Trotskyist *Militant* on 12 December 1942.

> Truth to tell, these organisations, like the Joint Distribution Board and the Jewish Congress, and the Jewish Labor Committee, feared to make themselves heard because they were afraid of arousing a wave of anti-Semitism here as a result. They feared for their own hides too much to fight for the lives of millions abroad.[44]

Certainly the former leaders of the Emergency Committee have tried to expose their old enemies, but since the war they have also been critical of their own efforts and they readily admit that they started too late. They did not understand the significance of the massacre reports until after Wise's announcement in November 1942. However, a broader criticism of the committee relates to their original demand for a Jewish army. This was pure Zionism and of no relevance either to the plight of the Jews or the fight against Nazism. A second criticism must be their failure to put the Jews directly on to the streets. A mass march to the immigration service in New York by many thousands of Jews would have been far more worrisome to the administration than the mobilisation of 450 rabbis. A hunger strike organised by the committee would have propelled the movement forward. The activists criticise themselves today for not having done so, and explain this omission in terms of their own political personalities. They were in America as the representatives of the Irgun, a military organisation that had always preached against 'Jewish Gandhism'.

The Irgun Revolt in 1944

The American Irgunists were to commit many worse mistakes when the Irgun began its revolt in Palestine in January 1944. After Begin arrived in Palestine in May 1942 he found Revisionism in total disarray. He called for the reorganisation of the Irgun and was eventually appointed its commander. At no time was the Irgun representative of more than a small minority of the Jews in Palestine. Most Palestinian Jews saw them as crazy Fascists, who brought disaster to the Zionist cause by attacking Britain while she was fighting Hitler. They were even repudiated by the old-style Revisionist political apparatus. They were a tiny force; a few full-time members and a few hundred more part-time. The Haganah, which saw them as Fascists, started rounding them up in collaboration with the British, although the Irgun refused to strike back against the Haganah as they knew that after the war they would join together to try to drive out the British. They also did not attack military targets, so that they should not appear to be interfering with the war effort.

In most respects therefore the revolt was largely symbolic, but in the United States and Britain it diverted attention from the Jews of Europe to the Jews of Palestine. Wise had a chance to regain credibility, and he accused the Emergency Committee of backing terrorism. However, the Americans — now calling themselves the Hebrew Committee for National Liberation — as well as the Emergency Committee, did not see the revolt as drawing attention from Europe, but rather as enhancing awareness of the Jewish plight. Peter Bergson still stoutly defends the revolt and the committee's relation to it:

> I know that there are some historians who say that in the end we were no better than the establishment, that we also diverted our energies from rescue work to presenting the case for the Irgun. They are wrong. You are supposed to revolt if the British are not rescuing your own kin in Europe. I would be ashamed for the Jews of Palestine, as people, if there was no one in the country that rose up.[45]

Shmuel Merlin maintains that the revolt upset some Jews more than it did the Gentiles.[46] Only Jews read the Jewish press and they were more influenced by the publicity put out by the establishment against the Irgun. However, once the Irgun revolted, the committee started back down its own road to political fanaticism. Hecht and others began to rant against all Germans in the columns of their organ, *The Answer*:

'Where ever a German sits or stands, weeps or laughs – there is abomination. The years will never clean him.'[47] Their inspiration became Hecht's pathetic *A Guide for the Bedeviled*:

I consider the Nazi government not only as suitable for Germans, but ideal from the point of view of the rest of the world as a German government. It should be left to them, after they are defeated, as a gift from Tantalus. They should be allowed to remain Germans in the open, with a good spiked fence around them such as is used in rendering a zoo harmless. Within this Nazi zoo maintained by the world for the diversion of philosophers, the Germans could listen to Beethoven and dream of murder and inconvenience no one . . . Locked firmly in the middle of Europe as Nazis (with storm troops, concentration camps, hangmen and Gestapo intact) the Germans would handle their own problems of extermination their own way. Their massacre would not have to be on our conscience . . . But such sensible things never come to pass in the world. Our statesmen will insist . . . that the enemy resume its masquerade as members of the human race. Thus we will reap from the victory the reward of allowing the Germans to delude us again.[48]

That the American Irgunists did more than all other Zionists to help the Jews in occupied Europe is clear. That Begin's revolt did absolutely nothing to help those same Jews is also clear. The American Irgunists pushed for Begin to start his campaign; therein lay their strength and their weakness. They did not expect the British to give them Palestine; they had broken with them before the war and fully expected to fight them during and after the war. They saw themselves as having to tear what they wanted from out of the hands of the imperialists, and that psychology carried over into their approach to rescue. They outflanked Stephen Wise because they represented the 'little Jews'. The ordinary Jews wanted 'Action not Pity' and they supported the Emergency Committee because it articulated their own outrage at what was happening to the Jews of Europe. But in Palestine Begin did not have the sympathy of the ordinary Jews. Had the Irgun mobilised the Jewish masses in a direct challenge to Gruenbaum, it is possible that they could have overturned the supremacy of the WZO. As it was, the cause of Palestine was once again a distraction.

'We Must Not Disturb the War Effort . . . by Stormy Protests'

It is impossible to excuse the delay on the part of the leaders of the WZO to acknowledge publicly the Nazi extermination, although, again, Wasserstein has attempted to defend them:

> Given the nature and extent of the terrible reality it is hardly surprising that it was only when the early, uncorroborated, and incomplete reports were confirmed beyond doubt that the Jews in the West could bring themselves to face the grim truth.[49]

Others had brought 'themselves' to foresee the likelihood of the extermination of millions of Jews even before the war. After Kristallnacht, on 19 November 1938, a statement was issued by the National Committee of the Socialist Workers Party (SWP). 'Let the Refugees into the US!' it read. 'The Brown-shirted monsters do not even bother to conceal their aim: the physical extermination of every Jew in Great-Germany.'[50] Again, on 22 December 1938, Trotsky foresaw the annihilation of the Jews.

> It is possible to imagine without difficulty what awaits the Jews at the mere outbreak of the future war. But even without war the next development of world reaction signifies with certainty the *physical extermination of the Jews* . . . Only audacious mobilisation of the workers against reaction, creation of workers' militia, direct physical resistance to the fascist gangs, increasing self-confidence, activity and audacity on the part of all the oppressed can provoke a change in the relations of forces, stop the world wave of fascism, and open a new chapter in the history of mankind.[51]

While the American Jewish Congress was co-operating with the State Department in suppressing the Reigner report, it was divulged from Stephen Wise's office and on 19 September 1942 the Trotskyist *Militant* ran an article obviously based on the information.

> The State Department has meantime — so we are informed — suppressed information that it received from its consular agents in Switzerland. This information has to do with the treatment of the Jews in the Warsaw Ghetto. Evidence of the greatest atrocities has occurred there in connection with the renewed campaign to exterminate all Jews. Rumor even has it that the Ghetto no longer exists,

that the Jews there have been completely wiped out. The reason this report has been suppressed by the State Department is that it does not wish any mass protests here that will force its hand on policy.[52]

It was not merely the State Department that was suppressing the report, and it was not merely the State Department that had no wish for protests in America. The final verdict on the record of the Zionists in the rescue of European Jewry should be left to Nahum Goldmann. In his article 'Jewish Heroism in Siege', published in 1963, he confessed that:

we all failed. I refer not only to actual results — these at times do not depend on the abilities and wishes of those who act, and they cannot be held responsible for failures resulting from objective considerations. Our failure was in our lack of unwavering determination and readiness to take the proper measures commensurate with the terrible events of the times. All that was done by the Jews of the free world, and in particular those of the United States, where there were greater opportunities than elsewhere for action, did not go beyond the limits of Jewish politics in normal times. Delegations were sent to prime ministers, requests for intervention were made, and we were satisfied with the meagre and mainly platonic response that the democratic powers were ready to make.

He went even further:

I do not doubt (and I was then closely acquainted with our struggle and with day-to-day events) that thousands and tens of thousands of Jews could have been saved by more active and vigorous reaction on the part of the democratic governments. But, as I have said, the main responsibility rests on us because we did not go beyond routine petitions and requests, and because the Jewish communities did not have the courage and daring to exert pressure on the democratic governments by drastic means and to force them to take drastic measures. I will never forget the day when I received a cable from the Warsaw Ghetto, addressed to Rabbi Stephen Wise and myself, asking us why the Jewish leaders in the United States had not resolved to hold a day-and-night vigil on the steps of the White House until the President decided to give the order to bomb the extermination camps or the death trains. We refrained from doing this because most of the Jewish leadership was then of the opinion that we must not disturb the war effort of the free world against Nazism by stormy protests.[53]

Notes

1. Robert Sherwood, *Roosevelt and Hopkins,* p. 717.

2. Anthony Howard, 'Duplicity and Prejudice', *New York Times Book Review* (16 September 1979), p. 37.

3. Yoav Gelber, 'Zionist Policy and the Fate of European Jewry (1939–1942)', *Yad Vashem Studies,* vol. XIII, p. 171.

4. Ibid., p. 170.

5. Ibid., p. 192.

6. Shabatei Beit-Zvi, *Post-Ugandan Zionism During the Holocaust,* post p. 251 (unpublished English translation).

7. Joseph Tanenbaum, 'A Final Word Regarding Packages to Poland', *Der Tog* (10 August 1941) (unpublished English translation).

8. Gelber, 'Zionist Policy and the Fate of European Jewry', p. 190.

9. Yehuda Bauer, 'When Did They Know?', *Midstream* (April 1968), p. 51.

10. Gelber, 'Zionist Policy and the Fate of European Jewry', p. 191.

11. Eliyhu Matzozky, 'The Responses of American Jewry and its Representative Organizations, November 24, 1942 and April 19, 1943', unpublished Masters thesis, Yeshiva University, app. II.

12. Walter Laqueur, 'Jewish Denial and the Holocaust', *Commentary* (December 1979), p. 46.

13. Bauer, 'When Did They Know?', p. 53.

14. Laqueur, 'Jewish Denial and the Holocaust', p. 53.

15. Gelber, 'Zionist Policy and the Fate of European Jewry', p. 195.

16. Ibid.

17. Ibid.

18. Beit-Zvi, *Post-Ugandan Zionism During the Holocaust* (unpublished English synopsis), p. 1.

19. Yehuda Bauer, *From Diplomacy to Resistance,* pp. viii–ix.

20. Yitzhak Gruenbaum, *Bi-Mei Hurban ve Sho'ah,* pp. 62–70.

21. Alex Weissberg, *Desperate Mission* (Joel Brand's story as told by Weissberg), p. 206.

22. Michael Dov-Ber Weissmandel, *Min HaMaitzer* (unpublished English translation).

23. Ibid.

24. Ibid. (Hebrew edn), p. 92.

25. Ibid., p. 93.

26. Bernard Wasserstein, *Britain and the Jews of Europe 1939–1945,* p. 207.

27. Chaim Greenberg, 'Bankrupt', *Midstream* (March 1964), pp. 5–8.

28. Ibid., pp. 7–10.

29. Matzozky, 'The Responses of American Jewry', p. 45.

30. Sarah Peck, 'The Campaign for an American Response to the Nazi Holocaust, 1943–1945', *Journal of Contemporary History* (April 1980), p. 374.

31. Ben Hecht, *A Child of the Century,* p. 540.

32. Wasserstein, 'The Myth of "Jewish Silence" ', *Midstream* (August 1980), p. 14.

33. Peck, 'Campaign for an American Response to the Nazi Holocaust', p. 384.

34. Author's interview with Peter Bergson, 27 February 1981.

35. 'On the Question of Rescue', *Congress Weekly* (10 December 1943), p. 3.

36. Arthur Morse, *While 6 Million Died,* p. 79.

37. Wasserstein, 'The Myth of "Jewish Silence" ', p. 14.

38. 'Attitude of Zionists Toward Peter Bergson', memorandum of conversation, 867N.01/2347, Department of State (19 May 1944), pp. 3–4.

39. Ibid., pp. 2, 4.

40. Morse, *While 6 Million Died,* pp. 257, 307.

41. Eliyhu Matzozky (letter), *Midstream* (March 1982), p. 44.

42. Author's interview with Shmuel Merlin, 16 September 1980.

43. Wasserstein, 'The Myth of "Jewish Silence" ', p. 15.

44. A. Roland, 'The Slaughter of the Jews', *Militant* (12 December 1942), p. 3.

45. Interview with Bergson.

46. Interview with Merlin.

47. Ben Hecht, 'My Dark Prayer', *The Answer* (1 May 1944), p. 7.

48. Ben Hecht, *A Guide for the Bedeviled* (1944), pp. 126–7.

49. Wasserstein, 'The Myth of "Jewish Silence"', p. 10.

50. National Committee of the Socialist Workers Party, 'Let the Refugees into the US!', *Socialist Appeal* (19 November 1938), p. 1.

51. Leon Trotsky, 'Appeal to American Jews Menaced by Fascism and Anti-Semitism', *On the Jewish Question*, pp. 29–30.

52. A. Roland, 'The Plight of the Jews and the Democracies', *Militant* (19 September 1942), p. 3.

53. Nahum Goldmann, 'Jewish Heroism in Siege', *In the Diaspersion* (Winter 1963/4), pp. 6–7.

25 HUNGARY, THE CRIME WITHIN A CRIME

The destruction of Hungarian Jewry is one of the most tragic chapters in the Holocaust. When the Germans finally occupied Hungary on 19 March 1944, the leaders of the Jewish community knew what to expect from the Nazis, as Hungary had been a refuge for thousands of Polish and Slovakian Jews, and they had been warned by the Bratislava working group that Wisliceny had promised that Hungary's 700,000 Jews would eventually be deported.

The Nazis summoned the Jewish community leaders and told them not to worry, things would not be so bad if the Jews co-operated. As Randolph Braham has written, 'History and historians have not been kind to the leaders of Hungarian Jewry in the Holocaust era.'[1] For as Braham admits, many 'tried to obtain special protection and favors for their families'.[2] Some did not have to wear the yellow star and, later, were allowed to live outside the ghettos and were permitted to look after their property. In post-war years the roles of two Hungarian Labour Zionists — Rezso Kasztner and Joel Brand, leaders of the Budapest Rescue Committee — were subjected to detailed scrutiny in Israeli courtrooms. Kasztner had been accused of betraying the Hungarian Jewish masses.

'They . . . Begged Them to Hush up the Matter'

On 29 March 1944 these two Zionists met Wisliceny and agreed to pay him the $2 million he had previously mentioned to Weissmandel, if he would not put the Hungarian Jews in ghettos or deport them. They also asked for transport along the Danube of 'some hundred people' with Palestine certificates, saying that it would make it easier for them to raise the cash from their people abroad.[3] Wisliceny agreed to take their bribe and to consider the transport, but was concerned that it be done secretly in order not to antagonise the Mufti who wanted no Jews released. The first instalments of the bribe were paid, but the Nazis nevertheless set up ghettos in the provinces. Then, on 25 April, Eichmann summoned Joel Brand and told him that he was to be sent to negotiate with the WZO and the Allies. The Nazis would allow a million Jews to leave for Spain in exchange for 10,000 trucks, soap, coffee and other supplies. The trucks were to be used exclusively on the eastern front. As a token of Nazi good faith, Eichmann would allow the Zionists the preliminary release of a Palestine convoy of 600.

Brand was confirmed by the Rescue Committee as their representative and the Germans flew him to Istanbul on 19 May in the company of another Jew, Bandi Grosz, a German and Hungarian agent who had additional contacts with various Allied intelligence services. Grosz was to conduct his own negotiations with Allied intelligence about the possibilities of a separate peace. On arrival, Brand met the local representatives of the WZO's Rescue Committee and demanded an immediate meeting with a Jewish Agency leader. The Turks, however, refused to grant a visa to Moshe Shertok, the head of the Agency's Political Department, and the Istanbul committee finally advised Brand to confer with him in Aleppo, on Syrian territory, which was then under British control. On 5 June, when Brand's train passed through Ankara, two Jews — one a Revisionist, the other an Agudist — warned him that he was being lured into a trap and would be arrested. Brand was reassured by Echud Avriel, a leading WZO rescue figure, that this warning was false and motivated by factional malice.[4] However, Brand was in fact arrested by the British.

Shertok interviewed Brand on 10 June in Aleppo. Brand described the encounter in his book, *Desperate Mission* (as told to Alex Weissberg):

> Moshe Shertok withdrew into a corner with them [the British], and they talked softly but vehemently together. Then he came back to me and laid a hand on my shoulder . . . 'You must now go on further south . . . it is an order . . . I cannot change it' . . . 'Don't you understand what you're doing?' I shouted. 'This is plain murder! Mass murder! . . . You have no right to seize an emissary. I am not even an emissary from the enemy . . . I am here as the delegate of a million people condemned to death.'

Shertok huddled with the British and returned again: 'I will not rest until you are free once more . . . you will be set free.'[5] In fact Brand was escorted by a British officer to imprisonment in Egypt. They stopped in Haifa, where he strolled around the harbour:

> I even considered the possibility of escape. But only those who have belonged to a party held together by the strongest ties of ideology will understand . . . I was a Zionist, a party member . . . I

was bound by party discipline . . . I felt so small, so insignificant – a man thrown by chance into the boiling cauldron of history – that I dare not take on my own shoulders the responsibility for the fate of a hundred thousand people. I lacked the courage to defy discipline, and therein lay my true historical guilt.[6]

Brand never had any illusions that the Eichmann proposition would be accepted by the Western Allies. However, he believed that, as with the earlier negotiations with Wisliceny, some serious SS officers wanted to invest in their own future. Live Jews were now a negotiable currency. Brand hoped that it would be possible to negotiate for more realistic arrangements or, at least, to decoy the Nazis into thinking that a deal could be made. Possibly the extermination programme would be slowed down or even suspended while an accord was being worked out. However, the British were not interested in exploring the possibilities of Eichmann's scheme and notified Moscow of Brand's mission; Stalin naturally insisted that the offer be rejected. The story reached the press and on 19 July the British publicly denounced the offer as a trick to divide the Allies.

On 5 October Brand was finally allowed to leave Cairo and he rushed to Jerusalem. He tried to go on to Switzerland, where Rezso Kasztner and SS Colonel Kurt Becher had been sent to negotiate further with Saly Mayer of the Joint Distribution Committee. The Swiss were willing to allow him entry, providing the Jewish Agency would sponsor him. The British gave him a travel document under the name of Eugen Band, the name Eichmann had given him for reasons of secrecy. He went to Eliahu Dobkin, head of the Jewish Agency's Immigration Department, who was supposed to represent the WZO at the negotiations, to get his sponsorship paper; Dobkin refused:

'You will understand, Joel,' he said, 'that I cannot vouch for a man called Eugen Band, when your name is Joel Brand.' 'Are you aware, Eliahu, that many Jews in Central Europe have been sent to the gas chambers simply because officials have refused to sign documents that were not absolutely correct?'[7]

Late in 1944, at a Tel Aviv Histadrut meeting, Brand was introduced, as ' "Joel Brand, the leader of the Jewish workers' movement in Hungary. He has brought with him the greetings of Hungarian Jewry" . . . I wondered where this Hungarian Jewry was.' He tore into the meeting:

'You were the last hope of hundreds of thousands condemned to death. You have failed them. I was those people's emissary yet you let me sit in a Cairo prison . . . You have refused to declare a general strike. If there was no other way, you should have used force .' . . . They hurried up to the reporters who were present and begged them to hush up the matter.[8]

An inquiry commission was hurriedly set up to appease Brand, but it met only once and decided nothing. Weizmann arrived in Palestine and Brand asked for an immediate interview. It took Weizmann 'a fortnight' to reply.[9]

29 Dec. 1944, Dear Mr Brand: . . . As you may have seen from the press, I have been traveling a good deal and generally did not have a free moment since my arrival here. I have read both your letter and your memorandum and shall be happy to see you sometime the week after next — about the 10th of January.[10]

They finally met, and Weizmann promised to help him get back to Europe; Brand never heard from him again.

'Hardly likely to Achieve the Salvation of the Victims'

The WZO approach to the crisis in Hungary had been timid throughout. On 16 May 1944 rabbi Weissmandel had sent detailed diagrams of Auschwitz and maps of the railway lines through Slovakia to Silesia to the Jewish organisations in Switzerland demanding 'absolutely, and in the strongest terms', that they call upon the Allies to bomb the death camp and the railways.[11] His proposal reached Weizmann in London, who approached the British Foreign Secretary, Anthony Eden, in an extremely hesitant manner. Eden wrote to the Secretary for Air on 7 July:

Dr Weizmann admitted that there seemed to be little enough that we could do to stop these horrors, but he suggested that something might be done to stop the operation of the death camp by bombing the railway lines . . . and bombing the camps themselves.[12]

A memorandum by Moshe Shertok to the British Foreign Office, written four days later, conveys the same hangdog scepticism:

> The bombing of the death camps is . . . hardly likely to achieve the
> salvation of the victims to any appreciable extent. Its physical
> effects can only be the destruction of plant and personnel, and
> possibly the hastening of the end of those already doomed. The
> resulting dislocation of the German machinery for systematic
> wholesale murder may possibly cause delay in the execution of those
> still in Hungary (over 300,000 in and around Budapest). This in
> itself is valuable as far as it goes. But it may not go very far, as other
> means of extermination can be quickly improvised.[13]

After setting out all the reasons why the bombing would not work,
Shertok then elaborated on the theme that 'the main purpose of the
bombing should be its many-sided and far-reaching moral effect'.[14]

The Jews of occupied Europe, through Weissmandel and Brand, were
imploring immediate action. The bombing of Auschwitz was not only
possible, it happened by mistake. On 13 September 1944 American
pilots, aiming for an adjacent Buna rubber works, hit the camp and
killed 40 prisoners and 45 Germans. In July, when Eden had asked if
the question could be discussed in Cabinet, Churchill had replied: 'Is
there any reason to raise these matters at the cabinet? You and I are in
entire agreement. Get anything out of the Air Force you can and in-
voke me if necessary.'[15] Nothing happened. It was felt the cost to the
attacking planes would be too high. Weizmann and Shertok continued to
petition the British to bomb the camps, but lost the initiative.[16]

The British Zionist leadership likewise faltered in its reaction to
the Hungarian crisis. When the Germans occupied Budapest, Alex
Easterman, Political Secretary of the British section of the WJC, went
to the Foreign Office; when the officials asked that the establishment
not organise any street demonstrations, of course he agreed. Again, on
11 July, Selig Brodetsky, a member of the WZO Executive and the
President of the Board of Deputies, rejected a call from the Palestinian
Vaad Leumi (National Council) that they should put on a mass march
in London.[17] Lady Reading, Eva Mond, was the President of the British
section of the WJC, and she came out against 'nagging'. 'Don't let us
drift into continental Jewish habits,' she admonished on 23 May, when
the death trains were still rolling.[18]

'He Agreed to Help Keep the Jews from Resisting Deportation'

The destruction of Hungarian Jewry took place at a time when the Nazi structure was showing all the signs of collapse. Canaris's Abwehr Intelligence had concluded that the war was lost; it therefore started making its own contacts with Western Intelligence, and had to be taken over by the SD. Count Klaus von Stauffenberg's bomb on 20 July 1944 came in the middle of the Hungarian crisis and almost destroyed the Nazi edifice. The Germans had invaded the country because they knew that Admiral Miklos Horthy was planning to pull Hungary out of the war. The neutrals, under the prodding of the War Refugee Board, protested against the new murders, and some made efforts to extend diplomatic protection to some of the Jews. From the beginning Eichmann, who had responsibility for the deportation of the Hungarian Jews, was concerned that Jewish resistance or attempts at escape over the border to Romania, which by then was unwilling to hand over Jews to the Nazis, would trigger off political shock waves that could slow down his operation.

When Eichmann first went to work for von Mildenstein, the fervent philo-Zionist gave him Herzl's *Judenstaat*. He liked it. He was also fond of Adolf Bohm's *Die Zionistische Bewegung* (The Zionist Movement) and once, in Vienna, he recited an entire page of it by heart during a meeting with some Jewish leaders, including the mortified Bohm. He had even studied Hebrew for two and a half years, although, he conceded, he never really spoke it well. He had had many dealings with the Zionists before the Second World War. In 1937 he had negotiated with the Haganah's representative, Feivel Polkes, and had been their guest in Palestine. He had also had close contacts with the Czech Zionists. Now, again, he would negotiate with the local Zionists.

In 1953 the Ben-Gurion government prosecuted an elderly pamphleteer, Malchiel Gruenwald, for having libelled Rezso Kasztner as a collaborator for his dealings with Eichmann in 1944. The trial had considerable international coverage throughout 1954. Eichmann must have followed it in the press, for he described his relationship with Kasztner at length in taped interviews he gave to a Dutch Nazi journalist, Willem Sassen, in 1955, parts of which were later published in two articles in *Life* magazine after his capture in 1960. Gruenwald had denounced Kasztner for having kept silent about the German lies that the Hungarian Jews were only being resettled at Kenyermezo. In return, he was allowed to organise the special convoy, which ultimately became a train to Switzerland, and place his family and friends on it. Further, Gruenwald claimed, Kasztner later protected SS Colonel Becher from being hung as a war criminal by claiming that he had done everything possible to save Jewish lives. Eichmann described Kasztner as follows:

This Dr Kastner [many sources Anglicise Kasztner's name] was a young man about my age, an ice-cold lawyer and a fanatical Zionist. He agreed to help keep the Jews from resisting deportation – and even keep order in the collection camps – if I would close my eyes and let a few hundred or a few thousand young Jews emigrate illegally to Palestine. It was a good bargain. For keeping order in the camps, the price of 15,000 or 20,000 Jews – in the end there may have been more – was not too high for me. Except perhaps for the first few sessions, Kastner never came to me fearful of the Gestapo strong man. We negotiated entirely as equals. People forget that. We were political opponents trying to arrive at a settlement, and we trusted each other perfectly. When he was with me, Kastner smoked cigarettes as though he were in a coffeehouse. While we talked he would smoke one aromatic cigarette after another, taking them from a silver case and lighting them with a little silver lighter. With his great polish and reserve he would have made an ideal Gestapo officer himself.

Dr Kastner's main concern was to make it possible for a select group of Hungarian Jews to emigrate to Israel ...

As a matter of fact, there was a very strong similarity between our attitudes in the SS and the viewpoint of these immensely idealistic Zionist leaders who were fighting what might be their last battle. As I told Kastner: 'We, too, are idealists and we, too, had to sacrifice our own blood before we came to power.'

I believe that Kastner would have sacrificed a thousand or a hundred thousand of his blood to achieve his political goal. He was not interested in old Jews or those who had become assimilated into Hungarian society. But he was incredibly persistent in trying to save biologically valuable Jewish blood – that is, human material that was capable of reproduction and hard work. 'You can have the others' he would say, 'but let me have this group here.' And because Kastner rendered us a great service by helping keep the deportation camps peaceful, I would let his groups escape. After all, I was not concerned with small groups of a thousand or so Jews.[19]

André Biss, Joel Brand's cousin, who worked with Kasztner in Budapest, and who supported his policy, nevertheless corroborated Eichmann's statement in part in his book, *A Million Jews to Save*, when he described who boarded the famous train which reached Switzerland on 6 December 1944:

Then came the most numerous group, Kasztner's pride — the Zionist youth. These were composed of the members of various organisations of agricultural pioneers, of extreme right-wing 'revisionists' who already possessed immigration certificates, and a number of orphans . . . Lastly came those who had been able to pay cash for their journey, for we had to collect the sum the Germans demanded. But of the 1684 in the train 300 at the most were of this category . . .

Kasztner's mother, his brothers, sisters and other members of his family from Klausenburg [Kluj] were passengers . . . Members of the families of those who had fought for the formation of this convoy formed at the most a group of 40 to 50 persons . . . In the confusion that ensued about 380 persons managed to clamber into the train which left Budapest, not with 1300 passengers as expected, but crammed full with more than 1700 travellers.[20]

The Israeli Labour Party got more than it bargained for when it set out to defend Kasztner. Shmuel Tamir, a former Irgunist, a brilliant cross-examiner, appeared for Gruenwald. Later, in 1961, Ben Hecht wrote his book, *Perfidy*, a remarkable exposé of the Kasztner scandal, and he presented many pages of Tamir's masterly demolition of Kasztner's defence.

Tamir How do you account for the fact that more people were selected from Kluj [Kasztner's home town] to be rescued than from any other Hungarian town?

Kastner That had nothing to do with me.

Tamir I put it to you that you specifically requested favoritism for your people in Kluj from Eichmann.

Kastner Yes, I asked for it specifically.

Kastner . . . All the local Rescue Committees were under my jurisdiction.

Tamir Committees! You speak in the plural.

Kastner Yes — wherever they existed.

Tamir Where else except in Kluj was there such a committee?

Kastner Well, I think the committee in Kluj was the only one in Hungary.

Tamir Dr Kastner, you could have phoned the other towns, just as you phoned Kluj?

Kastner Yes, that's right.

Tamir Then why didn't you contact the Jews of all these towns on the phone to warn them?

Kastner I didn't because I didn't have time enough.[21]

There were 20,000 Jews in Kluj and only a limited number of seats on that train. Judge Benjamin Halevi began pressing Kasztner and he blurted out his criteria for choosing who to save:

Kastner . . . the witnesses from Kluj who testified here — in my opinion, I don't think they represent the true Jewry of Kluj. For it is not a coincidence that there was not a single important figure among them.[22]

Levi Blum, also from Kluj, had attended a dinner for Kasztner in 1948, which had been arranged by the train passengers; he had spoiled the occasion by suddenly leaping up and calling the honoured guest a collaborator and daring him to take his accuser to court:

Blum . . . I asked him, 'why did you distribute post cards from Jews supposed to be in Kenyermeze?' Someone yelled out, 'This was done by Kohani, one of Kastner's men.' Kohani was also in the hall. He jumped up and yelled, 'Yes, I got those post cards.' I asked him, 'Who were they from?' He answered, 'That's none of your business. I don't have to explain what I do to you.'

Judge Halevi All of this happened in public?

Blum Yes, several hundred people were there.[23]

Kasztner was also involved in the affair of Hannah Szenes which was described at the trial. Szenes was a brave young Zionist from Hungary, whom the British finally allowed, together with 31 others, to parachute into occupied Europe to organise Jewish rescue and resistance. She landed in Yugoslavia on 18 March, one day before the German invasion of Hungary; she smuggled herself back into Hungary in June and was promptly caught by Horthy's police. Peretz Goldstein and Joel Nussbecher-Palgi followed her in and they contacted Kasztner, who conned them both into giving themselves up to the Germans and Hungarians for the sake of the train. Both were sent to Auschwitz, although Nussbecher-Palgi managed to saw through some bars on his train and escape.[24] Szenes was shot by a Hungarian firing squad. Kasztner's admission in court that he had failed to notify the Swiss, who represented Britain's interests in Budapest, of the Hungarians' capture of a

British officer and spy — 'I think I had my reasons' — outraged the Israeli public, many of whom had read her poetry and knew of her bravery in the Hungarian prisons.[25]

'Are We Therefore to be Called Traitors?'

On 21 June 1955 Judge Halevi found there had been no libel of Kasztner, apart from the fact that he had not been motivated by considerations of monetary gain. His collaboration had crucially aided the Nazis in murdering 450,000 Jews and, after the war, he further compounded his offence by going to the defence of Becher.

> The Nazis' patronage of Kastner, and their agreement to let him save six hundred prominent Jews, were part of the plan to exterminate the Jews. Kastner was given a chance to add a few more to that number. The bait attracted him. The opportunity of rescuing prominent people appealed to him greatly. He considered the rescue of the most important Jews as a great personal success and a success for Zionism.[26]

The Israeli Labour government remained loyal to their party comrade and the case was appealed. Attorney-General Chaim Cohen put the fundamental issue before the Supreme Court in his subsequent arguments:

> Kastner did nothing more and nothing less than was done by us in rescuing the Jews and bringing them to Palestine ... You are allowed — in fact it is your duty — to risk losing the many in order to save the few ... It has always been our Zionist tradition to select the few out of many in arranging the immigration to Palestine. Are we therefore to be called traitors?

Cohen freely conceded that:

> Eichmann, the chief exterminator, knew that the Jews would be peaceful and not resist if he allowed the prominents to be saved, that the 'train of the prominents' was organized on Eichmann's orders to facilitate the extermination of the whole people.

But Cohen insisted:

There was no room for any resistance to the Germans in Hungary and that Kastner was allowed to draw the conclusion that if all the Jews of Hungary are to be sent to their death he is entitled to organize a rescue train for 600 people. He is not only entitled to do it but is also bound to act accordingly.[27]

On 3 March 1957 Kasztner was gunned down. Zeev Eckstein was convicted of the assassination, and Joseph Menkes and Dan Shemer were found guilty of being accessories on the basis of a confession by Eckstein. The assassin claimed that he was a government agent who had infiltrated a right-wing terrorist grouping headed by Israel Sheib (Eldad), a well-known right-wing extremist.[28] However, the matter did not end with Kasztner's death. On 17 January 1958 the Supreme Court handed down its decision in the Kasztner–Gruenwald case.

The court ruled, 5 to 0, that Kasztner had perjured himself on behalf of Colonel Becher. It then concluded, 3 to 2, that what he did, during the war, could not be legitimately considered collaboration. The most forceful argument of the majority was put forward by Judge Shlomo Chesin:

He didn't warn Hungarian Jewry of the danger facing it because he didn't think it would be useful, and because he thought that any deeds resulting from information given them would damage more than help . . . Kastner spoke in detail of the situation, saying, 'The Hungarian Jew was a branch which long ago dried up on the tree.' This vivid description coincides with the testimony of another witness about Hungarian Jews. 'This was a big Jewish community in Hungary, without any ideological Jewish backbone.' . . . The question is not whether a man is allowed to kill many in order to save a few, or vice-versa. The question is altogether in another sphere and should be defined as follows: a man is aware that a whole community is awaiting its doom. He is allowed to make efforts to save a few, although part of his efforts involve concealment of truth from the many; or should he disclose the truth to many though it is his best opinion that this way everybody will perish. I think the answer is clear. What good will the blood of the few bring if everyone is to perish?[29]

Much of the Israeli public refused to accept the new verdict. Had Kasztner lived, the Labour government would have been in difficulty. Not only had he perjured himself for Becher, but, between the trial and the Supreme Court decision, Tamir had uncovered further evidence that Kasztner had also intervened in the case of SS Colonel Hermann Krumey. He had sent him, while he was awaiting trial at Nuremberg, an affidavit declaring: 'Krumey performed his duties in a laudable spirit of good will, at a time when the life and death of many depended on him.'[30]

Later, in the 1960s during the Eichmann trial, André Biss offered to testify. Because of his involvement with Kasztner he had more contact with Eichmann than any other Jewish witness – 90 out of 102 had never seen him – and it was apparent that his testimony would be important. An appearance date was set, but then the prosecutor, Gideon Hausner, discovered that Biss meant to defend Kasztner's activities. Hausner knew that, despite the Supreme Court's decision in the case, had Biss tried to defend Kasztner there would have been an immense outcry. Hausner knew from the Sassen tapes of the Eichmann interviews how Eichmann might implicate Kasztner. Israel had gained great prestige from Eichmann's capture and the government did not want the focus of the trial to shift away from Eichmann towards a re-examination of the Zionist record during the Holocaust. According to Biss, Hausner 'asked me to omit from my evidence any mention of our action in Budapest, and especially to pass over in silence what was then in Israel called the "Kasztner affair" '.[31] Biss refused and was dropped as a witness.

Who Helped Kill 450,000 Jews?

That one Zionist betrayed the Jews would not be of any moment: no movement is responsible for its renegades. However, Kasztner was never regarded as a traitor by the Labour Zionists. On the contrary, they insisted, that if he was guilty, so were they. Kasztner certainly betrayed the Jews who looked to him as one of their leaders, despite Judge Chesin's opinion:

> There is no law, either national or international, which lays down the duties of a leader in an hour of emergency toward those who rely on leadership and are under his instructions.[32]

However, by far the most important aspect of the Kasztner-Gruen-wald affair was its full exposure of the working philosophy of the

World Zionist Organisation throughout the entire Nazi era: the sanctification of the betrayal of the many in the interest of a selected immigration to Palestine.

Notes

1. Randolph Braham, 'The Official Jewish Leadership of Wartime Hungary', (unpublished manuscript), p. 1.

2. Randolph Braham, 'The Role of the Jewish Council in Hungary: A Tentative Assessment', *Yad Vashem Studies*, vol. X, p. 78.

3. Alex Weissberg, *Desperate Mission* (Joel Brand's story as told by Weissberg), p. 75.

4. Ibid., p. 158.

5. Ibid., pp. 163–5.

6. Ibid., pp. 165–6.

7. Ibid., p. 207.

8. Ibid., p. 210.

9. Ibid., pp. 208–9.

10. Moshe Shonfeld, *The Holocaust Victims Accuse*, p. 38.

11. Michael Dov-Ber Weissmandel, 'Letters from the Depths' in Lucy Dawidowicz (ed.), *A Holocaust Reader*, p. 326.

12. Bernard Wasserstein, *Britain and the Jews of Europe 1939–1945*, p. 311.

13. Ibid., p. 310.

14. Ibid.

15. Ibid., p. 311.

16. Ibid., p. 313.

17. Meir Sompolinsky, 'Anglo-Jewish Leadership and the British Government', *Yad Vashem Studies*, vol. XIII, p. 213.

18. Ibid., pp. 217–18.

19. Adolf Eichmann, 'I Transported Them to the Butcher', *Life* (5 December 1960), p. 146.

20. André Biss, *A Million Jews to Save*, pp. 92–4.

21. Ben Hecht, *Perfidy*, pp. 112–14.

22. Ibid., p. 118.

23. Ibid., p. 110.

24. Weissberg, *Desperate Mission*, pp. 236–47.

25. Hecht, *Perfidy*, p. 129.

26. Ibid., p. 180.

27. Ibid., pp. 194–5, 268.

28. Yitzhak Heimowitz, 'On the Kastner Case', *Middle East and the West* (31 January 1958), p. 3; Mordechai Katz, 'As I See It', ibid., (24 January 1958), p. 3; Katz, 'On Kastner and his Assassins', ibid., (7 February 1958), p. 3.

29. Hecht, *Perfidy*, pp. 270–1.

30. Ibid., p. 199.

31. Biss, *A Million Jews to Save*, p. 231.

32. Hecht, *Perfidy*, p. 272.

26 THE STERN GANG

Until Begin's election victory in 1977, most pro-Zionist historians dismissed Revisionism as the fanatic fringe of Zionism; certainly the more extreme 'Stern Gang', as their enemies called Avraham Stern's Fighters for the Freedom of Israel, were looked upon as of more interest to the psychiatrist than the political scientist. However, opinion toward Begin had to change when he came to power, and when he eventually appointed Yitzhak Shamir as his Foreign Minister it was quietly received, although Shamir had been operations commander of the Stern Gang.

'The Historical Jewish State on a National and Totalitarian Basis'

On the night of 31 August/1 September 1939 the entire command of the Irgun, including Stern, was arrested by the British CID. When he was released, in June 1940, Stern found an entirely new political constellation. Jabotinsky had called off all military operations against the British for the duration of the war. Stern himself was willing to ally himself with the British so long as London would recognise the sovereignty of a Jewish state on both sides of the River Jordan. Until then, the anti-British struggle would have to continue. Jabotinsky knew that nothing would make Britain give the Jews a state in 1940, and he saw the creation of another Jewish Legion with the British Army to be the main task. The two orientations were incompatible and by September 1940 the Irgun was hopelessly split: the majority of both the command and the ranks followed Stern out of the Revisionist movement.

At birth the new group was at its greatest strength for, as Stern's policies became clearer, the ranks started drifting back into the Irgun or joined the British Army. Stern or 'Yair', as he now called himself, (after Eleazer ben Yair, the commander at Masada during the revolt against Rome) began to define his full objectives. His 18 principles included a Jewish state with its borders as defined in *Genesis* 15: 18 'from the brook of Egypt to the great river, the river Euphrates', a 'population exchange', a euphemism for the expulsion of the Arabs and, finally, the building of a Third Temple of Jerusalem.[1] The Stern

Group was at this time a bare majority of the military wing of Revisionism but by no means representative of the middle class Jews of Palestine who had backed Jabotinsky. Still less was the fanatic call for a new temple attractive to ordinary Zionists.

The war and its implications were on everyone's mind and the Stern Gang began to explain their unique position in a series of underground radio broadcasts

> There is a difference between a persecutor and an enemy. Persecutors have risen against Israel in all generations and in all periods of our diaspora, starting with Haman and ending with Hitler . . . The source of all our woes is our remaining in exile, and the absence of a homeland and statehood. Therefore, our enemy is the foreigner, the ruler of our land who blocks the return of the people to it. The enemy are the British who conquered the land with our help and who remain here by our leave, and who have betrayed us and placed our brethren in Europe in the hands of the persecutor.[2]

Stern turned away from any kind of struggle against Hitler and even began to fantasise about sending a guerrilla group to India to help the nationalists there against Britain.[3] He attacked the Revisionists for encouraging Palestinian Jews to join the British Army, where they would be treated as colonial troops, 'even to the point of not being allowed to use the washrooms reserved for European soldiers'.[4]

Stern's single-minded belief, that the only solution to the Jewish catastrophe in Europe was the end of British domination of Palestine, had a logical conclusion. They could not defeat Britain with their own puny forces, so they looked to her enemies for salvation. They came into contact with an Italian agent in Jerusalem, a Jew who worked for the British police, and in September 1940 they drew up an agreement whereby Mussolini would recognise a Zionist state in return for Sternist co-ordination with the Italian Army when the country was to be invaded.[5] How seriously either Stern or the Italian agent took these discussions has been debated. Stern feared that the agreement might be part of a British provocation.[6] As a precaution, Stern sent Naftali Lubentschik to Beirut, which was still controlled by Vichy, to negotiate directly with the Axis. Nothing is known of his dealings with either Vichy or the Italians, but in January 1941 Lubentschik met two Germans — Rudolf Rosen and Otto von Hentig, the philo-Zionist, who was then head of the Oriental Department of the German Foreign Office. After the war a copy of the Stern proposal for an alliance between his movement and the Third Reich was discovered in the files of the German Embassy in Turkey. The Ankara document called itself a 'Proposal of the National Military Organisation (Irgun Zvai Leumi) Concerning the Solution of the Jewish Question in Europe and the Participation of the NMO in the War on the side of Germany.' (The Ankara document is dated 11 January 1941. At that point the Sternists still thought of themselves as the 'real' Irgun, and it was only later that they adopted the Fighters for the Freedom of Israel — *Lohamei Herut Yisrael* — appellation.) In it the Stern group told the Nazis:

The evacuation of the Jewish masses from Europe is a precondition for solving the Jewish question; but this can only be made possible and complete through the settlement of these masses in the home of the Jewish people, Palestine, and through the establishment of a Jewish state in its historical boundaries . . .

The NMO, which is well-acquainted with the goodwill of the German Reich government and its authorities towards Zionist activity inside Germany and towards Zionist emigration plans, is of the opinion that:

1. Common interests could exist between the establishment of a New Order in Europe in conformity with the German concept, and the true national aspirations of the Jewish people as they are embodied by the NMO.

2. Cooperation between the new Germany and a renewed volkish-national Hebrium would be possible and

3. The establishment of the historical Jewish state on a national and totalitarian basis, and bound by a treaty with the German Reich, would be in the interest of a maintained and strengthened future German position of power in the Near East.

Proceeding from these considerations, the NMO in Palestine, under the condition the above-mentioned national aspirations of the Israeli freedom movement are recognized on the side of the German Reich, offers to actively take part in the war on Germany's side.

This offer by the NMO . . . would be connected to the military training and organizing of Jewish manpower in Europe, under the leadership and command of the NMO. These military units would take part in the fight to conquer Palestine, should such a front be decided upon.

The indirect participation of the Israeli freedom movement in the

New Order in Europe, already in the preparatory stage, would be linked with a positive-radical solution of the European Jewish problem in conformity with the above-mentioned national aspirations of the Jewish people. This would extraordinarily strengthen the moral basis of the New Order in the eyes of all humanity.

The Sternists again emphasised: 'The NMO is closely related to the totalitarian movements of Europe in its ideology and structure.'[7]

Lubentschik told von Hentig that if the Nazis were politically unwilling to set up an immediate Zionist state in Palestine, the Sternists would be willing to work temporarily along the lines of the Madagascar Plan. The idea of Jewish colonies on the island had been one of the more exotic notions of the European anti-Semites before the war, and with France's defeat in 1940 the Germans revived the idea as part of their vision of a German empire in Africa. Stern and his movement had debated the Nazi Madagascar scheme and concluded that it should be supported, just as Herzl had initially backed the British offer, in 1903, of a temporary Jewish colony in the Kenya Highlands.[8]

There was no German follow-up on these incredible propositions, but the Sternists did not lose hope. In December 1941, after the British had taken Lebanon, Stern sent Nathan Yalin-Mor to try to contact the Nazis in neutral Turkey, but he was arrested en route. There were no further attempts to contact the Nazis.

The Stern plan was always unreal. One of the fundamentals of the German–Italian alliance was that the eastern Mediterranean littoral was to be included in the Italian sphere of influence. Furthermore, on 21 November 1941, Hitler met the Mufti and told him that although Germany could not then openly call for the independence of any of the Arab possessions of the British or French – out of a desire not to antagonise Vichy, which still ran North Africa – when the Germans overran the Caucasus, they would swiftly move down to Palestine and destroy the Zionist settlement.

There is rather more substance to Stern's own self-perception as a totalitarian. By the late 1930s Stern became one of the ring-leaders of the Revisionist malcontents who saw Jabotinsky as a liberal with moral reservations about Irgun terror against the Arabs. Stern felt that the only salvation for the Jews was to produce their own Zionist form of totalitarianism and make a clean break with Britain which, in any case, had abandoned Zionism with the 1939 White Paper. He had seen the WZO make its own accommodation with Nazism by means of the Ha'avara; he had seen Jabotinsky entangle himself with Italy; and he personally had been intimately involved in the Revisionists' dealings with the Polish anti-Semites. However, Stern believed that all of these were only half-measures.

Stern was one of the Revisionists who felt that the Zionists, and the Jews, had betrayed Mussolini and not the reverse. Zionism had to show the Axis that they were serious, by coming into direct military conflict with Britain, so that the totalitarians could see a potential military advantage in allying themselves with Zionism. To win, Stern argued, they had to ally themselves with the Fascists and Nazis alike: one could not deal with a Petliura or a Mussolini and then draw back from a Hitler.

Did Yitzhak Yzertinsky – rabbi Shamir – to use his underground *nom de guerre*, now the Foreign Minister of Israel, know of his movement's proposed confederation with Adolf Hitler? In recent years the wartime activities of the Stern Gang have been thoroughly researched by one of the youths who joined it in the post-war period, when it was no longer pro-Nazi. Baruch Nadel is absolutely certain that Yzertinsky-Shamir was fully aware of Stern's plan: 'They all knew about it.'[9]

When Shamir was appointed Foreign Minister, international opinion focused on the fact that Begin had selected the organiser of two famous assassinations: the killing of Lord Moyne, the British Minister Resident for the Middle East, on 6 November 1944; and the slaying of Count Folke Bernadotte, the UN's special Mediator on Palestine, on 17 September 1948. Concern for his terrorist past was allowed to obscure the more grotesque notion that a would-be ally of Adolf Hitler could rise to the leadership of the Zionist state. When Begin appointed Shamir, and honoured Stern by having postage stamps issued which bore his portrait, he did it with the full knowledge of their past. There can be no better proof than this that the heritage of Zionist collusion with the Fascists and the Nazis, and the philosophies underlying it, carries through to contemporary Israel.

Notes

1. Geula Cohen, *Woman of Violence*, p. 232.
2. Martin Sicker, 'Echoes of a Poet', *American Zionist* (February 1972), pp. 32-3.
3. Chaviv Kanaan (in discussion), *Germany and the Middle East 1835-1939*, p. 165.
4. Eri Jabotinsky, 'A Letter to the Editor', *Zionews* (27 March 1942), p. 11.
5. Izzy Cohen, 'Zionism and Anti-Semitism', (unpublished manuscript), p. 3.
6. Author's interview with Baruch Nadel, 17 February 1981.

7. 'Grundzuege des Vorschlages der Nationalen Militaerischen Organisation in Palastina (Irgun Zwei Leumi) betreffend der Loesung der juedischen Frage Europas und der aktiven Teilnahme der NMO am Kriege an der Seite Deutschlands', David Yisraeli, *The Palestine Problem in German Politics 1889-1945,* Bar Ilan University (Ramat Gan, Israel) (1974), pp. 315-17.

8. Kanaan, *Germany and the Middle East,* pp. 165-6.

9. Interview with Nadel.

INDEX

271